No Turning Back

The South American Expedition
of a Dragon Slayer

by

Benjamin "Coach" Wade

Shapato Publishing
Everly, Iowa

Published by: Shapato Publishing, LLC
                PO Box 476
                Everly, IA 51338

ISBN: 978-0-9833526-0-0
Library of Congress Control Number: 2011922706
Copyright © 2011 Benjamin Wade

First Printing August 2011

FOREWORD

On September 13, 1996 I was still a boy: alone, afraid and without a clue as to who I really was. Six months later, almost to the date, in late February of 1997, I had become a man.

In a small, 18-foot kayak, I traveled from Baja, California, on the beach of San Felipe; more than six thousand miles later I landed in Colombia, South America.

It was the stuff of fairy tales, or maybe legends. It was an epic trip of endurance, romance, heartbreak, danger and survival. At times it ripped my guts out. It brought me face-to-face with my own inadequacies, showed me my weaknesses and forged in me an incredible inner strength that stays with me to this day.

One of my favorite pictures from that trip is when I had just finished the six months of hell and was on my way back to the United States. I did a press conference in Mexico City, in a nightclub, and was there with the Minister of Sports and other bigwigs. It was a festive photo, with cigars and booze and whatnot— lots of people around in the background. But what I love most about that photo is the look on my face. It's the look of a man who has conquered death, who has faced his fears and come out on the other side victorious. It's the look of a man who can accomplish anything.

Since then I've taken the wisdom and inner strength from this voyage—a voyage beyond reason—and applied it to my everyday life. It's given me a confidence that has been unshakable and unbreakable, unbending and unyielding. I've set and accomplished other goals since then, each larger than the last: to coach a championship soccer team, to start and conduct my own orchestra, to write classical symphonies, to film a movie and star in the lead role (the film *180*) and to be on the CBS reality television show *Survivor*.

Many people have asked what happens on *Survivor*; they ask if it's real, and if it was the hardest thing I've ever done. My response usually goes something like this: "It was a once-in-a-lifetime opportunity that I had the privilege of doing three times."

Was it hard? Yes, absolutely. Was it the most difficult thing I have ever done? Absolutely not. What was harder, much more so, and that made me the person I am today, what brought me to the valley of the shadow of death, face-to-face with my own mortality, was the journey of which you are about to read.

If you let it, this story of the kayak trip I took in 1996 might change your life, as the journey itself changed mine. I dared to dream. I dared to undertake the impossible, something that had not been done before. My family and friends thought I was crazy. But I was on a quest for inner knowledge and peace; I had a goal and nothing short of death would stop me from reaching it.

Fourteen years later another dream has come true—to see the turmoil and triumph of that epic journey revive itself in the words and poetry in this book. It's come straight from the journal that I took with me and wrote in on a daily basis.

Plunge into the depths of my despair, my frailty and my delusions. Share in my desire for self-gratification, my successes, my failures and all it was that possessed me to kayak for six months alone on the open ocean. I hope that it will change you, as it did me.

Bon Voyage!
Benjamin "Coach" Wade

To my mother and father, and my brother Peter, who have endured so much on the home front, praying for my success and survival every step of the way. And to Cheryl Cranston, Tom Gauthier, William R. Wade and Jean Tennant for reading and editing and believing in my journals and keeping this flame alive.

TABLE OF CONTENTS

No Turning Back

The South American Expedition
of a Dragon Slayer

ONE
The Pages Of An Atlas

I have always been drawn to the ocean—transformed by its beauties, afraid of its powers, changed by its pleasures and mesmerized by its mysteries. The massive bodies of water that surround us have a magnetic passion, full of life and energy that defies logic. With a mind of its own, the ocean gives us a glimpse of its storied and well-told past.

I have seen its raw power, with churning surf and raging swells, destroying anything that dares defy it. So, too, have I experienced its calm beauty and splendor, on a quiet night, in a secluded cove, reflecting the moonlit sky, waves pattering softly against the sandy shore. With all of the focus today on man's progressive achievements, the ocean gives us an insight into how ruggedly beautiful is the hand of God.

Some of my fondest memories as a child took place near the water. I remember one day, many years ago, standing on top of a grassy sand dune on the coast of Florida, with my brother Peter at my side. It was the spring of 1979. We stood holding hands, feeling proud of our new matching shorts and shirts, looking out over the vast expanse of water that stretched before us as far as we could see.

Our dad had taken us out of school for a week of vacation, which only added to the thrill and wonder and excitement of standing before such a creature. I sensed, even then, that the ocean carried with it a soul, a mind, and a personality of its own. Before us stood a living, breathing, powerful being. The pull was inevitable. The wind whispered in my ears, beckoning for me to partake of its challenges. The surf roared through my soul, daring me to ride its thunderous currents.

I looked over first at my brother, and then my dad, who both seemed to be struck with the same sensations as I was.

"Daddy," I said, "what countries are on the other side? I mean, if you took a boat and headed straight from here, where would you land?"

"Actually," my father replied after a moment of thought, "we're not too far from Cuba, and once you get past Cuba, you can go all the way to South America. Colombia, probably." Dad knew the answers to everything.

"Are there sharks swimming around out there?"

"There sure are, but they won't bother you if you stay close to the shore."

We talked for a while before Peter and I decided we'd play around in the surf. After we tired from swimming we built a magnificent sandcastle. Its spires seemed to reach toward the deep blue sky. The late afternoon sun shone bright on the top of our new creation, casting long shadows over our heads and toward the hotels.

The beach was covered with seashells of all shapes and sizes, and I was amazed at the variety of treasures that flourished near the ocean. Already I was beginning to discover the rush of excitement that nature and the ocean had to offer. I would never forget the feelings of awe and excitement that filled my mind that day at the rumble of the waves and the cries of the seagulls.

Though we lived more than a day's drive from the Atlantic Ocean, we vacationed there frequently. My father taught mathematics at the University of Tennessee and was often asked to travel abroad to give lectures on equations that I, even later in life, couldn't begin to comprehend. Nonetheless, our father and mother deemed it fit that, as a supplement to our education in a foreign embassy school, Peter and I would see the world.

Included in many of these excursions were the sights and sounds that accompany the coasts of various continents, from the chalky White Cliffs of Dover at the narrowest part of the English Channel to the tranquil, mystic blue waters of the Caribbean Sea. The differences in color, intensity, surroundings, and the creatures within constantly astonished me. By the time I graduated college, I could not bear to be far from the beloved shores of an ocean.

I chose the Pacific, and thus began a dance that would start with a slow, waltz-like movement, followed by a thunderous, frenzied tango that I could scarce foresee. I began this quest, the relationship that would develop between the two lovers, the sea and myself, without the slightest hint as to how deep and intense this romance would become.

My new job took me away from the green hills of East Tennessee, to the coast of California. It was there that I learned to quiet my soul. There where I found solace from my everyday life, escaping the crowded cities to walk along the beaches, talking softly to myself and to God. It was there, among the rocks and sand, listening once again to the seagulls' cries, that I would begin to think clearly of my problems, my past, and my path yet taken. I felt the breath of God in the wind, and saw His powerful hands in the waves.

As I discovered that I had a talent for discerning the patterns and moods of the Pacific Ocean, my relationship with this great body of water took on new meaning.

For example, when I walked along the shore, mostly at sunset, I sometimes sensed when the ocean was about to become restless. Maybe it was a change in the wind, or a difference in the break of the waves, but deep inside I could feel the beast awakening. And sure enough, the waves would surge forward, pressing the sand where I stood as though to penetrate and perhaps madden my soul.

At other times, however, the ocean would roll lazily about, and I felt only the calm reassuring rhythm of the surf, calming my thoughts and paving the way for a more intimate relationship with its Creator—the same Creator that would give me peace in times to come.

It's somewhat ironic, then, that my vision—if you'd call it that; some might label it a call to death—came to prepare me for this impossible journey when I was nowhere near that familiar shore just south of Newport Beach. Instead, I was alone in the middle of the Mojave Desert, 100 miles north of Los Angeles, getting ready to see some customers for my new boss, business partner and friend, Allan Perry. The barrenness of the windswept desert might have assisted in exposing my discontentment.

Mulling over the last few years of my life, sifting through my decisions step-by-step, much like the sands that parted beneath my boots, I knew that something was missing. As I climbed up the steep slopes that crawled up the mountain, long after the road had run its course and expired, I was restless, unhappy with work, and in a spiritual rut. Simple solutions seemed out of reach. Money, which I had so desperately sought before coming to California, seemed pointless. My goals had changed. I was no longer the hard-driving graduate with a degree in business who had sought fortune and fame. My soul had taken on a freer spirit, and had shed the stuffy old shirt of corporate determination and success. Life was not as simple as it had been in college. I'd been dealt a different hand, and my mind was struggling to make something of it.

The date was March 13, 1996.

It hit me then and there, in the middle of the desert. As clear and concise as anything I'd experienced, it was as though the mountains had opened up to reveal the secret, and a goal so far out of reach that my mind reeled with the danger and soared with the anticipation of success.

My hands began to sweat. I ran back to my truck and tore through the pages of an atlas that I kept there. Despite the lack of pictures and clarity of detail that it displayed, my mind began to imagine the challenges that lay ahead. Dangerous surf, rocky coastlines, and miles and miles of endless ocean.

Yes, indeed, it was as if the message had been written just for me. The hand of nature that I loved and respected so much was beckoning, calling to me. I knew then, as I stood in the desert, alone and uncertain of what future my career was going to take, that I was going to South America.

TWO
"It's just something I have to do."

The following day, upon my return to Fullerton, California, I quit my job, broke up with my girlfriend, and bought a sea kayak. At this point I had never been kayaking on the ocean a day in my life, and in fact had never owned a kayak of my own—but I wasn't about to let small details like that stop me.

I began a daily training schedule that involved an early morning regimen of four hours of kayaking on the Pacific Ocean, an hour of jogging and two hours of weight training. I began to distance myself emotionally from my friends, who, for the most part, thought I was crazy.

I spent hours, long into the night, wondering about the times to come, weighing the pros and cons of the trip. Sometimes I would close my eyes, take a deep breath and try to imagine what it would be like to travel alone, in an eighteen-foot kayak, six thousand miles from San Felipe beach to Colombia, South America.

Often, in the dark of the night, I had nightmares. I would wake up screaming, drenched in sweat, as though the ocean itself had crashed down on my soaked sheets. But for all my visions and dreaming and wondering just what the ocean would bring to me on the expedition, I still had no real idea what I was getting myself into.

* * *

The next order of business, meshing with my rigorous hours of physical and mental preparation, was to hire an agent who would contact different companies around the United States. Every company except one, Nike, rejoiced at my madness, and offered everything from advice to products to personal photography sessions.

I would have preferred to begin the expedition without any assistance, but as my agent and friend, Christian Serino, pointed out, I had enough problems and obstacles to worry about, and "money should not be one of them." As I watched my bank account dwindle down to almost nothing, I had to agree. Because my training was taking the place of work, I was glad for the assistance these sponsors provided.

Finally, after only a few months of work and many letters, I had all of the equipment I thought I would need to complete my long journey. A few of the items included a beautiful new kayak from the Seattle-based Easy Rider Canoe and Kayak Co., enough PowerBars to feed an army, sunglasses from the Oakley headquarters in Orange County, shirts and hats from the National Sports Bar and Grill in Fullerton, California, and a promise from Photomation, another Orange County-based operation, to develop all of the pictures I took during my expedition.

* * *

Behind me on that fateful day of Friday, September 13, 1996, the day of my departure, stood a young woman. She was tall and beautiful, with golden hair that shone like the sun as it tumbled halfway down her back. Her name was Heather. Whether she felt it an obligation, a responsibility, or had just plain been conned into driving me, along with my kayak and 400 pounds of supplies, to the beach of San Felipe, I was glad of it. Glad to have her with me.

The expression on her face was a mixture of admiration, sorrow and fear. Her arms hung limp at her sides. I felt a little guilty leaving her there on the beach. She would possibly be my last contact to the life I had grown accustomed to in Southern California, and possibly the last person to see me alive.

We'd met only two weeks prior, introduced by a mutual friend, my roommate, Richard. Heather really was a beautiful girl, just twenty years old but already with more class than most women ever possess. She was very independent, worked at a modeling agency in Hollywood and had her own place. Just my type, and since I didn't want to get involved with anybody before I left—even going so far as to sever a current relationship the day after I started training—I figured there'd be no harm in asking Heather out.

It had been on our first date, as we were sitting in a restaurant across from each other, that she decided to broach the subject she'd been hearing so much about in the last few weeks.

"I can't believe you're actually going to Kayak to South America!" she said, her eyes looking intently into mine.

"It's just something I have to do. I've been training for the last six months," I replied, lowering my eyes in feigned modesty. Then, looking back into her steady gaze, I added, "I love going into challenges like this. I feel it makes me a better person. You probably think I'm crazy, like everybody else."

She nodded slightly, smiling.

I smiled back. "It's just too bad that we had to meet so close to my departure."

Her smile broadened and she reached across the table to slip her hand into mine.

The attraction I felt toward her troubled me a bit, and I attempted to brush off the rush of emotion by reminding myself of the task at hand. In the back of my mind, though, I knew that this could turn out to be more complicated than I'd originally anticipated.

"Listen," I continued, "I'm having a going away party next Sunday. I'm sure you already know about it from Richard. I thought I'd personally invite you to be my date. What do you say?"

"I'd love to," Heather replied, and then added, "I was hoping you'd ask."

And with that simple question, I took a step forward that put me in way over my head.

The next Sunday, sure enough, Heather showed up, as well as about fifty other close friends of mine. The people that attended could still scarcely believe that I was actually going to do it. Many of them told me I was making a mistake, and most were convinced I harbored a death wish. Though they continued to question my sanity, their love and concern, exhibited by their show of affection and gifts, was overwhelming that night. It made me a bit sad that I was about to leave all of this behind. I looked around at the smiling faces of my friends and felt a steadying warmth spread throughout my body, strengthening my resolve.

Allan Perry, my former boss, close friend and owner of the house, had graciously insisted that the party be held on his property. Though the majority of attendees were from our church, he'd bought and tapped a keg, adding to the festivities. Christian Serino, my agent, was busy in the kitchen, preparing the food that his restaurant had donated. I glanced around the room and out at the patio, searching out new guests and chatting with those around me. Merriment abounded.

The general consensus was that I had gone off the deep end, yet the two paddles that I would use in the upcoming six months were being signed by one and all. The festivities were unparalleled to any other party I'd attended that year. The food was good, the drinks were better, and everyone seemed happy.

Everyone, that is, except me. Perhaps reality had started to set in. I was beginning to wonder just how I would react to being mostly alone for the next six months or so. The faces of my friends reminded me that I was loved by many. It was a love and attention I knew I needed and longed for. As I stood outside on the patio of the house, the lights from the city of Brea twinkling in the night, I wondered just how detrimental the loneliness would become.

I would soon find out.

I pushed those gloomy thoughts from my mind, however, excused myself from my current conversation, and made my way over to Heather. A woman's companionship would cheer me up, I told myself.

Unfortunately, I had made the mistake of inviting most of the people I knew, including several ex-girlfriends, to the party, and I felt the glares from them as I reached Heather's side and took hold of her hand. Several ogling, testosterone-filled males had already begun to above like birds circling their prey. Perhaps a bit jealous myself, I decided it was time to make my move.

"Can I have a moment of your time?" I whispered into her ear.

"Of course," she said.

I guided her to a more secluded place, one of the bedrooms in the house.

"I know it's difficult for us to talk right now," I began, sitting down on the bed and facing her squarely. "What with everyone vying for your attention and mine. I don't want you to think I'm blowing you off. It's just that I have a lot of people who want to say their farewells, one at a time. Could you hang around until after everyone leaves? I'd like to talk to just you for a while."

"No problem." Again she smiled, and I felt my insides twist in a flurry of jubilation.

And talk we did, until four in the morning. The party, the people, and even the trip seemed to fade and I couldn't help but feel lucky sitting beside this magnificent woman, on this late night—or early morning, I should say—perched at the precipice of one of the most triumphant and disastrous times of my young life.

One of the highlights of the party had been the shaving of my head by another friend, Aaron Booth. He had used a disposable razor to bring it down right to the scalp, while everyone stood around and watched as the true shape of my scull emerged. The bumps and scars from previous injuries that stood out in various places, almost like the tattoos on an old pirate, added to the oddity of this man that sat before them. If any had questioned my sanity before then, there were certainly no doubts now.

On the back of my newly shaven head, I told Heather to draw a design with permanent ink. After she'd finished "Marking her territory," so she said, I looked at my watch.

"I wonder if the newspapers are out yet," I said. "Let's go down to the nearest store and see. I'd really like to read that story."

The story was an exclusive interview that I'd given the *Orange County Register*, and it was expected to appear in the morning edition of the Monday newspaper. Heather and I hopped in the car and drove to the local convenience store. The paper was printed and ready, so we bought two copies and took them back to the house.

We sat on the sofa, arm-in-arm and read the article. We were caught in the moment, snared by our own passions for life, adventure and each other. This was only the beginning of an unexpected relationship.

The following week Heather and I went out three more times, and at the end of the third date she suggested that she should be the one to drive me down to San Felipe. I readily agreed, happy that my last contact with civilization would be from this gentle and compassionate new friend.

* * *

The night before I was to leave, we went down to the beach near the city of Newport, so I could look out one last time upon the body of water I would soon embrace. The moon had not yet risen and the water was as black as ink.

I looked at Heather, and then at the ocean. My stomach muscles tightened in fear, and I turned to her.

"I have no idea what I'm getting myself into, do I?"

She shook her head, unable to answer my question.

* * *

And so, the next day, September 13, six months after my unexpected vision in the desert, I stood again at the ocean's edge. At the age of twenty-four, holding the rudder lines of my one-man kayak firmly with my left hand, I looked out over the Sea of Cortez, wondering just what it was that had possessed me to attempt such an expedition. I was headed for shark-infested waters, passages known for lawless drug smugglers, dangerous surf and rocky coasts.

I was also crazy enough to have purposely planned my departing date to coincide with hurricane season in Mexico—a decision I would later regret. And in a few months, just in time for my arrival, monsoon season would begin in the Southern Hemisphere.

My mind was filled with fear, excitement, and a burning desire to succeed. My emotions were running high, and my body was tense and rigid. Anticipation seemed to be clutching at my throat as my breath came in short, ragged gasps. This was the moment I had been waiting and preparing for during the past six months. Indeed, I felt like this was a time I had been waiting for my entire life. This was it. It was time to put words to rest, to live up to and far beyond any of the expectations and fears of my fellow man. Even the last conversation with my dad could not discourage my mounting excitement.

"Benjamin, you're going off half-cocked," he'd warned. "You don't know what you're getting into. People get killed out there on the ocean. It's a very dangerous place and you don't know the first thing about it."

His love for me no doubt clouded the issues, and all he could think about was the possibility of losing one of his sons. But in his attempt to discourage, he'd driven the stake for success deeper into my soul.

Challenges were what I lived for, and I wasn't about to let anything stand in my way. The excitement of the moment continued to increase as my heart pounded furiously within my chest. Adrenaline rushed from my heart, to my brain, and then back through my entire body, shocking my senses and sending jolts of energy to my taut muscles.

I stood waist deep in the brown waters of Baja, California, my kayak floating faithfully at my side. As the sun beat down on my brow, I squinted against its glare, out across the sea to a world that seemed ready to open its mouth and swallow me whole.

On the beach were a few tourists and fishermen. It didn't take long before most of them were watching me with open curiosity.

With a final push and a yell that was harsher, more primal than I thought humanly possible, I shoved the kayak into the waves, climbed aboard into the cockpit, thrust my paddle in the water, and began my journey. The people behind me faded. The noise—their voices and laughter—was drowned out by the roar of the challenge that lay ahead. After looking around at a society I already felt separated from, I faced the Sea of Cortez.

I turned back around, raising my hand in a farewell salute, but it was too late. Already my quick stroke had carried me far out to sea. Heather and the other spectators were but specks on the horizon, and then faded away altogether.

With heavy heart, I turned and continued to paddle.

THREE

"Assumption is the mother of all screw-ups."

Right away I received my first shock. My so-called training and mental preparation were nothing compared to what the ocean had in store for me. I had expected the waters in the Gulf of Baja, California, to be fairly calm, protected from the path of the hurricanes and stronger swells of the Pacific Ocean. I had planned to hug the coast from Baja to La Paz, 900 miles to the south, then cross over to the mainland of Mexico, a good month's journey. Plenty of time to mentally adjust to a life of solitude on the water and the prospect of increasing dangers. By that time I expected to be fit enough to tackle the twenty-foot waves, strong winds and continuous storms.

Was I ever wrong. I found the currents in the Gulf extremely strong and often unpredictable. At the end of the first day I was more exhausted than I'd ever been.

I woke up early on the third day, September 15. Stretching my limbs after a night of cramped sleep in the kayak, and began to paddle at an even pace. The water was blessedly calm, unlike the day before, and my spirits rose with the sun. By occasionally looking over to the shore for landmarks that I could identify on my map, I could tell that my progress was substantial. Focusing on the bow of my kayak, which parted the small swells and sent the fragments of water rushing by, I settled into a decisive rhythm.

I moved in such a state of bliss and concentration, that when a sandbar emerged directly in front of me I was mildly surprised. I easily pressed my right foot on the rudder controls inside the cockpit and steered around the obstacle. Once clear of that first strip of sand that stretched toward me like a knife, I noticed another to my left.

Confused, I stopped paddling. I knew that I was far enough from shore that I shouldn't be encountering any outstretching piece of the coastline. Looking around, I saw dozens of little islands dotted across the horizon. My kayak was currently in only a few feet of water and my paddle occasionally scraped the bottom sand.

It dawned on me then that the tide must have gone out rapidly, dropping the water level in the Sea of Cortez a good thirty feet. This early in my voyage, I was still unfamiliar with how suddenly the water along this stretch of coast could change.

I shook my head and smiled as the islands slowly connected to each other, until I was surrounded by one continuous ring of sand. Soon the crystal-clear waters receded so much that my paddle buried itself in the sand, and I climbed out of my kayak to stand in only a few inches of water.

From the front storage compartment I retrieved some dried fruit, and then sat down on the sand with my feet resting in the cool water. A few miles from shore, eating a light lunch and taking a break from the monotony of paddling all morning, I smiled in contentment and leaned back, soaking up the sun and stretching out my weary back.

This isn't so bad, I thought to myself. *It's so quiet here; I think I like being alone.*

My old job, friends, bills. They all seemed to float carelessly by, part of another world. It was a world I would return to eventually, but for now, miles from the nearest human interference, I could, for a while, forget my past.

This sense of peace would soon end. At first the distant sound of crashing waves was barely audible, almost like a buzzing in my ears, far away, intertwining with the visions that swirled through my head. I lay there basking in the sun, oblivious of what was yet to come, that day, as well as over the next six months.

Had I known the ferocity of the ocean, I might have thought twice about confronting her power. But through sheer naiveté and stubbornness, I'd plunged blindly ahead. I would pay a price for my stupidity. Like many of the lessons we learn in life, I was about to learn the hard way.

* * *

The northern coastline in the Sea of Cortez is affected by extreme levels of tide. The water comes rushing up along this slender area between Baja and the mainland of Mexico with much intensity and force. Second only to the Bay of Fundy on the Atlantic Coast, the distance between high and low tides can fluctuate as much as forty yards near the tip where the Colorado River once dumped its mighty contents into the sea.

At low tide the water level remains constant for only fifteen minutes, and then begins to work its way up the beach, sometimes at a speed of more than fifteen miles per hour. Each day, the hour for high and low tides advance one hour per day in accordance to the rotation of the moon around the earth. During a full moon, for four days, the difference between high and low tide is the least among the days in the cycle. The water will oftentimes become tranquil, almost lazy.

This is a perfect time to travel on its surface.

After this short period of rest, as if to make up for its lack of activity, the distance gap between high and low tide widens steadily for fourteen days. During this time the ocean becomes more and more restless. Vicious storms, winds and currents can arrive in a manner of minutes. At times, in some areas along the peninsula of Baja, California, the tide can be overwhelming, consuming and capsizing small crafts, swallowing their cargo, leaving little or no remains.

Every fisherman and boater that I talked to along this route knew well of the dangers on this perilous sea. Their schedules coincided strictly with the tidal flow and during some seasons, such as the ones approaching, wouldn't be caught dead in the middle of the Gulf. Unfortunately, I had to learn most of this by experiencing the power and tenacity of the Sea of Cortez myself, instead of simply opening a book beforehand and reading the information there.

This particular day that I was out, the tide happened to be at its greatest variance. To intensify the already hostile ocean, Hurricane Fausto was, at the same time, petering out to the south, near La Paz. The aftermath had quickly made its way up to where I paddled, causing more mayhem than usual for that time of year.

Perhaps it was the buzzing of the tide that caused me to get up and look around. That, or the insanity that continued to push me onward. Regardless of which it was, I eventually noticed that the water had risen up past my knees and was rapidly climbing higher. I climbed inside the cockpit again, finished swallowing my last bite of lunch, and dipped the paddle into the water.

At first there was no place to go, but then, up ahead, I could see an area of deeper water angling out towards the main part of the sea, between the various islands. I headed straight and then banked hard to the port side to pick up the current. It was then that I distinctly heard a distant crashing.

Farther ahead I saw several huge sets of breakers battering the sand of an island. I could hardly believe my eyes as the water around me continued to rise at an alarming rate. The islands disappeared from view, and I was once again in the open sea. The tide was coming in and it was not waiting for me.

Before I had a chance to react, the waves had leapt over the sandbanks and were pounding across my bow and into my lap. Jamming the rudder with my feet into the direction of each new wave, I avoided the water that wanted to turn my kayak sideways.

Unlike the Pacific Ocean, where one or two breakers might turn into white water, there were hundreds of waves crashing in front, to the sides, and on top of me, with no relief in sight. Several of the waves were more than seven feet high from trough to crest, and, as I maneuvered through and over what seemed to be hundreds of these monsters, I began to worry that I would capsize.

The compartment I was sitting in, called the cockpit, was half full of water, adding another hundred or so pounds to the already supply-laden kayak. It was not yet full enough of water to sink, but I wasn't going to take any chances. I steadied the kayak, aimed it at the next wave, and reached behind my seat. There, mounted between two brackets, was an automatic bilge pump.

I quickly grabbed the soft foam handle and set the pump between my legs. My arms strained as I tried to pull not only the weight of the kayak and its supplies, but the water inside as well. The water was already well past my stomach, sloshing around and making the boat less manageable. To make matters worse, I found I couldn't use the bilge pump and paddle to keep the nose of the kayak straight at the same time.

My training had not prepared me for such additional weight, and I knew my muscles couldn't comfortably keep up with the added strain. I tried splashing some of the water out by hand, but that didn't work. Every time I stopped paddling, the kayak would turn sideways in the crashing waves. I felt the strength of the current forcing me backwards, and every few seconds a new wave would come overboard, threatening to completely flood the cockpit. I wondered how much more weight it would bear without sinking.

Hopefully, I wouldn't find out.

Desperate for a faster method of bailing, I looked around my seat. I spotted the handle of an aluminum cooking pot sticking out from behind the seat on my left side. I picked it up and began to hastily bail the water out, forgetting again about the strength of the current. Unaccustomed as I was to such conditions, my mind balked and I forgot one of the first rules I'd learned during training: Never take your eyes off of the ocean.

As the boat suddenly surged downward, I looked up just as another towering wave crashed against the kayak. I threw all of my weight against the side on which the wave was breaking and thrust my oar into the water for balance. Ocean water poured into the cockpit again, filling it almost three-quarters of the way full. The kayak was sinking down closer to the water level. I had to do something—fast!

Holding the paddle in one hand and the aluminum pot in the other, I began to bail and paddle at the same time. Fortunately I was able to bail enough water out of the kayak in a short period of time to give it some stability and lighten the load. Enough, at least, to ease some of the strain from my aching arms. That bought me enough time to put on my spray skirt, a waterproof device in the shape of a skirt that fits around the waist of the kayaker at one end and the cockpit opening at the other end, allowing for a minimal amount of water to seep through. There were still several inches of standing water in the bottom of the cockpit, but at least for now I wouldn't take on any more.

For the next three hours, as the tide continued to rise, I battled the wind and the waves. The muscles in my arms, back, and legs ached beyond belief, and I felt the pain of blisters forming on my hands where I gripped the paddle. My legs cramped from having to steer the kayak's rudder in so many directions at once. My breath came in short, rapid gasps, and I wondered how much longer I could hold up before heading for shore.

As the sun began to set over the hills of Baja, I knew that I didn't want to spend another night on the water.

Up to this point I'd considered it a waste of time to look for a cove, head for shore and paddle the three or four miles it would take to reach the beach. Then it would take another hour to pitch the tent and lay out my sleeping bag, only to repeat the entire process again the next morning.

I'd been in such a rush, especially in the beginning, that my main thoughts had been to travel as many miles as humanly possible in a day, every day, until I ended this ridiculous trip. This feeling would change gradually over the next several months, and if it hadn't been for a few people whom I would meet along the way, and some miraculous experiences that God brought to me, I might not have enjoyed any of it.

For now, though, I was too tired to care. A small cove formed on my right, so I headed for the quiet waters as quickly as I could. As the night air grew colder, stiffening my relentlessly tired muscles, I realized that I'd spent five and a half hours fighting a losing battle against the current. I didn't know how much progress I'd made, but I assumed it wasn't much.

The kayak scrapped against the sand in a small, nameless bay, uncharted on my map. It was not pretty enough to sit and admire, but at that moment I could not have cared less. I wearily crawled out of the boat, happy to be on solid ground. I hadn't seen another person or boat for two days, but as a precautionary measure I strapped a knife around my leg and another around my waist. I had been warned of the bandits that roamed the wilds of Mexico. No point in taking any chances.

By the time dusk had fallen, and the light around me dwindled and then blew out like an extinguished candle, I was wet, exhausted, and more than a little frustrated. It was annoying to have traveled such a short distance, especially early on in my journey. For all of the effort and energy I'd spent over the past twelve hours, I figured I should be halfway to Central America by now. Surely it had to get easier.

Yeah, right.

I lit a candle, climbed into the tent, and brought out the map to study my course. It wasn't a very good map that I'd brought with me. A landlubber would have smiled, and a boater would have laughed or scoffed, whichever was to their liking, at the sight of the absurd little map I carried. I chuckled a little myself, but for now it would have to do.

As I squinted my eyes, adjusting to the light of the candle, I found myself looking at a Triple-A road map. Can you believe it? Beginning a 6,000 mile journey across vast stretches of ocean and shore, and I didn't even have a decent map.

I shook my head and laughed, remembering a line I'd heard someone say in a movie once: "Assumption is the mother of all screw ups."

Was that a premonition?

I figured, don't ask me how, that I'd gone twenty-one miles in two days, which wasn't bad. But it wasn't good, either. I lay restlessly awake on the hard sand that night and tried to keep myself from becoming discouraged. The weather had to get better, I told myself, and the tides had to weaken.

Surely, tomorrow would give me calmer seas.

FOUR
Continuing On With This Madness

The faint orange glow that crept across the sky at the horizon was like a mother awakening her child. I stirred from my sleep and rolled over, looking at my watch. It was 5:15 AM, Monday, September 16.

Brushing the sleep from my eyes, I climbed from the tent and stood up to stretch. When I extended my limbs I cried out in pain. I retracted quickly, sat down next to my kayak and gently rubbed my sore arms. My every muscle burned, not only on the outside, but deep inside the delicate tendons and joints that had borne so much work the day before. If someone had taken a sledgehammer to my bones I don't think I would have fared much worse.

The sand beneath was cool to the touch, and I lay back gingerly, stretching my back and willing my body to relax. The morning air was already starting to warm as I listened to the small waves pattering against the shore. I had no idea where I was, or when I would reach the next city, but for the moment I didn't care.

After a while I sat back up and looked out at the sea. Maybe I'd take it easy today, I told myself. What was the rush, anyway? I couldn't quite put a finger on it, but there seemed to be a dangerous undercurrent within me, causing me to always drive onward, relentless in the pursuit of success. It would go against my nature to hold back, but I knew I had to learn to pace myself.

I shrugged my shoulders and stood, cautiously stretching my taut muscles. The pain was still so great that I wondered if I'd last even a couple of hours, but as I looked again at the sea, it seemed to beckon me. There wasn't a whitecap in sight. Even the wind scarcely stirred, tempting me to continue.

A few deep breaths calmed my nerves. I quickly packed up my tent and belongings, and within a few minutes had shoved off, hunched over in the cockpit a little to ease the pain in my back and arms.

The water was calm and serene, almost like a huge lake. Yesterday's plight seemed a bad dream. Not knowing if the ocean would keep its peace, though, I began to paddle at a faster pace than the previous day, trying to gain as much ground as possible in case the weather decided to again turn sour.

So much for pacing myself.

Gritting my teeth against the pain, I paddled on. By nine o'clock I'd found my rhythm, and my muscles had warmed up and relaxed somewhat. I estimated my travel that morning to be around fourteen miles. The city of Puertecitos was a distinct possibility by nightfall. My frustrations were dwindling, my muscles increased their pace, and I felt stronger, mentally and physically, with every stroke.

Of course the weather would not remain calm. By mid morning the wind began to pick up, and in the distance I saw the tide, with its ominous whitecaps, returning. Ironically, the sky above remained a perfect topaz, without a cloud in sight. The seagulls adjusted slightly to the increase in wind, but continued to cry out in search of fish, as if nothing were the matter. Everything around me was unchanged and unmoved, as it should be on any normal day. Everything, that is, except the unexceptional strength of the incoming tide.

Today, however, would not catch me off guard. As soon as I saw the waves crashing several hundreds yards ahead of the kayak, I set about putting on and adjusting my spray skirt. It was fortunate I had reacted so quickly, because within minutes the first of the whitecaps began smacking the front of my bow.

The waves were a little smaller than they'd been the previous day and I was confident that I could maneuver past anything the ocean had to offer. The waves continued to toss me like I was a mere speck on its surface, but the skirt was doing its job and the cockpit remained relatively dry.

The current was so strong coming in that at times it felt like I was paddling up a river. Looking over my right shoulder, directly ninety degrees to the shore, I spotted a lighthouse perched on the rocks. I was about three miles off shore, and the water created an illusion that made it seem I had stayed in one spot now that I was going against the tide. Early that morning, when the tide had been going out, and I with it, the miles had seemed to fly by.

I looked at my watch and silently counted the hours, telling myself I would not look over to the shore until two o'clock. It was hard to avoid a glance over to the land that passed by, but I didn't want to be discouraged by the seemingly lack of gained ground.

After about an hour my head lowered slightly and my eyes narrowed. I was so focused on the waves ahead that I saw only one at a time. For the next three hours I paddled without stopping or looking around, keeping my head bent forward, lulling myself into a trance-like state with the continuous rhythm of motion my arms produced.

My mind began to wander. I thought of my friends, my home, and my family. The waves ahead fell slowly out of focus. Then even my kayak gradually faded out, like the dimmer switch of a light bulb, first gray, then hazy, and then black. I kept one eye on the ocean, while the other went subconsciously to my past, a trick I'd learned earlier while making trial runs in the Pacific Ocean. It was a good way to break the monotony of time and reflect on the memories that pushed their way to the surface of my mind . . .

* * *

The salt-filled air seemed to grow sour. I smelled the rank stench of cigarettes. Machinery hummed and clanked around me. As the scene grew clearer, I saw my boss walking directly toward where I sat, huddled on a stool. The look on his face told me I was in for another one of his tantrums. I sat back and braced myself, waiting for the coming abuse.

"I thought you were done with all these parts," Mike, my boss, yelled. "These needed to be done by this afternoon. I thought I told you that."

I looked up from my workbench into his anger-filled eyes, then back down to my desk, setting the piece of metal I'd been measuring down on its surface. "I'm going to get them done as soon as I can," I said slowly. "What do you think I'm doin' back here?"

"Why are they all different colors?" he asked. "These here are darker than all the rest."

"I don't know," I said. "That's just the way they're coming out of the machine."

"Well, can't you fix it?" he asked, but didn't wait for my reply. "You're probably going to tell me that you can't. It's out of your control, right? I don't give a damn about your college degree if you can't get these stinkin' parts right, do you hear me? You were supposed to learn all about this machine in training school. What in the hell did they teach you over there, anyway?"

I felt my neck turning red with embarrassment and anger. I clenched my fists, resisting the urge to hit him across the face. It would be easy. One punch and he'd be lying on the floor. I saw that he took a cruel joy in maligning my education. Just another typical day in the office. I hated it. Every day, for one reason or another, Mike would make me feel useless, even stupid. And recently the verbal abuse had turned personal, ripping into the girls I dated, the car I drove, even the vacations I took. I woke up every morning and dreaded going in to work. On that particular day, as he ranted and raved about the different colors of different parts, I would rather have been anywhere other than in that machine shop.

"Listen, Mike," I said as I stood up to look him in the eye. "I'm really getting tired of your coming back here."

"Just fix the damn parts. Can you do it, or have you not learned that much yet? Am I not making myself clear? Am I mumbling? Why can't I make it plain enough so that you'll do what I say?" And with that he threw the part down on the table and stormed from the room.

I stood there, shaking with rage. All I'd ever received from this man were insults. I was sick and tired of it, and I knew what I had to do.

An hour later, I asked Mike to come into the back room.

"Listen," I said, my voice surprisingly calm. "Things aren't working out. We're not communicating, and I certainly don't like the way you've been treating me lately. I think that I'm—"

"How have I been treating you lately?" he interrupted. "You're not being one of those extra sensitive types now are you? You gettin' soft on me?"

Ignoring this attempt to bait me, I continued, "Anyway, I think it would be best if I leave for a few days and think about my future here. I'm leaving today at noon. Okay?"

"That's ridiculous!"

"Of course you think it is. But I'm still taking off at noon. I'll let you know what I decide."

Seeing that I was serious, he said, "You don't have to leave at noon." He was calmer, his voice taking on a conciliatory tone. "If you want to leave, you can, but that's not the way to handle this situation. I don't see anything wrong with our working relationship."

Of course you don't, I thought, but held my tongue.

"I'll see you tomorrow," Mike said, walking away from where I stood.

"No, you won't," I said softly to myself.

I never set foot in that shop again.

The next morning I woke up relieved to realize that I wouldn't have to go back to work, back to where I'd felt lower than the dirt I swept off the floor. Back to a boss I'd grown to dislike so much. I picked up another job a week later. The previous job became a bad memory. Life moves on, I told myself. Or did it?

As time progressed, I found myself looking back at that situation and wondering if there'd been anything else I could have done. Maybe I could have been more patient, or found another way to get along with Mike. Anything other than quitting. I began to wonder if I'd really made the right move. Was I so insecure that I couldn't take a few harsh words?

I remembered what my grandmother had said upon hearing of my resignation. "Ben, don't you have more of a backbone than that?"

That hurt. Was I indeed spineless?

And I realized, then, while hypnotized by the rhythm of paddling on the open sea, that those words were at least part of the reason I'd taken on such a dangerous expedition.

To prove that I was not a quitter. To be able to say that I could tackle any obstacle without giving up and throwing in the towel.

There would be plenty of time to see if I was right.

* * *

A wave came over across the bow, slapping my face and stinging my eyes. Jolted, I looked ahead and brought everything back into focus. My arms were still moving forward. The art of paddling had become as natural as walking, requiring only a fraction of my brain to transmit the signals to keep going, at the same pace, same rhythm and strength.

I looked at my watch and saw that another three hours had passed. Time to take a break. Letting my muscles relax, I set the paddle across my lap, resting just inches above the swirling water. I looked over toward the shore and, to my surprise, spotted another lighthouse in front of me. I looked over my shoulder to see how far back the previous lighthouse stood, and realized, with a shock, that the one in front was the same one I had set my bearings upon some three hours before. I had not only failed to gain ground, I had gone backwards. Indeed, in the few minutes of rest that it took to realize this, the tide had already pushed my kayak backwards a couple of hundred yards.

Discouraged, I hung my head. Then I grabbed the paddle tightly with both hands and shook it in the air, resisting the urge to scream out loud with frustration and anger.

I prayed to God that he give me strength to overcome the current with new vigor. Again, I put my head down and paddled as hard as my weary muscles would allow. The blisters that had formed during the first few days had now popped. Blood and puss ran down my palms, mixing with the salt water and stinging the open wounds.

For another hour I battled the current. But finally, I was forced to give up, exhausted by my efforts. Still I had not reached the lighthouse, which had been so near and almost behind me that morning, some five hours prior. It was obvious that with the impact of the hurricane still being felt from the south, and increasing the tide's strength to greater limits, I would be foolish to stay out in the middle of the Gulf. Continuing on with this madness would only increase my frustration and waste my strength.

For the second time in two days, I reluctantly headed for shore.

FIVE
The Mighty Hand Of Nature

Because the tide was coming in, the waves for once were breaking in the same direction I was headed, and I neared the shore rather quickly. So preoccupied and distraught was I with the lack of progress I'd made that, if not for the abrupt difference the sound of the breaking waves made upon the shore, I wouldn't have seen the rocks that loomed ominously in front of my bow. At the last minute, I looked up to see the white foam dashing up and over the jagged faces of the rocky shore.

I fought panic and the urge to jump overboard, knowing that if my kayak were to be dashed upon the rocks, my trip and my life could possibly be over. Instead I swung the kayak around with all of the force I could muster, pressing hard against the rudder until it would turn no more. I dug my paddle furiously into the sea in the opposite direction as the waves thundered against the rocks. I tasted salt on my lips, joining with the bitter taste of fear on my tongue and the cold sweat of terror on my brow. My bow sliced through the charging breakers, and it looked at first as though I'd adjusted too late. But as the tide continued to push me toward the rocky shore, it seemed as though God Himself opened up a small stretch of sand among the rocks. The area of safety was a mere ten yards wide, but it was enough to maneuver my kayak through with only a couple of hard, jostling bumps.

As I felt the sharp nose of my boat cut through the sandy bottom, I clambered out of the cockpit and grabbed the front end, hauling it safely above the tide line. I was shaken but not hurt, thankful for my escape.

I looked out over the ocean and saw only the white tops of the thrashing waves. This was no place to be in a small boat, alone, and miles from the next town. I had been wise to turn in.

After securing the kayak, I fell to the sand beside it. The saltwater that covered my body began to dry. The sun reflected sharply off the sand and, despite its heat, a chill crept up my spine. Stunned by loneliness and the fury of the sea, and the thought of perhaps never again seeing home, I put my head in my hands and cried.

Once the tears came I could hold onto my pride no longer, and, after drawing my legs to my chest, I wept like a baby. Giant sobs wracked my body and I shook like a leaf in the cold November wind. I felt incredibly alone, tossed about at the expense of the mighty hand of nature, and powerless to stop the imminent fall.

With the progress I'd made earlier in the day having been nullified by the strength of the tide, I heard the words of several of my friends all at once: "You'll be back in a week. You'll never make it."

Maybe they'd been right. Maybe I had no business being out here on this great ocean. I felt as though I'd already failed. Nothing was working out as planned, and I surely didn't have the strength to travel for another week, let alone the next five months.

I began to hate myself for being proud. For taking on this miserable and lonely trip. What in the world had I been thinking? I wondered for a moment what would happen if, when I made it to the next town, I just called home and had one of my friends come and pick me up?

But then a stronger voice sounded, cutting through the weaker ones: *I am not a quitter.*

I'd taken on this trip and I aimed to finish it, no matter what the cost. I wouldn't throw in the towel after just a few days. Quitting now would prove the naysayers right. I'd begun this journey to search my soul, and regardless of the time, the sacrifice or the pain, there would be no turning back!

I stood up and wiped away the tears and snot that had accumulated on my cheeks. I let out a yell, shaking my fists at the sea and then pounding them furiously against my chest.

"No way!" I yelled. "You're not going to get the best of me. I'm not going to give up!"

I scolded myself for blubbering all over the place like a two-year-old.

"Are you some kind of a quitter?" I demanded as the unilateral conversation continued. "Absolutely not. Now is the time to put up or shut up. I can do this. I just need to pray." Then I quoted from the Bible: "I can do all things through Christ who strengthens me."

And with this I was able to get a hold of myself and get refocused.

I thought about the positives. I was alive and well. My boat was still in one piece, and even if it took me two years I was gonna complete this expedition.

After wiping away the final tear that had somehow loosened itself from my eyelid, I gave a halfhearted smile to no one in particular, except maybe the ocean, and wiped the sand from my shorts and legs. I looked around and for the first time noticed several houses up on top of the nearby hills. Most of them were boarded up and abandoned for the hot summer months.

I felt a strong urge to see something familiar. I was still lonely and in need of companionship, so I climbed up the steep sand dunes in the hope of finding someone to talk to. The houses were all empty, as I had suspected, but when I turned a flash of something shiny caught my eye. Three houses down, an old station wagon pulled up into a driveway.

With a cry of joy, I began to trot down the small cobblestone road that connected the houses, wondering what kind of people I was about to meet. Probably they didn't speak English, but I really didn't care. These were the first people I'd seen since leaving, and whether we could communicate or not I was confident that it would not matter.

I yelled out a greeting in Spanish, and the small Mexican family looked up in surprise. There were four of them—an older couple I assumed were the parents, and two boys. We greeted each other by shaking hands, and I told them as best as I could by pointing at the ocean and then to the kayak, that I was in the beginning stages of a long trip. Finally, after a few minutes of complete and utter miscommunication, I took out a newspaper clipping, water proofed by lamination, that showed me kayaking in the Harbor of Newport, California.

Finally, a big grin passed over the man's face and he grabbed my right arm, as if testing the strength needed for such a voyage.

Whether he was making fun of my puny arms or not, I smiled back and flexed a little.

I couldn't tell why this family was out on such a hot day, but it didn't matter. One of the sons, Abraham, as he'd given his name to me, motioned that we all sit down on the front porch, out of reach of the scorching midday sun. There were no tables or chairs, just the hard stone floor of the porch, but it felt cool to the touch and we spread out across the area in a random, haphazard way.

I could see the sons looking curiously at my light skin, and the dark blue tattoo, a crown of thorns representing Jesus on the cross, which streaked around my right arm. They looked to be about eighteen and twenty, Abraham being the older one, with tan skin and broad smiles. Their clothes were worn but modernized, and their stomachs were beginning to show the signs of good eating. It looked like I had run across a middle class Mexican family on a simple outing to the beach.

The mother wore a long dress made from a heavy cloth that must have been nearly unbearable in the heat. She smiled at me every time our eyes met, and I could tell she was not uncomfortable by my presence. Neither was the father, who wore a once-white cowboy hat that shadowed most of his dark, weathered face. Brown stains along the rim near the base where his skull held the hat in place, told of countless hours of hard work and sweat in hot weather. His hands, folded calmly around his knees, were knurled and callused, more lined even than his brow.

I'd heard all sorts of warnings about the native inhabitants of Mexico. Bloodthirsty bandits. Liars. Unfit for the civilized world. But as I would learn on that day and the months that followed, these were some of the nicest and most generous people I would ever meet. If an entire family had only one piece of bread they would divide it equally among the members present, including any strangers or guests.

When I'd stepped out of the kayak an hour earlier I'd strapped one of the knives I carried for safety to the back of my leg. My experiences during the next six months would destroy my preconceived prejudices against this country, and teach me to love this land and the people within. This family proved to be the first stepping-stone for the journey my mind took to release its stronghold of fear and disdain for a society I knew little about.

The first thing that Abraham did after I sat down on the patio was to reach in the back of the station wagon and pull out an ice cold quart of Tecate beer. It was the last thing I wanted to drink on a day as hot and as dry as this. I could still taste the salt water on my lips and tongue. But I didn't refuse. I didn't want to start off on the wrong foot by appearing rude.

We all settled down with our backs to the house and looked out over the sparkling blue ocean. The whitecaps continued their magical dance, and I was thankful that I wouldn't have to participate in their festivities for the rest of the afternoon.

After about an hour, Abraham's mother opened up the ice chest from which Abraham had earlier taken the beers, and pulled out a grocery bag filled with tortillas, *carne asada*, onions, and salsa. The father pulled out a grill, from where I could not tell, maybe from the front of the station wagon for it looked like something off of a '57 Chevy.

Feeling idle, I jumped up and helped Abraham haul the steel grill over to the sand in front of the house. Soon the smell of the cooking meat made my mouth water in anticipation. I hadn't eaten a hot meal in four days and couldn't wait to begin. There was plenty of food for everyone, the spicy meat washed down with more of the Tecate.

I had already guessed that real meals on the kayak would be few and far between, and I'd decided to thoroughly enjoy those that came my way. Aside from my other supplies, the food I carried in the front compartment comprised of more than two thirds of the load. I had enough food to last for three months, give or take a few days, and in order for it to keep without spoiling it all had to be dried. The food that I had brought on this trip consisted of 160 PowerBars, 64 Pop-Tarts, 100 servings of dried mashed potatoes, three pounds of trail mix, a pound of animal crackers, several bags of dried fruit, beef and turkey jerky, one loaf of bread to be eaten before the mold set in, Tiger's Milk bars, the occasional candy bar and a gallon of Gatorade. I also had a 10-pound box of vanilla flavored weight-gainer, a dietary supplement.

Even on the first day of the expedition, after eating three consecutive meals of the above-mentioned delicacies, I'd found myself daydreaming of home-cooked meals.

This meal with the Mexican family lived up to its expectations, enhanced by the scenery and the company, and I was happy to keep my share of the leftovers.

After we were finished with our plates, Abraham's mother cleared away the remains. His father then went over to the station wagon and, to my surprise, pulled out an old guitar. He sat back down next to me, tuned up the strings and began to play.

His voice was deep, rich and powerful, and I found myself lost in the music. My foot tapped to the rhythm, the mood in the air, stirred by the gentle breezes of the sea, was relaxed. Everyone was full, and the music seemed to blend with the sound of the waves below.

As the sun began to set, it struck me then how the simplest aspects of nature could make me happy. I thought back to the times in Los Angeles, where the water had been my haven and how it had quieted my soul. Now I again felt its gentle pull. I was being called back into the relationship we had once shared of joy, and not grief. I was quickly learning, though, that like most relationships, one of the two would have to take a bow sooner or later. I realized that it was I who needed the humbling. And though it was a newfound position, I accepted my role with a renewed mind.

SIX
There Were A Lot of Holes In This Plan

The variance between high and low tide on September 17 was still more than twenty yards. The night before I had tried to pull the heavy kayak above the watermark, but due to its weight, could only move it a few inches. I looked around for a tree or large boulder at which to tie the safety line that ran from the front nose of the kayak to the rudder in back, but all I could see was barren desert. I had no type of anchor and was worried that the tide would sneak up at night and steal away all that I possessed on this trip.

Subsequently, I ran the rope that was tied around the front of the kayak up to my tent, leaving a gap in the opening just wide enough for the safety line to run through. Inside the tent I tied the end of the rope around my leg so that if the tide came up suddenly in the night while I was asleep, I would feel the tug.

Indeed, that night the tide did come up past the original water line and I felt the rope cutting into my ankle, waking me up at once. I slipped out of the tent and pulled the boat several more feet above the tide and waited. Thirty minutes later the water had risen substantially and I had to move it again. This continued for a couple of hours, until the tide finally began to recede and I was able to go back to sleep, the rope still tied around my ankle.

When I woke up again, early in the morning, I felt hundreds of tiny bugs crawling all over my skin. I jumped out of the tent, ran down to the water's edge, and jumped in, scratching and rubbing my entire body. Some of the insects were on my scalp, in the stubble of hair that had begun to grow out, and it was several minutes before I was able to get rid of them all. I grimaced in disgust as I checked my arms and legs for signs of the pests that had probably slept better than I, warm and dry in the various crevices I had provided. I spat on the sand. I hated insects.

I walked back up to the tent and peeked inside. There were hundreds of little black bugs, slightly larger than fleas, crawling all over everything. My sleeping bag seemed to be the most concentrated area for their nesting.

After shaking out my sleeping bag and the inside of the tent, I packed them back into the storage compartments. I hoped that I had seen the last of the bugs. From then on, I vowed, I would be more careful not to leave a gap in the zipper flap of the tent opening. The bugs had either sensed the warmth of my body or had smelled food.

I shoved off with the ocean again smooth and calming, reassuring my soul. Without further incident I reached the small town of Puertecitos at 11:00 AM. The wind had begun blowing again from the south, and the sea began to grow restless, waiting for another dance with me.

This time I graciously bowed to my partner and allowed her to show off her power and majesty without me.

I pulled in among some jagged rocks surrounding the entrance to a bay and climbed ashore. Everything in the cockpit was soaked with water so I took all of the stuff out to dry. Saltwater had penetrated the supplies that were strapped along the insides of the cockpit. The two waterproof compartments, thankfully, were still dry, but in the end I had to throw away my safety manual, some batteries, food, two flashlights and one of the Triple-A road maps, the latter one not so much of a disappointment. This would be a common occurrence throughout the trip, the loss of supplies.

I sat down under a big palm tree and rested my back against its wide trunk. I looked out across the tiny beach to the small, U-shaped cove that stretched out a half mile to the ocean. Above the surrounding rocks of the bay stood the winter villas of Americans, each with windows overlooking the ocean. The quaint little town beyond was quiet, awaiting the return of the tourist season. A warm breeze ruffled the branches of the palm tree and the water lapped quietly against the shore.

The wind continued to blow from the south, but the sea had grown calm, as if disappointed by my lack of participation. I acknowledged this silence by nodding slightly in her direction, telling myself that tomorrow would be another day. Naturally, the first day I took to the shore early would be the day that she decided to grow silent.

I resisted the urge to throw everything back into the kayak and shove off. I needed to make a few phone calls, anyway. I was sure everyone back home was anxious to know if I was still alive. Hopefully there was a phone in this small town.

On board the kayak I did not have a VHF radio, a GPS or an emergency locating beacon, and in this remote area of Mexico, where the cities stretched out weeks apart from one another, finding a phone could prove to be difficult.

In order to somewhat ensure my rescue in case of an accident, Christian, my agent, and I had devised a plan. Every week I would call him to check in, and let him know my exact location on the map. We had identical maps, and I would tell him where I expected to be within a week's time. If he had not heard from me within a week, he would know the approximate location of where to send the Coast Guard to look for the wreckage or any signs of life.

There were a lot of holes in this plan, but it was the best we could come up with. One of the problems with our rescue plan was that there was only one Coast Guard ship the Mexican government employed on this coast that stretched for more than a thousand miles. Subsequently, if an emergency did arise, a week or two might be too late for a rescue. But, though I found all this out after the journey began, it gave me comfort to know that if I did get into trouble there would at least be some type of search and rescue attempt.

I took out another map, studying the next hundred miles of coastline. The map showed some detail, and I could make out that the coast ahead was rocky and barren. The next city, Gonzaga Bay, was fifty miles to the south. If the weather remained calm, and the tides receded somewhat, I hoped to make it there in three days.

The nearest phone after this, however, would be in Bahia de Los Angeles, past Gonzaga Bay. A long road ahead, as it were, with few beaches to rest on and fewer towns in which to get water. Better to wait, stock up on water, and leave the next day before sunrise. I knew that I needed to find a phone, but for the time being I sat back, turned on a small portable tape player I had brought along, put in a tape and closed my eyes.

SEVEN
The Dolphins Approached My Kayak Cautiously

Jay Panama—a nickname—was the only permanent, English-speaking resident in Puertecitos. He was quite a character—loud, lively, and sometimes obnoxious. He was also the only mechanic for a hundred miles around, so everybody knew the name Panama. After my nap I walked down a small dirt road and found him fixing a flat tire on an ancient school bus.

That night, I learned all about how Jay Panama had come to live in this tiny town.

Eleven years earlier, he told me, he'd come to visit his grandmother, who owned one of the villas overlooking the bay. After seeing the beauty and tranquility of the area, he never left. A machinist by trade, it was only a matter of time before he found his niche. Working on the local school busses and an occasional broken-down traveler's automobile, he became known as the local *taller*, or mechanic. He picked up the language and the women. Once settled into the community, he built a small shack from the remains of an old trailer. The garage, where he now worked on hundreds of cars a year, was in front of the house. This led to an open patio where he ate, drank, and slept.

Everyone in the town knew Panama. His was the place to go for gossip, a drink, or with a broken-down vehicle. He had seen a lot, you could tell it by his eyes. Some times they twinkled, showing some merriment he found that others didn't. Once in a while, I could see he was in another world, perhaps in some faraway place he had ventured across before.

At one time he'd traveled the world, living in Panama for three years, where he learned the language and found his dog. Ten years prior he'd hiked the entire Andes trail barefoot. His face was an ageless golden brown, with wrinkles only around the eyes, and a smile that showed just the right amount of teeth. With a beer in one hand and a wrench in the other, he told tales so numerous and wild that this book could not do justice to them all.

After visiting with him for a few hours, I walked back to the beach and crawled into my sleeping bag. A small family had set up a camping spot next to mine, and it was amazing the comfort and security I felt just knowing I was close to other people.

I fell asleep quickly, with all the companionship I needed.

* * *

The one phone in town had been out of service the night before when I'd gone to check. I decided to wait around for another day, and went to pay Panama another visit.

The day was September 18, which happened to be my birthday. I didn't really want to spend the day by myself. It was bad enough not being with my family. So I went up the dusty road to Panama's place and walked into the garage. He was sitting on the concrete floor beneath a giant yellow school bus, changing one of the front tires.

"Hey there, Jay," I greeted him, "How's it goin' today?"

"Same old stuff. How about yourself?"

"It's too bad you're working. It's my birthday. I wouldn't mind goin' out for a beer." I knew already that there were no restaurants in this town of about 200. I was teasing him and it had seemed a good way to inform him of the importance of the day. Important to me, at least.

"It's your birthday?" He pushed back his cap. "Well, hell. Hop in the car. We'll go down to Speedy's Camp, the only place in town for a beer. Work's a bore, and I always have time for a beer. Let's go."

Soon Jay had washed his hands, and with a pat on my back, we were off.

On the way we picked up one of Jay's friends, and a few minutes later, a half-mile down the dirt road, we turned into a driveway with an old wooden sign marking the entrance to Speedy's Camp.

Old Speedy himself, half blind and mostly deaf, served us from his wheelchair. There was only one selection. You guessed it—quart bottles of Tecate. After a while, more of Jay's friends dropped in and before I knew it we were at a table of twenty, drinking beer and celebrating my birthday. They didn't know who I was, but that didn't seem to matter.

But it wasn't really my type of party. When one of the guys stood up to drink half a pint of tequila in one gulp, I knew it was time for me to go. I sat there for as long as I could, then excused myself and left, unnoticed amidst the cries and shouts of the partiers.

I walked back along the road that led to the beach and stopped again at the only store in town. The phone was working, so I made the three phone calls that were on my agenda—one to my parents, one to Christian, and the other to Heather. Heather surprised me by saying that she wanted to come down and meet me along the way. All I had to do was name the day and the place.

With high spirits, I walked the rest of the way down to the beach, thankful that I'd not been forgotten back home and ready to get on with the rest of the expedition.

* * *

The next morning, Thursday the 19, I woke before dawn, stumbled out of my tent and, eyes still half-closed from sleep, jogged down to the water's edge. There were some rocks I had to jump over before reaching the water, and I wasn't watching where I stepped. As a searing pain shot through my left foot and up my leg, I almost fell flat on my face. Blood was already staining the rocks beneath my feet as I yelled out in pain, limping around until I found a place on the sand to sit.

I saw with dismay that a sharp rock had sliced through a hunk of skin on the big toe on my right foot, leaving a painful, gaping wound. I crawled back to where my kayak rested, and poured saltwater over the cut. I opened the emergency kit that was strapped behind the seat in the kayak and cut away the extra flap of skin that hung loosely. I wrapped the toe with gauze, a sterile pad and some surgical tape. The wound really required stitches, but there was nothing I could do about it here. I hoped that it would not get infected.

At 10:00 AM, Jay came down to see me off. I sat gingerly in the kayak. It was difficult to steer the rudder with my injured foot. I winced as the pain shot up my leg, but finally I was off.

* * *

The day passed without incident. The weather was calm. At 4:30 I spotted a school of dolphins in a small bay two hundred yards off to my right. I continued to paddle, veering slightly in their direction, and took out my waterproof camera. I set it on my lap and hoped they would be curious.

Indeed, they were the inquisitive type. They changed course to see what strange creature was in their territory. Prior to this experience I had been in contact with dolphins a few times, either from a boat or from the shore, but I had never before been this close.

At first the dolphins approached my kayak cautiously, but when it was evident that I meant them no harm, they came dancing toward me, keeping even with my pace. I couldn't believe how close they were swimming. It was an incredible feeling to be almost eye level in the dolphins' own wild and untamed environment. Chills rolled up my spine.

There were about two dozen dolphins in the school and two of them swam on my right hand side, so close that I had to watch where my paddle hit the water. I could easily have reached out and touched their glossy backs.

They would surface briefly and the sound and spray of their blowholes seemed to reverberate across the water, filling my ears with their noises. The rush of water grew louder all around as they continued to follow my course. Their eyes, intelligent and observant, stared intently into mine. The dolphins' powerful bodies, some more than eight feet long, effortlessly parted the waves as they surfaced, breathed, and dove again.

I continued my pace, my heart racing. I tried to take a few pictures, but without a zoom lens I was unable to catch the creatures in their fullest glory. After a while they decided it was time to play, showing off their speed and agility by performing different acrobatic feats. They swam faster, racing out in front of me, leaping from the water. With the best seat in the entire ocean, I was an appreciative audience.

Some would roll over on their sides, lifting their fins out of the water to hit the surface with a resounding *whack*. Others swam out in front of the pack, leapt from the water, then turned back to where I was still paddling. At the last second, before a dorsal fin could hit my bow, they would dive beneath the surface, leaving a little ripple that broke across my bow. I felt an occasional bump underneath as they nudged the boat's slick surface.

I continued to watch these magnificent animals in awe. It was as though time had stopped, and the only things left on earth were these creatures, the ocean, and myself. A type of communication arose between us. I found myself talking out loud in soothing, coaxing words to the dolphins that played around my kayak that wonderful evening.

That day, to me, was a gift from the sea and her Creator. A belated birthday gift, perhaps.

Eventually the dolphins grew tired of my inability to take part in their festivities, and they dove off toward the horizon in search of better company and food.

After they were gone I stopped paddling and sat back, reveling in the beauty I'd briefly been a part of. The water around me grew still. All I heard as I resumed my stroke was the quiet whispering of my oar slipping into the waves. The sun by now had slipped beneath the mountains and the sky was turning from a soft pink to a vibrant crimson red. The ocean seemed to freeze in time, holding its breath for what I was about to experience.

Suddenly, directly in front of me, the waters parted and a dolphin leapt clear out of the water, across my bow and dove beneath the surface on the other side. His breath and movements shattered the stillness and I started in my seat with a jolt. I stopped paddling, my body tingling with delight, knowing that in their own way, the school of dolphins had just given me this final gesture of grace as if to say goodbye.

I saw them no more that night, but the memory of that intimate experience will live within my soul forever. Just another page in the growing experiences I was allowed to take part in.

Amazing what could happen when one lets go of his own world, and dances with the raw beauty created by our Lord.

* * *

There was a storm mounting to the east and heading my way. I saw the dark clouds on the horizon, piling up on top of the other. In the last rays of the setting sun, the pleasure of my experience with the school of dolphins still lingered in my mind like the aroma of a fine wine. Dark shadows colored the clouds, foreshadowing the heavy downpour to come. I was still tucked into that small bay where I had waved goodbye to the last of the dolphins. The water was calm, but I knew better than to head out into the main channel at night with a storm on the rise.

It was dark by the time I began to set up my tent and lay out my sleeping bag. After securing the kayak to my leg by the safety line, I took a moment to look up at the sky and marvel again at the beauty of nature as thousands of stars winked down at me. I was miles from the nearest town, and a hundred miles from the nearest paved road. The solitude was complete. I was beginning to feel the effects of my loneliness, so I looked to the stars, lifted my hands and began to sing.

As I lifted my voice to the Lord, filling the air with my song, I felt God's presence with me, His hands on my shoulders. I sensed His angels, protecting me from danger.

He is good to me, I thought. *No matter what I do, or how often I displease Him, He is there, Faithful to the end. Protecting, guiding and comforting me.*

My eyes filled with tears and my voice trembled. Alone in that quiet bay, miles from nowhere, I was filled with the spirit of God, through the wind and the waves and the sky. No longer did I feel alone. My body seemed wrapped in a parental blanket of love.

What a sensation. Alone with just myself and God.

EIGHT
"Don't see many kayakers in these parts."

I woke up with a start. My watch read 10:10 PM. Everything outside was shrouded in darkness.

I lay still and listened, knowing that something had caused my sudden alertness. Forcing myself to breath slowly and deeply, I heard a sound, not five feet from my head, outside of the tent. Footsteps. Someone was out there, walking toward my kayak.

My heart beat faster and my palms began to sweat. I quietly unzipped my sleeping bag and, as slowly as possible, reached over and unsheathed my 12-inch Bowie knife. I sat up and looked out of the tent.

It took a moment for my eyes to grow accustomed to the dark. Standing beside my kayak was an old man, half naked and with very dark skin.

I gripped my knife tightly, waiting for something to happen. But the old man just stood there, looking at my boat. I told myself that he was just curious. When he turned around I saw that he was an Indian, probably from one of the migrating tribes that I had heard of, which roamed the mountains of Baja, California. He wore a heavy cloth around his waist, and his body was lean and bronzed, as though accustomed to traveling long distances and hunting for his food.

I relaxed a bit, and watched as he walked around the kayak, muttering to himself.

The Indian looked out across the water, and then up at the sky. He turned and glanced over to where my head was peeking out of the tent. It was hard to tell in the soft moonlight, and maybe it was something I imagined, but I thought he looked at me and smiled knowingly. He bowed slightly, and then walked away.

I waited for a few moments before climbing out of the tent. I walked down to where the Indian had been. Everything was still intact.

Eventually I went back to the tent and tried to sleep, but I was filled with the restlessness of one not fully accustomed to his surroundings. When sleep finally did come to me, it was filled with many dreams. Dreams of forgotten pasts, legends, and the people—some of them my own ancestors—who had once populated the earth.

In the morning, when I awoke, I wondered if the dreams had blended with reality and I had imagined the Indian. Rain had fallen during the night, and when I walked outside I saw several smaller footprints in the wet sand, leading away from my camp and back into the hills. I looked up over the mountains and waved farewell, knowing that he was out there, watching me and protecting his bay.

* * *

It continued to rain all through the next morning. Everything around me and inside of the cockpit was soaked. The air was warm, though, as was the water, so I didn't feel too cold. One good thing about the storm was that, after it released its fury and decided to move on, the water became quite still.

I took advantage of this break in our dance, and I felt it was my turn to take the lead. I made good progress that day and it was getting late in the afternoon when I realized, by spotting several small islands ahead, that I had traveled more than thirty-two miles that day.

The five islands provided shelter from the open Gulf, and to my right I spotted a beautiful little cove. I checked the map and saw that I was in a bay just north of Punta Bufeo. As I neared the shore, I looked down through the crystal-clear water, some of the clearest I had yet seen, to the sand below some fifty feet down. Fish were swimming around in all directions, scurrying about as my long shadow glided by.

The bay stretched around in a wide arc so that both points marking the entrance to the bay were parallel. On the south side of the bay a mountain cast shadows upon the water below. Beside the rocks were about twenty houses, all stretched out along the shore. All of the houses looked deserted except one, right in the middle of the bay. Its lights shone brightly out toward me. There were several *palapas* on the beach (umbrellas made from dried palm fronds) so it was easy to tie up the kayak for the night.

I settled in, the light of the nearby house offering its distant comfort.

* * *

I was beginning to fall into a groove. A rhythm, you might say. My muscles were adjusting to the grueling daily workouts, and I was learning to discipline myself in a way that maximized my time and effort.

A normal day would begin like this:

Wake up with the sun at 5:30 AM. Pack the tent and my other belongings in the dry compartments. Eat one PowerBar and drink a cup of water. On the ocean by six o'clock. Though I would be hungry and thirsty within a couple of hours, I wouldn't stop until ten, when I would rest for two minutes and have a few gulps of water so as not to get dehydrated. More paddling until noon, when I would jump out of the cockpit, swim around to cool off, get back in the kayak, and have lunch. At 12:15 I would begin again. At two I would take another swim to keep cool. Most days the temperature would soar to above ninety-five degrees. For the rest of the day I would paddle forward until I found a suitable place to spend the night, usually around six o'clock.

My muscles screamed in agony after only a few hours of paddling, and I would have to push through the pain, driving toward my second wind. It did take some getting used to, but by the end of the first week, after seven days on the water, I was rewarded by feeling less pain and more comfort with this regime. My body had adjusted for the most part.

That Saturday, the 21st of September, I went through my routine, warmed up my not-too-sore muscles, and headed out. The water was still clear and I looked down again at the curious fish that followed my progress. More fish were jumping out of the water all around my boat, and some of the wiser, earlier-rising pelicans were enjoying a good breakfast as a result.

The wind kept still until noon, after I'd rounded Punta Bufeo.

Daily I prayed that the wind would change, as it was as much of a detrimental factor as were the tides. For now the tide seemed to be going out only at night, while I slept. Unfortunately, that meant that when I woke up early in the morning the tide was already coming in.

I had been paddling against a headwind since day one, and was wondering if it would ever change. Somewhere in my studies before leaving I had read that the wind would start to blow from the north in November, so for now I just had to set my jaw and put up with it. Sometimes though, my frustration would mount as the wind and tide allied their forces against me. Often it was difficult to take even the smallest break for lunch, because if I stopped I would be pushed northward, away from my eventual destiny. I continued to wait for the wind to help, not hinder, and my patience was being tested.

I reached Gonzaga Bay in the early afternoon, and decided to stop there for lunch. There were several more houses here that all faced the water; there were even a few boats sailing about on the far side.

When the afternoon wind began to pick up again, I was glad to be out of the way and on the shore.

I easily found a *cantina*, one with large bay windows trimmed with whitewash paint. It was the first building I'd seen for a while that looked American, and it was a welcome sight. The white wooden boards and glass windows almost gave the restaurant a New England, countryside lighthouse aura. I was the only customer, but that didn't bother me.

I ordered three burritos from the cook and went to sit down in front of one of the large windows to look out over the bay. I had hoped to make it to Punta Final by nightfall, but was beginning to have doubts as the water grew increasingly restless and the wind howled. Inside the cantina, however, the air was quite peaceful. Bringing my hand to my face to feel the rough stubble of a beard unshaven for four days reminded me of the less-than-fine points of traveling on the ocean. The abrasive nature of the water so irritated my face while shaving that I only struggled through that process twice a week, and then only my cheeks and upper lip. I had decided to let my chin go unshaven during my trip. I had shaved my head again recently, however, so it wouldn't be a bother for another week or so. Sea salt clung to my skin like a parasite, and the numerous swims in the salt water only seemed to further open my pores.

When my burritos were ready I sat at the bar to eat them. They were delicious, and when I'd finished I ordered another Coke, ice cold and quite a luxury. My throat had long since forgotten the feel of a cool liquid beverage, and this one seemed to refresh my taste buds all the more.

The front door opened and two men walked in, one slightly older than the other. They sat down next to me at the bar. One of them leaned over and said, "Was that you coming in to the bay a while ago in that kayak?"

"Sure was," I replied.

"You want a beer or something?"

"No, thanks," I said.

"Where are you headed to?" the other guy asked. "Don't see many kayakers here in these parts."

They both looked like they had been in the sun too long. I would have mistaken them for Mexicans if they hadn't spoken.

"To Colombia or Ecuador," I said shortly, attempting to avoid a lengthy conversation. I'd made up my mind to leave despite the windy conditions, and didn't want to sit around hamming it up with these two strangers.

"Ecuador?" the younger man said. "You crazy, or what?"

"Yeah," his buddy broke in, pointing at me. "You're that guy that was in all the newspapers a couple of weeks ago up in LA. You were on the radio too, weren't you?"

"Yep, that's me," I replied. It didn't hurt my ego any that I'd been recognized way down here. Maybe it wouldn't hurt to talk for a little bit, after all.

"Wow. You got major guts man. How long you been out?"

"Just a week. I won't be through for another six months. Got a long haul ahead of me."

"Where are you from, LA.?"

"Fullerton. I did my training in Newport Beach."

"No kidding. I think I seen you out there in the bay. I have a house out on the peninsula."

Sure enough, that's where I had done my training. After a bit of talking, I excused myself to leave. They wondered why I was going out with the wind so strong, but I just smiled and said I couldn't let any moss grow under my feet.

As I walked toward the beach, I could feel how strong the wind had grown and wondered as well if this was such a good idea.

I got in my kayak anyway.

The waves pounded toward the shore and the wind blew furiously as I started to paddle parallel to the coast. My efforts were less than successful. The waves tossed me about and I made the mistake again of not putting on the spray skirt before the cockpit was half full of water. There was a point up ahead, just north of

Punta Final, that looked safe enough to camp for the night, but it was obvious, after a couple of hours, that I would have to put in sooner. I was tired, and the burritos I had eaten for lunch were starting to give me indigestion. Living the life of luxury did not mix well with the intensity of an expedition.

NINE
"Damn, son. You tryin' to kill yourself?"

As I got closer to land, I spotted a couple of guys sitting on top of an old Jeep, watching my progress. I dug in harder with the oars, wanting to look like I knew a little something about what I was doing. One of the guys, sitting in the driver's seat, had on a bright pink baseball hat. Before I had even landed, the guy in the pink hat jumped out of the Jeep and strode over to the shore I was headed for, a big grin on his face.

"I bet you're good and ready for an ice cold beer!" he shouted as he extended his hand forward, waiting for me to grasp it.

Oh, boy, I thought, *here we go again with this beer thing. Doesn't anyone drink water down here?*

"Sure I'd love one," I responded, contrary to my thoughts. By this time the other fellow had made his way over to us, and he shook my hand as well.

"Where in the hell did you come from in this thing," the guy in the pink hat asked.

"Damn, this is heavy," the other muttered under his breath as we all three grabbed the kayak and lifted it up onto the beach.

"Tell me about it," I said. "I have to haul this thing up above the water line every night I come in to sleep."

"Where did you say you came from?"

"San Felipe," I said proudly.

"Man alive! That's a hell of a long way."

"Where you goin'?" the other asked.

"Never mind about that, Gary, let's get this old boy a beer. I'm sure he'll tell us all about it over supper. You hungry ain't you? We got a place up here behind this first row of houses and we got plenty of food." He took off his pink hat and wiped his brow. "By the way, I'm Carl and this is my brother Gary."

"I'm Ben," I said and we all shook hands again.

"You got a safety line?" Carl asked.

"Sure do."

"Good. Let's tie it on to the back of the Jeep and we'll tow it up on the beach twenty yards."

We walked up to the Jeep and I saw that it was a real beauty. A white, 1940 Willys Military edition. Original engine, I was told. Gary had even welded a metal luggage rack on top, similar to the ones you see in the African safari tours.

Carl turned the key in the ignition and seemed pleased to hear the engine rumble. We pulled up the kayak, unhitched the rope, and slowly crested the nearest sand dune. Minutes later two trailers came into view. They were twenty feet apart, their foundations long since cemented by the blowing sand. Between them, beneath an awning that connected the two, were three chairs, a table, a stove, and a refrigerator. Fishing gear, tackle, poles and nets were scattered everywhere.

"Have a seat there, I'll bet you're beat," Carl said. "We saw you comin' in. Been watchin' you for about an hour. Seemed to be makin' good progress at the end. Wind's a bitch today. I myself wouldn't be out there even in my fishing boat. Too dangerous. Freak wave come up and all, knock you smack out of the water. You must be crazy."

"A little," I admitted.

"Where you goin' again?" Carl asked, obviously the more gregarious of the two. Gary seemed content to sit across from me and listen.

"Colombia, or maybe Ecuador," I told them.

Carl handed me another beer, which I really didn't want but took anyway.

"I been comin' down here since 1965," Carl said. "Hauled these two trailers here myself. That was a trip in itself, coming down these roads that ain't worth a tinker's damn. Every road that leads to this place is filled with holes and washouts. One time the rains were so bad that I had to wait three days before I could cross the river that had washed out the road. Gary here didn't want to have anything to do with it. Thank goodness we don't have to drive here anymore. Built an air strip out back ten years ago and have been flying down ever since. I been flyin' planes for as long as I can remember. That's my Cessna 172 out back. Flew in a couple of days ago."

"Where did you fly in from?" I asked.

"Up in Snelling, California," Carl continued. "I've got a landing strip at my house. Own two hundred acres of ranch land. Beautiful country. Pretty convenient to fly straight down. Don't have to deal with customs or any of the airport bull. Gary here flies too, but I do most of the flyin' when we come down here. Only when the weathers calm, though. Don't like takin' off when there's a storm headed. I've flown all the way down this coast and over to the mainland. By the way, where are you gonna cross over to Mexico?"

"I don't know," I said. "Maybe from La Paz, maybe from Cabo. Depends on how the weather is and such."

"Damn, son. You tryin' to kill yourself? Have you ever been down there? The water is so choppy at the point that some of the big boats avoid it. And you're in a tiny kayak. It'll take you what, four, five days to cross?"

"More like eight."

"You're crazy, you know that? You'll never make it. Storm comes up and you'll never be heard from again."

Thanks for the encouragement, I thought. I asked, "Well, then, what do you suggest? I got to make it over to the mainland somehow."

"Well now, let me see. Mind you, I am not tryin' to scare you or anything. I just don't want you to get killed. I've flown all over this peninsula so many times I can't count. Know it pretty damn good. One thing you're doin' wrong is goin' down the Baja side. It's good for us 'cause it's easy to fly down here, but for you it's all desert. No water. You could go for weeks without seein' anybody, a town, or even a boat. What do you do for water anyhow?"

"I usually carry five gallons on board. Depending on where the closest town is. The weight is a problem or I'd carry more."

"My point exactly. Can't carry enough water to go for more than a week, probably. That ain't much. Not out here. Baja is too desolate. It's a good thing you happened along our beach, I'll tell you that. We're goin' to set you straight, give you some good advice, and all the help we can. What've you got for maps?"

"Well," I said, kind of sheepishly, "from Acapulco on south I've got some really good navigational charts. But I figured the Gulf of California would be flat, like a pancake. So I've only got a Triple-A road map for these waters."

"A road map?" roared Carl, and Gary joined in the laughter. I felt like crawling under the table. "Flat as a pancake? Whoever told you that should be shot. Damn! Look here, I don't want to see you get killed or anything like that. It can be pretty dangerous out there, like you've probably already found out. Thank goodness you came to Punta Final tonight."

I was a little unnerved by all the carrying on that was taking place. Carl seemed to be rambling on a bit, and maybe he'd already had a few beers before I came along, but when I looked up I saw genuine concern in his eyes. I was shocked. I didn't know these people from Adam, yet they were worried about my well-being.

That touched me. These guys wanted to help, not just with words of advice, but also later on with any supplies that I requested. I felt an instant attraction to the generosity of these two brothers, and I imagined my brother, Peter, and myself years from now doing a similar adventure.

I looked to each one in turn and said, "Thanks. Really, I mean it. I'm glad that I met you guys today."

"It's nothin'," Gary said looking down at his beer, then getting up to get another. " You want another while I'm up, Ben?"

"No, thanks. But have you got any cold water? I'm dyin' of thirst."

"Sure, no problem."

"Its nothin' all right," Carl said as he went over to the refrigerator to see what food was going to be prepared that night. "Down here its different from the states. Gotta stick together, look out for each other and all that. Like I said, it's desolate out here. We got things and you don't. We'd be either selfish or crazy not to share it with you." Handing me a glass of water, he continued. "Don't take it personal, but I don't think you're quite prepared for this trip. A road map? Gary, you know where my son's extra aviation map is?"

"It's in the front trailer, I think. I'll go get it."

I drank the water. Ahh . . . much better.

"We'll set you up, Ben. I'll bet that water tastes pretty good, huh? I give you credit for takin' this trip. It takes guts to do something like this. I don't know if I would've tried it even when I was younger."

"I just like to go for the gusto, I guess. By the way, how did you get this water so cold?" The water was even colder than the Coke I'd enjoyed earlier.

"Propane. That's the key down here. Everything we got runs on propane. Stove, refrigerator. Keeps everything cold and its not expensive. You got that map yet, Gary?"

"Here it is," Gary said, coming out of the trailer. He walked over to where we sat and spread it out on the table.

"Lemme see," Carl said opening up another beer. "We're here, Punta Final. You know why they call it that? Because its the last point of habitation of any kind until Bahia de Los Angeles. Well, except for Calamahue Fish Camp around the corner. But I mean, that's *it*. Nothin' but rocks along the coast. Not one beach. Mountains fall into the sea like they've been sheared off with some great big knife. After that it doesn't get much better, and the tides finally start lettin' up past the Bay of Conception. I know. I've flown over it a hundred times, haven't we, Gary?"

"Yep, sure have. You've said that already about a hundred times," Gary said, rolling his eyes and giving me a sidelong glance.

"Well, don't get snappy. And remember, Ben, no water. That's the key. Look here," Carl said and pointed to a couple of tiny islands that stood out in the middle of the Gulf. "I think it would be best if you cross right here, that way if things get bad, a storm comes up or somethin', you can head for the shelter of these islands. You know what a chubasco is?"

"Nope. What is it, a shark?" I said, laughing.

"No, it's a gale," Gary said. "A hell of a wind that can come up out of nowhere, without any warning. Sixty-knot winds. Blow your kayak right out of the water. The wind comes up any time, but usually in the summer and fall. In other words, right now. You don't want to get caught anywhere, especially in the middle of the Sea of Cortez, when that sucker comes up."

"So you think I should cross here?" I pointed again to the islands, getting his focus back on the map.

"Positive. We even go across that way when we're flyin' down to Puerto Vallarta, and we bring plenty of water, too. Here, study this map for a while, I'm gonna go make dinner. You hungry? I bet you are."

I nodded readily and then looked at the map. It really wasn't much better than my road map, but I appreciated the gesture. It didn't have one topographical feature and only listed the cities with airports. What I needed here, I realized, were the same types of charts I had for the southern part of the route. The kind that listed depths in fathoms, as well as currents, beaches and harbors.

I studied the map anyway, and then looked over at Gary. He sat there, silently sipping his beer and looking at the map once in a while. Carl was busy clanging pots and pans together and making supper so I decided to pick Gary's brain.

"You like it down here?" I asked.

"Oh, sure. It's the place to go to get away from everything."

"Are you married?"

"Yep. Same wife all these years. Got two kids as well."

"Do you live near Carl?"

"Close. A place called Linden, California. I own a hardware store there."

"Do you live on a ranch like Carl? You got an airstrip too?"

"No to both questions. But I've got two acres of land with cherry trees and a walnut grove. Its beautiful country, just like Carl said."

"Sounds like it. I love the countryside. Growin' up in Tennessee, I had to. I'll have to go up there after I finish my trip and visit you two."

"You damn well better," Carl shouted from the stove, where he was cooking. "If you make it through this trip in one piece, I'll come pick you up personally in my airplane. You can count on that."

Before long, dinner was ready. Chicken with lemon and other spices, grilled on the open flame grill, with beans, corn and bread. Carl was definitely a good cook.

I ate everything in front of me and then ate the legs of the table I was so hungry. It was amazing how good the food tasted and how much I could eat after a week and a half of dried fruits and nuts. The plates were cleared and we continued to talk about the best place to cross, where to get water and so on. Carl again reminded me that the mainland of Mexico had a lot more cities and pumped water. In the end he was beginning to convince me.

After a while he got up and brought out a large block of ice. "Where's a knife when you need one? I need some ice cubes for my after dinner drink."

"I got one," I said, pulling out a knife that was clipped to my shorts. I had been given a couple of knives from a hunting buddy, Dave McShane, before I left. They were terribly sharp, probably the best knives I'd ever seen and I was very proud to be their owner. Later, on my trip, the knives would begin to feel the wear and tear of use, and the salt water didn't help in keeping the rust away, but for now they were as sharp as razors. I opened the knife, displaying its edge in the candlelight.

"Looks sharp. Here cut this piece," Carl said.

I brought the knife down quickly and it cut through the hard surface of the ice like butter.

Carl held the ice steady with both hands. He said, "Give me a couple more chunks."

I did it again but this time the knife slipped and I cut more than just the ice.

"Yow! Son-of-a-bitch!" Carl yelled. "You about cut my finger off!"

He jerked his hand back and covered it quickly with a towel. I hadn't felt anything, and at first I wondered if he was joking. But I had underestimated the sharpness of the knife. Carl held up his hand to the light and a large stream of blood spurted sideways. The knife had cut through the skin and nicked a vein. He was bleeding badly and all I could do was just stand there, helpless. I felt like a real jerk. After all of his help, this was my way of repaying his kindness?

"Oh, man," I said. "I'm so sorry. Are you all right? Carl, I'm sorry, man. I didn't mean to. It just kind of slipped. Is there anything I can do?"

"Yeah, take off in that kayak of yours before I take that knife away." He took a deep breath. "No, just kidding. I just need to put a bandage on this. It looks like it really needs stitches, but that'll have to wait until I get back to the states."

He ran into the trailer and to the bathroom, still holding his towel-wrapped hand. He soon had the finger taped up but the wound was deep and continued to bleed. I felt terrible and could not offer enough apologies.

"No real harm done," he said, "But if you don't shut up and quit apologizing I'm really gonna get mad. Join me for a drink, and see if you can cut off a few more ice cubes without taking off my other hand."

I put my knife away and sat down to have that after-dinner drink, which I found I needed badly now.

The rest of the night was uneventful. By the time we got ready for bed the two brothers had piled up several items that they said I would need. They gave me thirty feet of floating line, two gallons of fresh water, maps, a twenty-pound test fishing line, and different kinds of sinkers and lures. Even some good luck trinkets.

I removed the gauze from around my big toe that had gotten cut. Carl had insisted that we look for signs of infection. There were none, but because the wound was not getting enough air it had not healed much. The skin was a ghastly white where it had been denied oxygen, and the wound continued to gape in an unsightly manner. We cut some of the dead skin away, and then poured alcohol on the rest of it. Then Gary gave me a pair of his own socks to protect the toe.

We settled in under the stars, Carl, Gary and I, on army cots. I felt satisfied from eating such a good meal, and at having made two new friends.

There was one more troubling incident in my stay with Carl and Gary. After falling asleep, Carl began to mutter. At first it was sort of funny. He'd drunk a lot that night. But soon his tone of voice became louder and more commanding. When I finally could understand what he was saying, his words sent chills up my spine.

"Ben, don't go," he said loudly, thrashing about. "Don't cross over to Mexico . . . don't go. On the second island, Ben . . . you're going to die. Death is waiting for you." He muttered something else incoherent, but that was enough to strike fear into my heart.

In the morning, I tried to put this behind me. Carl once again prepared a meal. After cleaning our plates and packing my new supplies into the kayak, Carl turned to me and said, "Are you in a hurry to get out of here?"

"No, not really," I said hoping that they wanted me to stay for another day. I needed the rest.

"Let's go out into the desert. What do you say Gary? We haven't been up to Los Palmas for a while. Let's take Ben out there and show him the palm trees and everything. Should be a good time of year to go, now that it's cooling off a bit."

"Sounds good to me," his brother said cheerily. "I'll make some sandwiches and pack the cooler full of ice and drinks."

It sounded good to me too, and I readily accepted the offer for a free tour.

In an hour we had everything packed and ready to go. We hopped into the old Jeep and took off. We took a dirt road that was just as bad as Carl had said it would be, a road that at times was almost invisible. We bumped and rattled straight across the desert floor, dodging bushes and cactus that appeared in our path. Thirty miles in, we neared the end of the barren plains of sand and slightly populated Joshua tree forests, and began to wind up through a canyon, with rock walls shadowing the road on either side.

The Jeep continued to find its way on the loose gravel and sand, and I was glad to have a couple of "natives" as my guides.

Eventually, after my butt and back had grown sore, Gary pointed ahead at what looked like a hundred palm trees sticking out above the other vegetation, Clustered together, they were a stark contrast to the canyon walls, which spread out accordingly to make way for the uncommon oasis within.

The meadow that spread out beneath the palm trees converged at the end, on a well, still used by the Indians, ranchers, and wild animals. The water stood in the middle of the great trees, some of which were more than a hundred feet tall. A makeshift barbed wire fence surrounded the well, discouraging the larger animals from getting too close, eliminating the possibility of a fall and a drowning that would poison the water source for the others that depended on it for their livelihood. An irrigation trench had been dug from the upper reaches of the well to another trough, fifteen yards away, allowing for another puddle of water to form for the other animals.

Carl pointed past the well, up the rugged mountains that rose sharply above our heads, to a summit that reached above the clouds. He told me that was where the original source of spring water began.

"There used to be a mission up there, when the Spaniards came and tried to convert the heathens. Ruins still remain, I hear, but it's an eight-hour hike straight up the mountain's face. There's supposed to be another spring up there too, with birds and all that. Sometimes even from here in the valley we can see the bighorn sheep climbing across the rocks. Wish I had the stamina to make it up there. Supposed to be quite a place, and hardly anyone knows about it 'cause it's so remote. Most of the year it's too hot to even think about."

I looked up, imagining the missionaries of long ago. What a hardship that must have been, to live in the middle of the desert, isolated from civilization. Much like this journey of mine, the spiritual strengthening must have been immense. We stayed for a couple of hours, ate lunch and then headed back.

It was late in the afternoon when I took off in my kayak, but I didn't mind the delay.

I paddled out with a different attitude than I'd come in with less than twenty-four hours prior. Up to that point my thoughts had been focused only on myself. How many miles I had to make each day, the books I was going to write after it was all over, my safety, my supplies, my time, my strength, and my courage. I'd come into Punta Final worried about the intensity and duration of the expedition, and how quickly I could get it over with, instead of worrying about my own personal fulfillment, enjoyment, and satisfaction in undertaking such a trip. I'd been losing sight of the forest for the trees.

Yes, it was mandatory, to a degree, to think about my safety, lest I risk personal injury, and about keeping up the pace, lest I get distracted and quit short of my goal. But it had become an obsession to cover as much ground as possible, with no more regard for the little pleasures and relationships along the way than I would have had working forty hours a week in a job in Los Angeles. I had begun to attack this challenge with the same mundane enthusiasm I would any everyday chore.

But after being embraced by the friendship of Gary and Carl, I was like a spring flower blossoming in the desert, and beginning to sense a change in myself. They had given their time, their efforts, their energy, food and shelter without expecting anything in return. I was suddenly filled with guilt for having wanted only to receive. It was time to look outside of my pride and self-focus, and seek out the needs of others.

I wanted to do more. I wanted to enrich other people's lives knowingly and substantially by putting forth that effort and sacrifice, enabling others to benefit from my gains. I made a mental note then to lessen the focus of my own accomplishments, and to be aware of other's needs and desires and dreams.

I turned the kayak around, pausing to look back upon the two brothers who stood on the shore, still waving goodbye. They had done everything in their power to assist me in my quest for safety, and I would be grateful to them forever. What they didn't know, however, was that they had helped me in a way far more beneficial to my mental health than anything physically listed among my supplies.

I smiled and waved back. This would be the first among a string of many such events that would interconnect with my own personal goals, increasing the satisfaction of this expedition and leaving all parties involved fulfilled with the knowledge that they had come away from the encounters with a broader focus on life, and the memories of an untainted, untouchable experience.

TEN
I Could Hear The Sharks In The Water

That night, after leaving Carl and Gary, I reached a small village that the locals called Calamahue Fish Camp. There were several sharks swimming around in the shallow waters near the small beach. The beach rose steeply from the water, at an angle of almost forty-five degrees, making it impossible for me to haul the kayak above the high tide mark. I could not even carry the entire kayak out of the water, so the lower half still rested in the sea. I looked for a rock or tree with which to tie the safety line to, but there was nothing in sight.

Among the various supplies that Carl and Gary had given me was an empty bucket, which they'd said to fill with rocks, giving it enough weight to act as an anchor.

I tied the safety line of the kayak to the handle of the bucket, and, filling it to the rim with rocks from the beach, dropped it into the gentle surf. On the other end of the kayak I tied another rope and climbed up the beach, wrapping it around a rock no larger than my head. I went to bed without much worry.

Fortunately, the rocks beneath my tent provided a restless sleep, and I woke up several times during the night. Just past one o'clock I woke again, instinctively listening for the sound of the Kevlar hull of the kayak gently scrapping against the rocks. I heard nothing. Sitting up in the tent, I unzipped the flap and looked out. It took a while for my eyes to adjust, but when they did I was shocked. The beach where I thought the kayak had been just two hours earlier was now empty.

I threw back the flap and stumbled out to the beach. Cursing beneath my breath, I half slid, half ran down the steep slope of the shore and across to the water's edge. As my eyes continued to adjust to the moon's pale illumination, I wondered what would happen if I'd lost my kayak.

My trip would be over, that's what.

I had assumed that the makeshift anchor would hold, but I'd been wrong. How could I go back to LA now, having botched the trip and missing my final destination by about, oh, let's say 5,500 miles?

Frantically I looked out over the water, in the hope that a glint of moonlight on fiberglass would show me the kayak.

Then, just when I began to despair, my eyes caught the faint silhouette of an elongated shadow, some fifty yards out in the middle of the bay. Flooded with relief, I recognized the shape of my kayak.

At that same time, I had a vivid mental picture of the sharks that had been swimming about in the bay when I'd paddled ashore hours earlier. I knew that when the fisherman brought their catches home from a day of fishing, they cleaned the fish on the shore, throwing the guts and other remains out into the water. Sharks, other fish, sea gulls and even a few crabs would wait all day in anticipation of this free meal.

I stood on the shore, wondering what to do. I had to act fast, but I could hear the sharks in the water, giving me cause for hesitation. Finally I let out a yell, hoping that this predatory scream might frighten away some of the closer sharks and bolster my own courage.

I jumped into the water.

I'm sure I swam faster than I ever had in my life. I made it a point to thrash about as much as I could, yelling as I paddled, hoping the movement and noise would turn away any predator. There were a few times when I felt something brush against my legs, and once I kicked hard and felt something as rough as sandpaper against my foot. My heart was in my throat but I reached the kayak unscathed and pulled myself up into it, gasping for breath.

I was still scared, sitting atop the kayak in the middle of the bay on this moonlit night. I was angry with myself for again taking the tide so lightly. I pulled up the bucket full of rocks and cut the line with my knife. So much for that bright idea.

In my haste to retrieve the kayak, I'd forgotten to bring out my paddle. Lying down flat on the bow, I paddled with my arms, like on a surfboard, back to shore.

My sleep was restless for the remainder of the night. I woke every few minutes to check on the kayak and my belongings.

* * *

Baja, California is a vast expanse of desert, rocky mountains, and unprotected beaches. For the most part it's uninhabited, unlike the mainland of Mexico, especially in the Southern region, which boasts of lush tropical rain forests, coconut groves, and sugarcane plantations. The peninsula of Baja is without a constant supply of fresh water. Desolate stretches of coast cover the inside area of the Gulf of California, also known as the Sea of Cortez. Few boats enter north past Bahia de Los Angeles because there are few cities and ports with which to stock up on fresh water and supplies.

Along the Sea of Cortez, the uninhabited, sparsely vegetated mountains of rock come tumbling down to the water from a thousand vertical feet. Boats find these stretches particularly hostile, with no room to cast anchor.

The area of coast between Calamahue Fish Camp and Bahia de Los Angeles is no exception to these hazards. The desert that stretched beyond Punta Final gave way to rugged stone mountains. The sight of these mountain ranges was intimidating. I found there to be not one single beach between the two points, only endless rock wall, some seventy-five miles in distance.

Looking at my Triple-A road map I could tell this was going to be a tedious part of the journey. I left earlier in the morning than usual, hoping to get as much of a head start as possible. Perhaps, I thought, I could cover the seventy-five miles in three days. There would be little time for sleep, drifting about in the open Gulf, and I would have to stay awake to take note of the currents and the possibility of drifting into the rocks. I had tried to prepare myself mentally for parts of the trip like this, but there was really nothing I could have done to be ready.

The first day was uneventful. By nightfall, however, I was exhausted, having put in fourteen hours of paddling. My neck was so stiff that I could barely turn around to retrieve the parachute anchor that would help deter the dangerous currents at night. The currents here were still too strong for the anchor to fully do its job, and I forced myself to stay awake for another two hours. Those were the longest two hours I had spent so far. My body cooled down rapidly in the night air, and my muscles cramped painfully.

The moon had not come out yet, and the surrounding blackness seemed to swallow the sea and my kayak along with it. The tall figures of the mountains above looked like giants. Every sound was magnified, and the smallest noise, even the break of a wave, made me jump. Several times I imagined I saw sharks, larger than my kayak, glide by.

At eleven the moon finally came out, forcing back the shadows. My eyelids were heavy, and I drifted off into an uncomfortable sleep, cramped in the cockpit. Before long my body had cooled down enough that I woke with a start, chilled and exhausted.

I paddled ahead for a while, embracing the madness that seemed to come with the uncertainties of the night. Eventually, too tired to lift the paddle for even one more stroke, I climbed out of the cockpit, and lay down on the flat bow of the kayak. After a bit of a struggle, I wrapped the rope and two bungee cords around my body, allowing for enough stability and security to close my eyes and sleep.

After an hour I woke once again, and unstrapped my body from the kayak. I had drifted a considerable distance from the shore. I paddled closer until I was satisfied with my location, strapped myself again to the front of the bow and fell asleep. But I was more restless this time, hearing the crash of waves upon the rocks, and I woke again after only a few minutes.

It was a miserable night. I lost track of the number of times I'd tried to sleep only to be jolted awake again. By morning, and the first glimmer of dawn, which rose above the eastern horizon, I was too tired to move, and I wondered if I would have the strength to eat.

But the rising sun brought with it the warmth and promise of a new day. The nightmares vanished, my sanity returned, and I could feel the rumblings of my stomach, ready for nourishment. After a delicious meal of two PowerBars, a bag of dried oatmeal, and water, I felt strong enough to continue, passing by the endless cliffs and faceless mountains.

* * *

The next night passed in much the same way as the one before, the nightmares and visions gleefully returning to haunt my mind and slow my progress. It was hard to tell at times if I was awake or asleep. Reality slipped from my grasp, and into darker shapes. When the new day came, it was harder to awaken from my trance. But eventually the sun cast away even the darkest shadows, and I felt foolish for entertaining the ghosts of the night.

ELEVEN
They'd Set Sail, Leaving Everything Behind

That day was harder than the last as exhaustion and fatigue set it. I knew that my muscles could not take much more abuse without resting. The lack of sleep also seemed to slow down my mind, and the minutes and seconds crept by. Twice that day I fell asleep while I sat in the cockpit, but it didn't matter much. I was afraid that I would not make it to the next city by nightfall. With the sun setting again, I could hardly bear to face another night alone.

I had no idea where I was. There were numerous coves, points, and cliffs that discouraged my calculations as I looked at my map, trying to locate my whereabouts in this maze of camouflaged wilderness. The sun was still casting its last bit of light over the mountains when I looked ahead and saw a break in the coastline. My heart leapt with hope, and ignoring the pain in my muscles, I paddled furiously. An hour later, I passed by the lighthouse that stood guard over the entrance to the Baja de Los Angeles. It was welcoming me into its quiet haven.

With relief, I saw the lights of houses and parks emerging one by one, like a string of Christmas lights. I could hardly believe it, but realized that I had made the seventy-five miles in three days.

There were a few sailboats anchored on the far side, and it was there that I made my way to beach my weary body. I could hardly see the waves in front, but the lure of solid ground beckoned. A warm meal, some company, and a good night's rest spurred me on past the sailboats and onto the beach.

One of the fishermen who sat along a stone wall came over to help me pull the heavy kayak on to the shore. Directly in front of me lay three cottages, which looked like rental units. The one to my left appeared vacant, the one to my right showed two men on the front porch, drinking beer. Much like Goldilocks, I found the last one to be just right. On the front porch was an older man, sitting in a chair, reading a book and drinking a cup of coffee.

I walked up to him and said hello. I told him quickly about my adventure, and asked where I could get a good meal.

"Well, we're from San Diego," he told me. "Down here fishing every day."

Three other men, all about the same age, came walking out of the front door of the cottage.

"I'm Roger," the first man said, "and this is Don, my brother Karl, and Phil."

We shook hands all around. They invited me to stay for supper, and I gratefully accepted.

"Do you happen to have a glass of water? I'm dying of thirst," I added.

"We got plenty of that," Phil said, and grabbed a cup off the shelf. He poured some water out of a twenty-gallon container that stood on the stone porch railing. "I've got a good map in the trunk of the van," he continued," I want to see just exactly where you've come from."

As I showed Phil and Roger the places I'd been, Don filleted the fish they had caught earlier and fried them in a skillet. The smell passed through my nostril and made my stomach rumble.

"Now, we want you to stay for dinner, all right?" Phil said. "We'd be honored to have you here."

"I'd be honored as well," I said.

Again, men willing to share what they had. God was continuing to bless me, providing points along the way for people to greet me and welcome me into their company.

I liked Phil. That night and through the next day we talked about the ocean, our faith and our families. Phil had a son about my age, and even though our time together was short I felt another bond forming as my respect for him grew with the passing hours.

Phil reminded me of my grandfather, and this took me back to a better place in time. A time when everything seemed to be going well, and my life had focus.

Years earlier I had spent a summer in Whittier, California, as an intern in the company that my grandfather had started in 1957. It was during that summer that my grandfather and I formed a powerful bond. Those were memorable times and some of my happiest in California. We'd sit and talk for hours every day after work on the porch swing by the side of the house. Grandma would bring us sodas and snacks. We studied blueprints, the backbone of the machines that the company owned. I hadn't known the first thing about blueprints at first, but my grandfather's patience and kindness motivated me to learn how to read the prints without error.

After graduating from the University of Tennessee, I had moved out to California to one day take over a business that my uncle owned. At least that was the excuse I gave. Looking back on that, I realized later it was my grandfather I was moving close to, and not the job.

The summer of 1993 seemed to hold the promise of a new life, moving close to the two things I cherished most: the ocean and my grandfather. Grandpa was nearly eighty, but I thought those times would last forever. He was my best friend in this new environment of financial responsibilities and hassles, and I confided everything in him.

In December, he began to weaken. Then came that fateful evening, as I was leaving to go out, that the phone rang. I picked it up and heard that Grandpa was in the hospital. He'd suffered a heart attack. I hurried to the hospital and sat beside his bed. Grandpa died later that night, with me still holding his hand.

My best friend was gone.

As I sat and visited with Phil and his friends, I was able to let go of some of the grief I still carried with me.

* * *

The next day was a day of rest and I took the opportunity to stock up on water and other supplies. I had made good time coming into the bay and was ahead of schedule.

That night I made some phone calls, again assuring everyone of my safety and whereabouts. Most importantly I told Christian Serino of the changes in route, so that if need be he could send out the coast guard. I now planned to cross from San Francisquito, a point forty miles south of the bay where I was.

I was sad to see the four older men leave early the next day. It was becoming a ritual, to make new friends only to have to say goodbye. I wondered if it would be better not to come ashore at all.

I knew that these thoughts were damaging my mental stability. I'd only been gone for twelve days, but it seemed so much longer. In looking at the map in front of me, I took some comfort in seeing the ground I had already gained. The distance ahead, though, seemed overwhelming, and I wondered how I could possibly survive in the months to come.

* * *

The next day, September 26, I started out early, but a mile or so out a ferocious wind came up and drove me back to the shore. I was only a couple of hundred yards south of where I had slept the night before. Eventually the wind died down, but the day was already spent and I could not hope to leave before the next morning.

I quelled the frustrations I felt at being forced to take another day of rest. I was still a day ahead of schedule. Yes, that was the ticket, I told myself, taking a deep breath. Slow down and enjoy this trip.

The sun was about to set when there came a sailboat, forty feet in length. It set anchor in the bay close to where I sat. I watched intently as the crew, a man, his wife and their baby, stepped on board a motor-powered dinghy and headed for shore.

Stuart, Dee, and Coral, their six-month-old daughter, were making their way down the same coast as I. Stuart was from Australia. They were planning to go by Costa Rica and through the Panama Canal, hoping to end up next year in the Bahamas. The couple had spent several years saving their money to buy a boat and sail around the world. They had set sail from Vancouver early the previous year in search of warmer waters and weather. Unexpectedly, the day before the departure, Dee had learned that she was pregnant. Without hesitation, they'd continued their plans and begun their adventure. They'd set sail, leaving everything behind.

They were only in the bay for one night to pick up supplies of food and water. I went to the town with them, helping them carry their groceries and enjoying the time to talk. I could only imagine the added difficulties of doing the simplest chores, with the presence and wanted attention of a baby. They told me they planned to cross the gulf to the very islands Carl and Gary had insisted I head for.

Over dinner, I asked, "What would you guys think about us leaving together? We could go over to the islands at the same time. I had planned the same route you're taking, and I could use your help if things got rough."

"That's an idea," Dee said.

But Stuart scowled. "I don't think you'll have any trouble. The weather is supposed to be smooth for the next couple of days."

He didn't seem to want me tagging along, but I pressed on. "Yes, but I'd feel much better if I had an escort along the way. At least for a little bit."

"I think it would be lovely," Dee said before her husband could say anything else. "We'd love to have you with us, right Stuart?"

Stuart still seemed reluctant, but I assured him that I would not be an intrusion. I'd eat my own food, sleep on the kayak, and they'd hardly know I was there.

My eagerness to tag along with Stuart and Dee stemmed, in part, from what had happened when I'd stayed the night with the brothers, Carl and Gary. The words of Carl's nightmare, "You're going to die," had stayed with me. Not normally a superstitious person, I couldn't help but be uneasy.

Now, sitting in that tiny restaurant in the Baja de Los Angeles, I felt an urgency to accept Dee's offer of safety. In the end they both consented. I headed for my kayak and they for their dinghy. Then Dee insisted that I come aboard their boat to sleep, and I hesitantly accepted.

I lay down on the cushions nearest to the steering wheel and closed my eyes, wondering if Stuart and I were going to get along. I hated to impose. My last thoughts before sleep were comforting, and I told myself that if things got uncomfortable between us, I would just leave and go it alone.

TWELVE
"And the moon shall be turned to blood."

The *Running Shoe*, the sailboat that belonged to Dee and Stuart, was a forty-foot craft trimmed in blue and white. It was a pretty boat, not too big. The galley had a small kitchen with two stoves, an icebox, and a sink. To me it seemed a paradise. In the front of the boat were the captain's quarters, with a queen-size bed. The cabin was littered with books, charts and pictures of friends and family long since left behind. It was a well lived-in boat, and I felt at home immediately.

On deck, Stuart had all kinds of fishing equipment, scuba gear and a wind surfer. We prepared for the crossing, and it wasn't a bad place or time to spend my days.

When we set sail we made our way to a hurricane hole (a small cove) at Puerto Don Juan, to stay out of the wind-tossed seas. There, with my kayak safely on board, we joined up with an entourage of other cruisers. The crews in the other boats had already heard the news that *Running Shoe* was accompanied by a kayaker on his way to South America.

As soon as Stuart let down the anchor, the others made their way over in dinghies to where his boat rested. Soon there were a dozen people on board the *Running Shoe*, all curious as to the tale of the newcomer. Dee kept busy down in the galley, fixing drinks and appetizers for the guests. The mood was so relaxing I decided to break out one of my hand-rolled cigars from Honduras. Even after everyone had left, I was still enjoying the mild taste of the cigar when I noticed that Stuart was eyeing the smoke.

"Do you smoke cigars?" I asked.

"No. Well, once, when Coral was born. But those were terrible."

"You ought to try this one. Good taste and very mild."

"Don't mind if I do," Stuart said.

I handed it over him and watched as his eyes lit up after an especially big toke. Any hint of tension between us dissolved. He began to show me where things went, and how the sailboat worked. Soon I felt like another part of the crew, which made the awkwardness of my intrusion more bearable.

He also showed me how to tie different knots, which I should have learned in Boy Scouts if I'd ever been to one of their meetings. He asked me to tie a bowline knot, which I botched miserably.

He laughed and said, "Look at this, mate, a granny slip knot, eh?"

Eventually I learned how to tie all of the required knots for sailing.

After Stuart and I finished the cigar, Dee took me crabbing. The cove where we were anchored provided a good sheltered area and a good variance between tides. The tide was going out, which, I was told, was the best time to go digging. We dug our toes into the soft sand where the water stood a couple of inches deep. I followed Dee's lead and found the clams to be easily accessible.

We took only as much as we would eat. Some of the clams were larger than my hand, and my mouth watered as we carried the bucket back to the ship. Stuart boiled and sautéed the clams. I ate close to forty of those tasty morsels, until I began to feel a little sick.

The canopy was up over the deck, shading us from the hot mid day sun. I propped my feet over the edge of the railing and let the sun warm part of my body. This was a life of relaxation I had not experienced over the last several weeks, and I knew it wouldn't last much longer. I relished every minute I was on board the small, peaceful sailboat.

* * *

That night was a big event. A lunar eclipse was about to happen, and all the cruisers in the area were going onshore to get a better view. We all climbed up the hills, a couple of hundred feet, through cactus and thorny bushes, to the top of the ridge where we could get a good look at the sunset as well as the eclipse. Each boat brought over a dish that added to a sort of potluck, and I had helped make our own dish, twice-cooked mashed potatoes in clamshells. Blankets were spread out and the food was eaten. Cameras were set on their respective tripods and we sat back and watched the sun set.

Finally, at nine o'clock, the moon came up and we could see the sun's shadow quietly and majestically engulf the entire moon. As the shadow crept along the surface of the moon, leaving only blackness behind, the remaining lighted portion turned blood red.

I couldn't help but think of the passage in Joel that read, "And the moon shall be turned to blood." A sign of the second coming of Christ. I thought of that return of the Savior and wondered if I would be ready. It would be an awesome sight, to see Him coming out of the sky, making this eclipse and anything else I had seen, small and inconsequential.

After the moon came back out from under the sun's shadow, we all made our way back down the hill to the harbor. We climbed back into the dinghy and set out for our own boat. On board, after putting Coral to sleep, Dee, Stuart, and I sat out under the stars, drank some rum, and shared another cigar. A wave of absolute serenity washed over my soul. I couldn't help the smile that slipped across my face. Stuart noticed my contentment and nodded.

That night, in my journal, I wrote:

> *My sojourn from needless worry and the stress of the expedition has changed this night to an attitude of peacefulness and serenity. I have ceased to worry about tomorrow, the time of day, or the mileage I can make. Even my final destination seems to be far away into the future, so far that I need not concentrate upon it. Now is the time to develop friendships with the people I have met here, and to add enrichment for both parties. The ocean is such a wonderful creature, and I enjoy it when she and I are not fighting. Her peace steals into my heart, giving me a serenity that few have experienced, and I love her for bringing together and strengthening all who fall within her grasp.*

On Friday, the 27th of September, the VHF radio alerted the boaters to two approaching tropical storms, which had the potential to turn into hurricanes. They were approaching our area from the south. Although the water outside was choppy and the wind whistled across the hills above, inside our cove the water remained calm and the mood optimistic. We decided to stay put and wait for calmer weather, and I thanked God once again that I had not tried to be a hero and cross on my own the day before, without the protection of an escort.

Several of the captains within our circle of boats remarked that they had heard news of my story on these common waters. Sometimes I felt odd, being amongst the older generations of the cruising world, but they made me feel like a celebrity.

* * *

The next morning, the radio reported that both storms had changed course and were on their way to the open waters of the Pacific Ocean. Relieved, we said our goodbyes and headed out. We ran into some pretty rough seas, once around the point. Up and down we rolled on the waves, some ten feet high. It was a hard day, but we were rewarded by actually seeing the results of our progress.

At 5:00 PM Stuart called out that we were going to go past the Isle of Partita, which had been in our sights for most of the afternoon. The next island was six miles away. At our present rate, we expected to land in just over an hour.

"We're traveling at three knots now, so it will only take us two hours to reach the next island," Stuart said. "Can you make it, mate?"

I told him I could. The currents between the islands, however, turned those two hours into five. Were it not for the patience of Stuart, who slowed the engines down to further control the sailboat, I might have gotten discouraged and headed back to the previous island. At 10:00 PM, after darkness had long set in, the island at last came into sight. But at the same time we all felt the currents underneath picking up their intensity. It almost felt as though we were standing still.

"We're not even going one bloody knot," Stuart yelled, his engines at full throttle. To make matters worse, *Sunward*, the other boat we were traveling with, was nowhere in sight. It was a bigger and far heavier boat than the *Running Shoe*, and it was struggling harder against the strong currents. Now and then we could make out the mast light, peeking out above the fog.

"*Running Shoe, Running Shoe*, this is *Sunward*."

"*Sunward*, this is *Running Shoe*," Dee said. "Over. Channel thirteen, over."

"We can't see anything out here right now, Dee," said Ron, the captain of the other ship. "I think it was a bad idea to come to the next island tonight. We should have camped for the night at Partita when we had the chance. The sea sure is rough right now, and I don't know if it's a fog or what, but the visibility is down. I wish we hadn't pushed it tonight."

Ron had wanted to harbor on the previous island but Stuart had urged us to press on. Thus the resentment in Ron's voice.

"Sorry about that, Ron," said Dee into the microphone. "Nothing we can do now, eh? Just keep coming towards our mast light. It's pretty rocky around the harbor, so we'll wait for you here at the entrance. Once you catch up you can follow us in. We've been here before and know the way."

Dee remained cool. Stuart and I were listening to the conversation over the VHF, slightly amused at the exasperation in Ron's voice.

"Okay, but I still say that we should have stayed on the other island tonight," Ron snapped.

The harbor was on the south side of the island, and from the looks of the chart, filled with treacherous, submerged rocks. It was now pitch black, the moon just starting to rise. Eventually *Sunward* caught up, but now he had a new complaint.

"*Running Shoe, Running Shoe.* We lost our damn dinghy back there. The waves were too big," Ron shouted. "We're going to have to go look for it right now."

Their dinghy, he said, was worth a pretty penny, so no one argued as *Sunward* turned around. We could hear them arguing about who'd tied the dinghy, just before they switched the radio off. We watched as their mast light slowly disappeared and they headed back into the night. By then Stuart was getting tired and irritable, and said he was not going to wait for the *Sunward*'s return.

Dee went to the front of the bow to look for exposed rocks with a flashlight, and Stuart told me to keep an eye on the depth meter.

"If that meter reads twenty-five feet, you'd better let me know, mate," he said. "Read out the numbers every ten feet, okay?"

"Aye, aye, Captain," I said, enthused to be a part of the crew.

The meter currently read sixty-seven feet, and we headed straight for the cove, into the shadow of the rock wall beyond. Dee and I shouted encouraging advice to the captain. The ocean was still rough and we held onto the railing.

Coral slept down below, oblivious and no doubt used to the commotion on deck.

The depth meter was now holding at a steady forty feet. Stuart had said he'd anchor the boat at thirty. Only a little ways to go. The hull of the ship, I'd been told, went into the water six feet.

The water grew less rough as we entered the protective stretches of the cove. Suddenly, the depth meter went crazy. The numbers jumped from forty, to thirty, to twenty-two in a matter of seconds. I shouted out the changes and I could hear Dee shouting her own warnings from the front. Stuart reacted to the strain in our voices, turning the wheel quickly in the opposite direction, and Dee yelled for him to back up. Jamming the throttle into reverse, he put the engine in gear and pulled down the handle for maximum power.

We were still drifting forward, and I called out the numbers as they continued to decrease. The boat was slowing down and would eventually move in reverse, but we didn't know if it would be in time.

"Ten, nine, eight, seven," I called out.

We all tensed and gripped the railing, waiting for the rocks below to rip open the hull. But the blow never came. We had caught it in time, and I yelled out the numbers triumphantly, as they began to go up again.

* * *

Sunward came dragging into the rocky harbor well past midnight. Stuart, tired from the long day, was in no mood to listen to Ron's continued complaints. They had not found their dinghy. After we'd all said goodnight, Dee switched off the VHF.

"How did they lose the dinghy, Stuart?" I asked as we got ready for bed.

"It was probably because Ron tied the old granny slip knot, and the boat just slipped away."

We chuckled over this one, keeping out laughter low because *Sunward* and its scowling captain were anchored just a few feet away. We switched off the lights and headed to bed, but not before Stuart and I shared a few smokes of the cigar.

THIRTEEN
Poisonous Barbs Of The Stonefish

The next day we agreed to stay in the harbor of San Esteban Island, and I didn't object. Dee wrapped Coral up in a light cotton shawl and put her into a jumper that hung around Stuart's shoulders. Soon we were traipsing about the tiny, uninhabited island, exploring its peaks and valleys.

The path we were on wound up around the point, giving us an excellent view of the ship and the cove in which it was anchored. From here we could see that the boat was surrounded by treacherous, submerged rocks.

"You were the *man*," I said to Stuart, "for getting us in safely last night,"

"I wouldn't have tried to get in there at night if I hadn't been here once before during the day, mate."

In another hour, we stood at the top of the mountain, which rose above the bay nearly five hundred feet. The last few turns of the trail had been very rocky, and at times perilous. I was amazed at Stuart's agility, making the same maneuvers as I, but with a fifteen-pound baby clutching at his chest.

We could see not only the ship in the harbor, but the island as well. Stuart pointed to a distant peak on the eastern horizon, and said that it was the next island we were headed for. The ocean spread out before us like a great carpet.

Stuart pointed. "Look, there's *Sunward*, the poor bastard. Doesn't look like he found his dinghy, eh?"

I took the binoculars out and confirmed what he had just said. The glint of light from the sailboat showed no smaller craft in tow.

"We better get down to our boat so we can be there when he starts complaining again," he added.

We headed back down the hill.

We were giving Ron a hard time about losing the boat, but he really wasn't a bad guy. He was a soft-spoken Canadian, on a budget, like the rest of us, who was just frustrated.

Ron suggested, after he recast his anchor and we joined him, that Stuart take us diving for lobster. He looked over at me and asked if I wanted to go. There was no question about it, so the three of us suited up and dove over board. There were only two spears, one for Stuart and the other for Ron. They did have an extra set of fins and a mask to use, so after they dove in, I followed, carrying a diving knife.

It was a beautiful spot to dive and an even better one for lobster. The rocks that lay underneath housed all sorts of beautiful fish. As we dove, my eyes were opened to a whole new world. Blue fish, yellow fish of many different types and colors flitted in and out between the rocks. Among the rocks were sea anemones, their tentacles extended, waiting for small fish to come by. I touched a few, and watched as they withdrew from my touch.

After Stuart had caught a few lobsters, he and Ron went to the surface. They stood on some rocks, half out of the water. Some giant crabs caught my eye, and I swam toward them. I scraped my knee on some hard coral. I took a look and realized that I would have to crawl on my hands and knees to reach the other side. Halfway across the shelf of rocks, I decided to again look at the beauty of marine life that lay hidden in some of the smaller niches. What I saw made my heart skip a beat in my chest.

A few feet from my outstretched hand peered the beady eyes of a stonefish. It was hidden, camouflaged among the rocks, its deadly barbs already fanning out along its back, waiting for my hand to settle on its lethal body.

The stonefish, or scorpion fish, as it's also known, is one of the deadliest species of fish in the ocean. It's armed with barbs, three inches long, on its back and belly. The skin is brown and gray, blending and changing to the colors of its surroundings. When a predator of any type is near, the spines spring out.

Once the poisonous barbs pierce the flesh, the victim is quickly paralyzed. The poison works its way to the heart, ending in a painful death while the heart palpitates furiously before collapsing.

I froze in mid-stroke and waited, hoping the stonefish would not come toward me. A prick from those three-inch spines would administer enough poison to paralyze my body. Being three days from the nearest city, I would not survive long enough to receive medical treatment from any hospital.

I slowly moved my hand away, and saw with relief that the fish would not attack. It was content to lie still, in wait for its next victim.

After a while, keeping my eye on the stonefish, I motioned for Ron and Stuart to come and have a look. Stuart himself, just three hours prior, had warned us of the dangers of swimming around the rocks. Now we all stood, half in and half out of the water, our masks held tightly against our faces, a respectful five feet away, anxiously looking down at the brown and gray tiger stripes on the back of the fish.

With its coloring and elegantly curved spines, I found it quite beautiful in a rugged way. Excitement buzzed through my head and I tasted the makings of a kill. I told Stuart of my intentions. He handed me his spear.

"You'd better hit that sucker dead between the eyes, mate," he said, "or the bloody thing will swim out and barb us all."

I put my head again under the water, lifted the spear and took aim. My hand shook a little as I gripped the handle. It was the first time I'd ever used such a weapon.

The stonefish sat there motionless.

I waited another second and then thrust the spear forward with all my might. I can't say that I saw the moment the three-pronged barbs entered my prey's head, because I blinked at the moment of release. But when my eyes flew open again, I saw I'd made a direct hit.

The stonefish jumped, as did Stuart, Ron and I. It attempted to wrench itself from the spear. The movement sent shock waves up along the length of the shaft still clasped in my right hand, and the water rippled. I gripped the shaft of the spear tighter and brought the fish above the surface of the clear water.

Stuart was yelling and clapping me on the back. I brought my capture over to the rocks. Taking out my Bowie knife, and being careful to avoid the barbs on the stonefish, I plunged the blade deep into its brain, splitting the skull with a sharp crack. With a final flop, the dreaded stonefish became still.

I looked at the other two and grinned.

Stuart reached over and again slapped me on the back. "Good job, mate! Don't get too close to it. Those barbs will kill you even after its dead."

Later I removed one of the three-inch spines as a souvenir, carefully storing it in a small glass jar. The deadly poisons held within could kill even years after the rest of the body had deteriorated.

That night we all converged on the tiny beach adjacent to the harbor. A bonfire was built for warmth and a smaller fire was lit to cook the food.

We ate lobster, scallops, grouper and stonefish. Once the poisonous barbs were moved, the meat of the fish is edible. Here, on this tiny island, far away from the luxury of automobiles, telephones, showers and computers, I felt completely satisfied. I was surrounded by friends, the hands of nature, and the majesty of the ocean. We had dined like kings on the noblest of foods, and relaxed in the comforts of an old world spa. What more could one possibly want on a night such as this?

Frankly, this was paradise. The way God meant for the world to be enjoyed.

FOURTEEN
Boaters, Avoid The Canal At All Costs!

The Seri Indians once traveled the island that our company was now traversing, migrating from one point to the next and then back again in a wide circle that encompassed the islands in the Gulf of California.

Early on, at the turn of the twentieth century, the Mexican government granted this tribe a state of autonomy, meaning that, at least on paper, they were an independent nation. The island that housed the main part of the tribe was called Isla Tiburon—Shark Island. Here they lived off the land, later to become famous for their wooden carvings. These statues were cut from native trees called ironwood, and can still be found along the coast of Baja and most parts of Mexico. The main themes of the carvings are of sharks, dolphins and lizards.

Their era of freedom lasted little more than half a century. The government began to grow weary of the peace the little tribe enjoyed, and began to publish articles stating that the Indians were cannibals. Though the reports were untrue, it was only a matter of time before society decided that the Seris must be integrated into the mainstream culture of Mexico.

By the late seventies and early eighties, the Seri Indians were forced off of the islands and into nearby cities in the mainland of Mexico. Soon the villages on the islands were completely abandoned.

* * *

The next night, we all camped in Dog Bay on the eastern tip of Isla Tiburon. Stuart informed me that they would be leaving the next day to go back to Baja and continue down the coast to La Paz. It was time to part company. I thanked them with heartfelt gratitude. The past several days had truly been an uplifting experience for me.

After following me out from the bay a few miles, Stuart lowered the kayak into the waters, holding the line.

"I really felt like I made some good friends here," I told him and Dee. I was standing at the edge of the deck, just beneath the blue awning, ready to climb into my kayak and set off.

"Likewise, mate," Stuart said clasping my hand firmly. "Don't forget all of those knots I taught you."

"I won't," I said, laughing.

"You take care," Dee exclaimed, giving me a hug. "Remember what we said. We're going to be in Mazátlan for Thanksgiving and there's going to be a great big feast. I want you to be there and feel welcomed as our guest."

I kissed little Coral goodbye, then said, "I will see you all for Thanksgiving turkey, you can count on that."

I climbed down and settled into the kayak. With yet another wave of sorrow, I pushed off through the waves and headed for the mainland.

That day was the first of October, and I floated aimlessly for the remainder of the day. It was the first time in five days that I'd been alone. As the sun set I could barely make out the Mexican coastline in the distance. I had not anticipated this sorrow at the departure of my new friends. I would miss them terribly.

When it was full dark I climbed out onto the flat part of the bow and strapped several bungee cords around my waist and legs. I stretched out just inches above the swells of water, feeling the rhythm of the sea beneath me. I had a restless night, adrift in the Gulf but far enough from land that I knew there would not be a problem of running aground.

The waves were choppy that night, and the following day as well. The wind picked up and it was difficult to keep a straight course. By now, though, I was used to the five-foot swells that crested over my head. It was the strength again of the current that worried me. My body swayed with the rhythm of the waves but the shore did not get any closer.

Looking at the charts with Stuart two days prior, I had learned about the Canal del Infiernillo that lay between Isla Tiburon and Bahia Kino, the closest port city in Mexico. I was told that the currents in that area were so strong that a visible wall of water, sometimes four feet high, could be seen at the changing of the tides. The maps of this area and their warnings were clear and concise.

Boaters, avoid this canal at all costs! the maps stated in several locations.

Some people say I'm crazy, and others say I'm adventuresome, but one thing I am not is stupid. I headed well to the south of those treacherous waters.

There was a stiff wind from the south, and headway was difficult. It was obvious that I was not going to reach the mainland by nightfall, so went about preparing the kayak again for the night.

Drifting at night was one cause for concern. Another was getting run down by larger boats that would not be looking out for a craft as small as mine. To compensate, I switched on a light I had strapped to my forehead to warn anyone who might be out that night.

Off in the distance, near the entrance to the Bay of Kino, I saw other lights from shrimp boats. The lights twinkled carelessly in the dark night. The moon had not yet risen, and the water was very dark. The slightest noise seemed magnified by the silence, and the lack of visibility again made my nightmares increase. The gentle slap of the waves against the hull was not a peaceful sound, but one filled with sharks and other creatures to disturb my rest.

Once or twice I felt the movement of something beneath my boat, possibly a shark. Nothing surfaced, and in the moments I held my breath and waited I believed the beasts that lurked below could hear the pounding of my heart and sense my fear. I felt small and helpless, a mere speck on the massive surface of an enormous, moving, mass of energy.

The waters I was paddling through were known for shark attacks, and I wondered just how long my luck would hold out. I stayed in the cockpit longer than usual that night, not wanting to put myself in a vulnerable position—easy to see, easy to eat.

Twice during the night I switched off my headlight to get my bearings by the glow of the city lights of Kino, and twice, to my dismay, found that I was drifting too far north, toward the mouth of the canal. Both times I paddled south, swinging the kayak around until the compass, which was mounted on the bow, pointed to the correct setting.

I had paddled pretty much nonstop since the day before, and when the sun peeked over the horizon I was so weak from the lack of sleep, food, and rest that my hands shook uncontrollably. I was exhausted and lightheaded.

With luck I thought I would reach one of the northern beaches by noon. The water around the kayak was a light brown, telling me I was in fairly shallow water. The waves had settled down and I was making good progress.

I was thinking of the lunch I would buy once I got on shore when I felt a sudden jolt. Startled, I thought I'd hit a sandbar. The kayak was still moving steadily forward, though, so I continued on, scanning the waters in every direction.

I heard a noise to my right, like water being sucked down a bathtub drain, and looked in that direction. The waves parted and a fin slowly emerged from the water.

Briefly I hoped this was another school of dolphins. The fin moved side to side, a few inches at a time as it came closer.

My breath caught in my throat, and I couldn't have screamed if I'd tried. Everything seemed to slow down. I stopped paddling and watched as the fin slowly sank back down into the water only a few feet from my outrigger. I could see the snout of what was clearly a shark. The water that was displaced by its close proximity slapped the kayak sharply, and I gripped my paddle between both hands.

Bracing myself for an attack, I felt the impact as the beast became more aggressive. With the second bump, as it passed beneath the kayak, I saw the brown streaks along its back and knew this to be a sand shark. Normally aggressive, sand sharks were known to attack just about anything. This one appeared to be more than nine feet in length.

Again the fin emerged, circling to my left. I fumbled for one of my knives, but in my panic I dropped it and almost lost hold of the paddle. I became aware of just how close I sat to the water, only inches above its surface, and I felt trapped.

I continued to watch the fin intently as it broke the surface just a few inches away. Wherever the shark went, the water moved and swirled, making room for this perfect predator of the sea. When the shark emerged a few yards to my left, I sensed it was getting ready to attack. I grabbed the paddle until my knuckles turned white.

When the shark was only a few feet away, I raised my paddle in anticipation. The shark lurched forward, and its mouth came out of the water, right beside me. I looked into the eyes of the beast, and with all my strength I thrust the oar forward into its open jaws. There was a sharp cracking noise, like a tree being splintered in two, then a moment of struggle. The shark's tail whipped around and slammed into the side of the boat, causing me to lose my balance.

Water sloshed into the cockpit. I took one hand from the paddle so I could grab the kayak and not be thrown out. With a jerk, the shark released the paddle and with a quick flick of its tail, turned and slipped back into the murky water from which it had come.

At first I was afraid the paddle had been broken, but on closer inspection found that only the tip had been split. I turned the paddle to take a closer look and saw, to my surprise, a shark's tooth lodged between the broken sections of the paddle. I pulled it free and looked at it, shuddering at the thought that this tooth would have sliced easily through my flesh.

Then that I noticed a gash in my left hand, just above the middle knuckle. Crimson blood trickled down over my wrist and into the water. I took out the medical kit from behind the seat and wrapped the cut in gauze. My hands shook so violently that I could hardly place the gauze on my hand and cut the tape.

After a while my nerves settled down, and I gave thanks to God for my continued safety. I slowly paddled on, my senses on high alert.

There were no other mishaps that morning, and I reached the shores of Bahia Kino a few minutes after noon. I was so exhausted and shaken that it was all I could do to tie the safety line to a nearby palm tree, crawl beneath the outrigger of my kayak, and sleep for the rest of the day.

FIFTEEN
"No agua, tres dias."

I woke up that evening feeling miraculously refreshed. I sat up, brushed the sand off of my back and tore into a PowerBar. There was a road several yards up the beach, and I walked over to it.

Half a block down to my left was a most welcome sight—painted yellow, half buried in the drifting sand, was a pay phone. It was the first I had seen since leaving San Felipe. Half of the people in Los Angeles got collect calls from Mexico that day. Most were surprised I'd made it across the Gulf alive.

I felt on top of the world. I'd traveled more than five hundred miles, and was still alive and healthy. Except for the cut on my hand and the older one on my big toe, I had no lasting injuries. I felt an extra wave of support from my family and friends who seemed to realize that I might make it through alive after all.

While I was making phone calls, a moped zoomed by and then stopped, the rider obviously shocked to see another white man in the city. He introduced himself to me as Frank. We talked a while, and then he invited me over to his place to clean up and spend the night. I was elated. God seemed to be putting people into my life every time I turned around.

After my last phone call, I walked down to the ocean's edge and looked out, feeling invigorated and refreshed. I untied the kayak from the palm tree and pushed off into the water. Frank had given me directions to his place just a half a mile down the beach. In a few minutes I pulled up on the beach in front of his house. Frank himself was out front, getting a tan and sipping a frozen drink.

Without saying a word, he pointed to an outdoor shower. It was the first time I'd washed in fresh water in nearly a month. Over the next two days I would shower as often as I could. It felt great to wash away of the sand, sweat and Aloe Vera lotion that had built up all over my skin.

* * *

Frank told me he had recently moved to Mexico. Like many *gringos* this side of the border, he seemed to be running away from problems in the states. Frank's weakness, I soon learned, was women. He was a mild-mannered, middle-aged man, bald and with a tan most locals would envy. He drove around town daily on his little scooter, looking for young, available Mexican ladies. He didn't drink much, which was a relief, but he was homesick and kept talking about his old life in California.

At first I felt sorry for him, but he continued to talk on and on about his boat he used to have, and the business he used to run. By the end of the day, I was a little sick of his chatter. After we watched the news on a color TV, the first I had seen so far, I decided to get out of the house for some fresh air.

I walked down the street to the pay phone I'd used before, picked it up, and dialed Heather's number. I hadn't called Heather during that earlier marathon phone-calling session because I'd wanted to devote a special block of time just to her. After a couple of rings, that soft, familiar voice was on the line.

"Hey, baby, it's me," I said, thrilled to hear her voice.

"Oh, my goodness, Ben? Are you okay?" The enthusiasm in her voice reached out through the phone to touch me.

"Yeah, it's me," I said happily. "I made it across the Gulf of California in one piece. I'm in a city called Bahia Kino." I knew I still sounded weary.

"Are you all right?" she asked.

"I'm okay, just tired. It took a little longer than I thought."

"I know. I've been worried about you. You said you'd call in six days, and when you didn't I thought something had gone wrong. I called Christian yesterday and he hadn't heard from you either. He was so worried, I think he even called the Coast Guard."

"That's what I heard," I replied. Christian had told me that when we'd spoken. I was sorry to have caused everyone so much worry.

"What happened?" Heather asked.

"Oh, the usual—strong winds, high waves. I did get some help from two sailboats. Met some really great people. I had to avoid a canal called Little Devil, so I paddled south several miles to get away from the currents."

I deliberately left out any mention of the shark attack. No sense in her getting more worried than she already was.

"It's so good to hear your voice," she said.

"I missed you, baby. Are you going to be able to come down and meet me somewhere?" I asked hopefully.

"That depends on whether you're going to be good or not."

"No problem," I replied. "I'll get a room with two double beds if I have to."

"That won't be necessary, just get two rooms," she said, and we both laughed.

"I can't wait to see you. I'll be in San Carlos in . . . let's say a week and a half to be on the safe side. Can you make it then?"

"I'll try," she said. "I'll talk to my travel agent tomorrow. But how will I know if you've made it?"

"I'll call you when I get there. If I haven't called before you leave, postpone the ticket."

"I can't wait to see you," she sighed.

"You don't even know," I said.

* * *

The next week would be a long one, but the thought of seeing Heather in just a short time made the days go by faster, each new dawn bringing with it a building excitement. I longed for her passion, and her love. The warmth of Heather's touch would soon be with me.

I left Frank's house the next day. Cutting across Bahia Kino, I spotted several shrimp boats heading toward me. As they got closer, I slowed down to see in which direction they would turn.

One of the boats, bearing down on me fast, was not changing its course. The water parted rapidly from the point of its bow, throwing up large amounts of white saltwater on both sides. When the boat was less than a hundred yards from me, I stood up in the cockpit and waved the paddle over my head. By then it was almost on top of me. I heard the growl of its engines shattering the morning calm.

I sat down and dug into the water with all my might, scrambling out of the way. The boat continued on its course, not slowing down for a second. Ten feet in front of my bow the shrimp boat plowed by, its wake almost knocking my kayak sideways. The other boats were approaching just as rapidly. I was in trouble and knew I'd better get out of the bay before they ran me over.

Two more boats came close, less than twenty yards away. One went in front of my prow, the other behind, sandwiching me in between.

It looked as though every ship in the harbor was coming in at the same time, and their line of passage was right through my kayak.

I paddled harder, attempting to reach the other side of the bay. It seemed that no matter which direction I turned, the huge shrimp boats, all more than fifty feet tall, were bearing down on me from all sides. The sheer helplessness of my situation was devastating. There was nothing I could do except to think that this would be the stupidest way to end my trip.

One boat had stopped. The captain was ordering the nets to be inspected, so I paddled over as close as I could get.

"Hello!" I called out. "Sir, could you tell the other boats to keep an eye out for me?" I fought to keep the fear from my voice.

The captain only looked at me in disgust, shook his head, and began to drop the nets on top of my head. In shock, I paddled out of the way, barely escaping the hooks and rope that dropped all around the kayak and into the water. I yelled out in frustration, but the man just motioned for me to get out of the way. He then revved up his engines, and drove away.

I paddled through his wake, doing the only thing I could—pray. "Please, God, don't let me end up dead. Not this way."

There were several more close calls, but finally I reached the safety of shore. I thanked God again for his protection. At the end of the day, Punta Baja was in sight.

* * *

On October 6 the waves, as I prepared to set out, were strong, rising five to seven feet. As I attempted to jump into the kayak, a wave slammed into it. The hard fiberglass shell crashed into my right hip.

When I finally got situated in the seat, I winced with the pain. By the next day my entire leg turned black, and ugly streaks crept down my leg, past my ankle. Weeks after, I would still be uncomfortable and unable to rest on that side. For a few months as well, I had to jump into the kayak on the other side to avoid further aggravation of my hip.

* * *

Frank, the man I'd stayed with in Bahia Kino, had given me an extra cooler in which to carry my water supply. After washing the inside out with soap and water, we'd filled it with purified water and a large block of ice. Frank had told me, after I asked, that the ice was not necessarily purified, but that he'd never had a problem with it in the past. Not very assured, I reluctantly put the cooler, filled with ten gallons of water, on the space between the outrigger and my seat. I then secured my new water container by strapping it down with rope and bungee cords.

At first, it was refreshing to drink cool water in the middle of the Gulf. The temperature still soared above ninety degrees, but as the ice began to melt on the second day the water developed an unpleasant taste. That night, before I went to sleep, I realized my gums had started to bleed. Since I hadn't really been flossing well lately, I figured that must be the reason.

The next morning, when I took a sip of water, I spat it out in disgust. It tasted and smelled like gasoline. I wondered what kind of bacteria it contained.

Water was a precious commodity. There were no cities in sight, and no other boaters to supply me with fresh water. I tried to drink some more of the cooler water with my breakfast, but it was horrible and I could only manage a few sips. I poured a five-gallon can of concentrated Gatorade powder into the cooler, hoping that would help the taste. It didn't. Next, I put some dried tealeaves in, but that only made it worse.

With no choice but to continue, I got in my kayak and paddled. By nightfall my gums were bleeding profusely and I felt lightheaded. I put ashore beside the backside of a mountain range, spit out another mouthful of blood in disgust, and shook my head. My water supply for the next week was ruined.

The fresh-water-maker that I had as a backup plan was not intended for regular use, but only in emergencies. I tried to pump some fresh water through the desalination kit, but after an hour gave up with only a few teaspoons in my cup to show for my efforts. I would have to take the whole day off, just to get enough water to carry for a day. I decided not to waste any time, and hoped there would be a small town nearby, one not listed on my trusty map.

Even though I'd only sipped a few ounces of the contaminated water that morning, I was feeling violently sick. I still tasted the bitterness in my mouth. A fever was coming on, and my muscles felt very weak. My stomach vomited everything I ate, and there was a strong taste of metal as the blood continued to flood my mouth. I fell asleep on another deserted beach that night and slept restlessly.

Throughout the night, I had dreams that were as poisoned as my water.

* * *

The next morning I poured the remaining water out onto the sand. My mouth was so dry I couldn't even swallow. It had been three days since I'd tasted good water. My fever was still high and my gums continued to bleed. Spots of blood were caked on my lips, but I couldn't bring my tongue far enough out of my mouth to clean them off.

As I paddled in my kayak, I felt almost delirious, and worried about poisoning, infection. Even the pain in my hip seemed minor compared to this new torture. But late that afternoon, October 7, a small fishing town came into view. All day I had forced myself onward, stroke after stoke, one arm forward, the other arm back. I shivered with fever chills, and prayed that the villagers would share their water.

I was weak from exhaustion, and the paddle seemed to weigh a hundred pounds. The tiny village was now only a few hundred yards away, but it was over an hour before I reached the beach leading up to the shacks that made up the community.

People were running out to see me, a strange man paddling into their little world. I could tell by the expressions on their faces that I looked terrible. When I fell out of my kayak and onto the sand, a man ran up to me. I grabbed him and pulled him down to where I kneeled. "*No agua, tres dias,*" I rasped.

He understood and motioned for me to follow him. It took the last reserves of my strength to get to my feet. A few minutes later we were standing in front of a makeshift store, and I ripped the lid from a gallon jug of water, pouring it down my throat. I gulped down half of the gallon, spilling some onto my chest. It was heaven.

When I came up for air I saw through half-closed eyes what appeared to be most of the people in town crowded around me. I sat down on the dirt patio of the store and drank the rest of the water in the jug. It filled my stomach and quenched my thirst, but it was too much, too quickly.

My stomach wrenched violently after only a short time, and I leaned over and threw up most of the water I'd drunk. I caught my breath, then took a more cautious sip of water. I began to feel better.

The man who'd given me the water sat down too. After a while he walked with me to the kayak—most of the townspeople following, staring at me with open curiosity—where I looked for something to trade. These people would have little use for *pesos*. He seemed interested in a length of heavy chain I had, so I gave that to him. We went back to the store. This time I traded some lures for several gallon containers of water. When I felt strong enough to continue on my way, the village people again followed me to the beach. Clapping and yelling their approval, they waved as I pushed off.

I waved back. They'd saved my life.

* * *

On Tuesday, October 8, Hurricane Hernan—though I didn't know the name at that time—was churning its way through the Pacific Ocean. In the distance, clouds were beginning to creep over the horizon, and I smelled the upcoming rain in the air.

Just as I was deciding to head for the shore and call it a day, the storm hit. Clinging to the paddle with both hands, I struggled to maintain control, squinting through the saltwater that whipped into my eyes. The wind was gusting so powerfully that I could see barely ten yards ahead. Despite my efforts to paddle to shore, the wind pushed me backwards, north at a frightful speed.

The rain, fat, heavy pelting bullets, slammed into me.

I dug into the water as the churning waves swept over my bow, threatening to overturn the boat. The kayak tilted sideways and, looking up in dismay, I saw a wall of water breaking overhead. Then it hit me, and for a moment I was completely submerged. The water swirled and rushed around my head like a freight train. I closed my eyes and held my breath, hoping to resurface quickly. The water continued to hammer into my ears like thunder, pounding my head and threatening to rip me from my seat.

Finally, the bow of the kayak broke above the waves, and I gasped for breath. Ahead, I could see a cluster of rocks jutting out of the foaming water, like teeth hungry to devour. I had gotten turned around by the last wave, and another wave loomed from behind. Its sickening strength pulled me. I had only a split second to grab onto the rudder. No matter what happened, I couldn't get separated from the kayak. Taking a quick breath, I felt the wave's power grab me. The rope cut into my hand, but I hung on. The rocks tore into my right hip, the one that had already been injured, and I fought the urge to open my mouth and scream.

Kicking forward, I pressed toward the surface and another breath of air.

I opened my eyes just in time to see another towering wave coming at me. I let go of the rope and dove into the wave at the last second.

This time I avoided the rocks. For the next ten minutes, which seemed to last for hours, I plunged into each new wave, fighting to keep away from the rocks.

In the distance, the sound of my kayak smashing against the rocks reached my ears, and I wondered what would be left when I eventually found it.

SIXTEEN
"This is a private club and beach, sir."

As suddenly as the gale began, it stopped. The wind slowed to a steady breeze, and the waves, after having nearly beaten me to death, settled down as well.

My right hip throbbed painfully. Blood that was nearly black seeped through my shorts and into the water. Afraid that the blood would attract sharks, I looked for the kayak. I spotted it some fifty yards from where I bobbed. I'd been certain it would be in a thousand pieces, smashed and strewn across the rocks. But as I swam toward it, it looked to be in one piece. The kayak had lodged between two rocks.

By the time I reached it twenty minutes later, I could barely drag myself aboard. There were some scratches and dents along both sides of the hull, but for the most part the kayak was in good shape. The Kevlar structure had held tough and lived up to its reputation.

The cargo and extremities of the kayak had not been so fortunate. The leeboard, a wooden attachment used for additional steering in rough water, was split in two, and the rudder had been completely torn off. Some of my supplies were floating nearby, but they were ruined so I let them go. I was thankful to be alive and still with my boat.

I wearily paddled to the nearest beach. With the last bit of strength I hauled the kayak onto the shore and tied it to a nearby palm tree. I lay down and closed my eyes, shivering from exhaustion.

* * *

The next day, paddling without a rudder proved to be difficult. At times I had to stop altogether and push my oar in a backwards motion, severely slowing my progress. It was the only way I could keep a straight course, though, and San Carlos was not far off.

When I did reach the city, I planned to call Christian first thing and tell him to make the necessary arrangements with the kayak sponsor, Easy Rider, to send down another rudder ASAP.

At mid afternoon I rounded a rocky point and saw an enormous bay spread out before me. In the distance was the lone white triangle of a sailboat coming into the bay from the opposite side, about four miles away. I watched its progress along the far rock walls and hoped I would reach it in time to ask for some water. My supply was already running low. The currents in the bay worked in my favor, and in an hour I was within earshot of the now anchored sailboat.

The captain was sitting on the deck, enjoying the weather. The sun was out and the clouds from the previous day were a distant memory. I shouted out to the man on board, and waved, asking if I could tie up to his side.

He stood up, surprised, and looked down at me in the water.

"How are you doing, Captain?" I asked in my most chipper voice.

"Just fine," he said, smiling incredulously. "Where are you coming from? San Carlos?"

I could tell by his handsome features that he was a man of good fortune, accustomed to living the life of luxury and relaxation. His smile was warm and friendly. He wore a white shirt, unbuttoned to his stomach, and he looked just like the kind of man you would expect to see on a weekend outing with the local yacht club.

"I came from San Felipe," I told him.

"Wow!" he exclaimed. "That's a long way."

"I'm going all the way to South America. I've been out for three weeks. You don't happen to have some extra water, do you?"

"Sure we do. Tie up and come on board. The deck's small but we have plenty of room for you. You came just in time."

He introduced himself to me as Bill Ronstadt. He was definitely enthusiastic about my trip, and we got out several maps to see where I'd been and where I would soon be going. I told him about the storm and the various mishaps along the way. After a while, his wife, Liz, came up on deck. She had long, black hair, streaked with gray, and her white summer dress flowed about her ankles.

After lunch we talked about our respective families, and again I fell right in step with the relaxed way of life on a sailboat. The Ronstadts were lovely people, kind and generous with their time and belongings. Bill was an amateur photographer, and took many pictures while I was on board their ship and in my kayak. Later on, I found that he'd also been kind enough to send copies of the pictures to my friends and family.

That night we camped out in a small bay. With the wind coming from the south, I was able to set up camp long before Captain Ronstadt's boat anchored into the soft sand of the harbor. I was invited again to dinner, and we had fresh fish and a salad, with wine.

Later Bill played his guitar in front of the candlelight and I sang some songs that we both knew. The boat rocked gently in the smaller swells of the ocean, creaking and adding voice to our music.

Before setting in for the night I took a look at my hip. The rocks had torn away a good piece of skin. I wiped it with a wet cloth from the medicine kit, and then bandaged it up.

I slept in my tent on the beach, careful not to lie on my twice-injured side.

Bright and early the next morning I joined Bill and Liz for breakfast before setting out. Before I paddled off, Bill reached over the side and handed me a heavy orange tube, about a foot long and six inches in diameter.

Seeing my puzzled look, Bill said, "This is an ELB—Emergency Locating Beacon. Inside the waterproof compartment is our address. We want you to write when you get done with your trip. This'll give us another excuse to see each other again after you're done."

"I can't take this from you," I protested. Those units, I knew, cost several hundred dollars.

"I insist," Bill said firmly. "We don't need it down here because we won't go very far from San Carlos. You need the ELB much more than we do. I'll be offended if you don't take it. Besides, like I said, you'll have to make a trip over to Arizona to give it back to us, and I'll enjoy your company again."

So, without further resistance, I accepted what was probably the most important and valuable piece of equipment on board, given to me by the memorable Ronstadts. I was very thankful, expressing my gratitude and promising to see them on my return.

* * *

Turning my focus ahead, I looked on the map and saw that Club Med was a few miles south from where I'd spent the night. The absence of my rudder was beginning to wear on my nerves as well as my muscles, so I pulled in at the first sight of the resort's illustrious beach. It would be nice to talk to more English speaking people.

A closer look told me that most of the people on the beach were women. Even better.

What luck, I thought cheerily to myself. My first thought was to put off the phone call for a new rudder, and talk to some of the women sunning themselves on the sand, but I knew better. Business first.

As I strolled into the lobby, I noticed that people were looking at me in a way that made me feel uncomfortable. Like I didn't belong there. I knew that I looked like I'd just crawled out of the depths of the sea, but I smiled at them anyway. The glares continued unabated.

Walking past the pool I found it too tempting to pass up. I dove in, letting the pure water rush over my body, washing away the salt that had begun to cake again on my exposed skin. There were gasps from several of the women closest to the pool, so I got out quickly and dried off.

I later learned that the club was catering only to lesbian couples. No wonder I'd seemed so out of place.

One of the women from the pool must have told the management on me, because before I could reach the phone an American woman approached me, looking very official in her neatly pressed suit. She asked if I were a guest. I said no, and she promptly told me to leave the premises. Immediately!

"This is a private club and beach, sir," she said, raising her eyebrows and looking me up and down. She was attractive, but her attitude showed an unpleasant side. "No one is allowed here without permission."

"I know," I replied somewhat defensively. "I just wanted to use the phone."

"I'm sorry. That just cannot be allowed. Only guests may use the phone. You really must leave at once!"

I felt like telling this woman just what I was doing in this part of the Sea of Cortez, but a month or so on the ocean was having its humbling effect on me. I only smiled and apologized for my presence, asking again, if I could just use the phone. "It'll only take a minute," I added. "It's very important.

"Absolutely not, young man," she said in an even fiercer tone. "Do I have to call security?"

It was hard not to be rude in return, but I just walked away, back to the beach. On the way four women, all young in age, stopped and asked me about the knife strapped to my leg. What a welcome relief to at last find some friendly faces. I told them about my journey, and soon we were all sitting under a *palapa*—a thatched, open-sided structure—on the beach. Two of the girls smuggled out plates of food from the buffet table and shared them.

We had a good time visiting, but by mid afternoon it was time for me to say goodbye. After a few pictures were taken, I headed down the short stretch of beach to the nearby Howard Johnson hotel.

The first thing I did after securing my kayak on the beach in front of the hotel was to head for the pool to rinse off more thoroughly. This time no objections were made by anyone around.

That night, as the sun set over the water, I spotted a man looking out over the railing opposite the pool. He was taking in the beautiful view.

"How are you doing tonight?" I asked, walking over to where he stood.

"Good. Just enjoying the scenery." He was Hispanic, but spoke English well, with very little accent. He was of medium height, with pleasant features. I guessed him to be in his early thirties.

"Are you by yourself?" I asked.

"Yes," he responded. "I'm on business. How about you?"

I told him my story, and he told me his. His home was Guadalajara, where he owned a company called Agra de Mexico, which imported grains of all types to Mexico from the U.S. and Canada. He was educated and had traveled extensively.

He said, "My name is Edward. What is yours?"

"Ben."

And with that we shook hands.

About that time two young women and a guy walked into the outdoor restaurant and took seats. Edward looked at me, and motioned for me to step over to another table, closer to the party that just walked in. We sat down adjacent to the three newcomers. They seemed to be about the same age as myself, mid-twenties.

Both women, by the way they talked and flirted with the waiters, appeared to be single. One in particular was beautiful, with medium-length blonde hair. Her skin was tanned a dark golden brown. Her smile that was friendly, yet somehow also distant.

This was going to be an interesting evening, I told myself.

Edward mentioned that he wanted to see the paddle where the shark had taken a bite out of it, so I hopped over the rail, onto the beach, and walked to my kayak. When I came back, Edward, that sneaky dog, had already pulled his chair to the other table and was engrossed in conversation.

Clever man, I thought. And quick, too.

Edward had already begun to tell them some of my story, so I needed no introduction when I sat down. They looked astonished when I brandished my paddle like a sword, showing them where I'd pulled the lone shark's tooth out from the shattered edge of the fiberglass. The guy sitting next to me reached out a hand.

"I'm Dan. Nice to meet you. This is Cyd and Sage."

Sage was the blonde, I made a note of that, and I lingered a bit longer than necessary when she put her hand in mine. She looked into my eyes. Her smile was fleeting.

Be patient, I told myself. I didn't want her to see how eager I was, so I pretended to look the other way. In the back of my mind were thoughts of Heather. I promised myself that I wouldn't do anything I'd later regret. Other than that, I was going to enjoy the evening.

When the waiter came over to take our order, Edward leaned over discreetly to tell me that I should order anything I liked. He definitely had style.

Sage, I learned, was originally from Florida. She'd recently moved to Arizona to finish college. She was almost as passionate as I when it came to the ocean, and told me that she went scuba diving nearly every day.

Dan and Sage had gone out that morning, she told me, on the rocky south side of the bay. Scuba diving was something that I'd always wanted to try, and would have gone the next morning with them had I not needed to be certified.

Dan's parents owned a house down the street and he invited Edward and me to come over later. After Dan, Sage, and Cyd left, Edward talked about the possibility of romance. I listened, but didn't seriously have any interest in anything of that sort. Heather would be coming down in a few days. For now I was just happy to be with people.

Edward, it turned out, was something of a Casanova. He bought two bottles of wine from the restaurant in the hotel.

We walked down the beach to the house. There the five of us sat up and talked well past midnight. When it came out that I planned to spend the night on the beach, Dan asked if I wanted to sleep on the sofa. I readily accepted the offer.

* * *

Sage, Cyd, Edward and I met early the next morning for breakfast. After we ate, Edward insisted on taking me down to the immigration office to get my Mexican Visa. There, with him working as an interpreter, we filled out the necessary papers.

He dropped me off at the hotel. It was time for him to leave and take care of business. I was sorry to see him go. He told me, while handing over his business card, to contact him if I ever had any problems in Mexico, and he would be glad to help. I didn't realize just how much I would rely on this offer in the months to come.

Later that evening, Sage and I got a chance to talk. We seemed to share several passions, but she had a man, and I a woman. Another time, another place. After a brief kiss on the cheek, we headed to our separate beds.

Dan and I had a chance to talk that evening. He offered to buy me a thick, juicy steak, and I wasn't about to refuse.

After we'd finished our steaks and were sitting back in the wicker chairs, looking out over the swimming pool, he said, "You're one of the most interesting people I've ever met. I wish I could go out and do something dangerous, too."

"Listen, Dan," I responded. "I don't want to look back on life and regret anything I have or haven't done. I'm chasing my dreams. If anybody asked me right now when was the most exciting time of my life, you know what I'd answer?"

"What?"

"Right this minute. Right now!" I said with emphasis as my finger pointed down at the table. "Life has a lot to offer, Dan. You just have to be willing to reach out and grab it."

"I wish I had something to do," he said. "Like you. You have your goals for this trip. I'm stuck in a rut."

"So get out there and do something."

Dan raised his eyebrows. "What am I waiting for?"

"For one thing, I think you're scared. Forget that! Just go for it. You might not ever get the chance again."

As I was giving him this pep talk, Dan seemed to be listening. He sat in silence for a few minutes, then looked up with a gleam in his eyes. "All right," he said, excited. "You've really got me thinking. But I wonder what kind of adventures are waiting for me?"

"I don't know, but at least you're thinking along the right lines. It's gonna happen. Just keep your eyes open."

* * *

The next morning, as they were leaving to go back to Arizona, Sage ran over to give me her address. She gave me a quick kiss on the cheek. We hugged briefly, before saying goodbye. I waved to all of them as they drove off, out of the parking lot, and down the dusty road.

Heather would be coming in on Tuesday, and so I had a few days to relax, and wait. I got a room in the hotel, and felt like I was in another world with the plush carpets, the clean sheets, and best of all the warm showers. I took so many that I began to loose track of how many bars of hotel soap I went through in a day. Sometimes I would let the clean, hot water run for an hour. Residue from the dried saltwater was finally off of my skin, my hair and my clothes, which I took the time to rinse off in the sink. I was a new man.

SEVENTEEN
Heather Looked Out Over The Darkened Water

Heather Stackhouse arrived in San Carlos right on schedule. I took a cab to the small airport outside of Guaymas. The twin-engine plane, which seated about ten passengers, landed in a cloud of dust on one of the two airstrips. Heather stepped out on the runway, looking terrific in a mid length skirt and denim top.

Once she'd been cleared through customs, I walked over and swept her in my arms, oblivious of the other people standing there waiting for their loved ones. I held her close for a long moment, and then pulled away, still holding her hands. "It's great to see you."

"You too," she replied, squeezing my hands.

"You look great, sweetheart."

"I am so glad I could come down." She gave me another hug.

"Same here."

Back at the hotel, she opened her suitcase to proudly display the supplies inside. She'd brought an entire suitcase just for me, and I was like a kid on Christmas day.

New clothes, a new rudder for my kayak, food, pictures, and another camera. Everything I could possibly need. I took everything out and laid it all aside. The suitcase would be full on her return, too, because I'd decided I needed to lighten my load of supplies. I had items that were luxuries in comparison to their weight. One of my two flashlights, a cooking pan, two dozen batteries, and a large boom box would all be going back with Heather.

The next few days went by more quickly than I would have liked. We played tennis, swam in the pool, walked around the town, and ate at all the best restaurants San Carlos had to offer.

The night before she left, we had a long talk. We were in the room and had just finished a dinner that room service had delivered. We were enjoying our last few hours together.

"Are you still glad you took on this expedition?" she asked, raising her eyebrows slightly as she sat across the table from me. There was a hint of sarcasm in her voice.

After a few moments of thoughtful silence, I said, "I don't know if I can answer that right now."

"Well," she said rather slowly, "are you happy out there when you're all alone? Do you find some peace and quiet?"

"Yes and no. Sometimes, it's just brown, ugly desert. It's been dangerous at times. One thing for sure, it's exciting. Very lonely, though. If I could only share some of the beauty, the experience, with someone else, I think it would be better. If I did have someone with me, though, I don't think I'd want to stop. Maybe I'd just keep going around South America until I reached the Caribbean."

"Why?" she asked, looking as though she really did think I was crazy.

"Well, for one I don't have to worry about a job, finances, traffic, or any of that stuff. It's just the water, God, and me. I like that part the best."

"I wish you'd hurry up and finish and come home. I miss you, and I worry about you. You don't know how many nights I've lay in bed, awake and wondering if you're okay." As she said this, Heather reached over and took hold of my hand.

"I know, baby," I said gently. "It's hard for me to go on, but I have to, even if I don't enjoy it at times."

"You mean you don't even like this crazy thing you're doing?" she asked incredulously.

"Sometimes, no." I said truthfully. "I might not even make it in five months. Maybe I won't make it at all!"

"Don't say that," she exclaimed, pulling her hand away from mine. "Why continue if you don't want to? Can't you just stop?" She sat back in her chair, refusing to look at me. I chuckled and she looked up. "What are you smiling at?" she asked.

I said, "You look cute when you're mad. But you know this is something I have to do. I'm not going to quit now. Too many people, including myself, are counting on me making it to South America."

"Most people didn't think you'd make it this far."

"I know," I replied. "But there's only one thing that will stop me from continuing."

"What's that?" she asked hopefully.

"Death. Or something close to it."

"That's so stupid," she exclaimed. Moving over to the window, Heather looked out over the darkened water. "Nothing is worth getting killed over," she added.

I went over to where she stood. I put my arms around her and held her close. "When I hiked all over the Sierras, I spent several days trying to make it to the highest peak. I didn't necessarily enjoy every minute of it, or the sixty-pound backpack that cut into my shoulders at every step, but I did it. The rewards at the end are greater than the pain. The view from the top, and the beauty of the wilderness is worth it all. Same thing here. If it weren't so difficult, I wouldn't enjoy the end result as much. When this is all over, I'll look back and be proud of myself. That's why I keep going."

"Just hurry up and finish so I can see you again soon. And in one piece, do you hear me?"

"I hear you," I said, still holding her in my arms. "Nothing is going to happen to me."

I kissed her gently on the lips. It would be hard to see her go. It felt good to be with her, but I wondered how long it would last. We were both independent, and there were still several months left in my trip. There'd been an unspoken agreement between us for those few days. We never talked of our future together, and no false promises were made.

One step at a time.

* * *

I watched sadly the next day as Heather walked to the small airplane. Our time together was over. It was time to move on.

That night, as I looked out of the hotel window, I saw storm clouds and lightening on the horizon. An overwhelming ache came over me, so deep that I had to sit down. I hated the fact that I was once again alone. Doubts clouded my head as I wondered if I truly knew the reason why I continued on with this expedition. Was it pride? Determination? Was this my destiny, or was I just running away from my past and the emotions that came with it?

I put my hand to my head and let the tears stream down my face, hating myself for my stubbornness.

* * *

By the next morning I'd gotten most of it out of my system and was ready to forge on. I was sad to leave San Carlos and the memories therein, but eager to get on with my journey.

As the clouds had promised the night before, there was a bit of a drizzle. The sea seemed to welcome my return with a flourish of activity. There was a strong headwind as soon as I left the bay and again entered the Gulf, and the water was extremely choppy. There were only a few boats. The wind howled and the sea continued to churn.

By mid afternoon I found shelter in a large bay just north of Guaymas. There was a small beach to my left, and what looked like a clubhouse behind the sand.

My muscles had quickly tightened, and were feeling quite sore. It would again take time to get used to the rigorous schedule that I needed to keep. I was not making good progress so I put to shore. I made camp, ate a meal, and slept without pitching my tent. Sleeping that night without the comforts of a mattress beneath, or a bedspread above, reminded me of the pleasures left behind.

The nights, for now, were not too cold, and my sleeping bag provided ample warmth. I curled up tightly, wondering where Heather was, and if she was thinking of me. The only solace I found that night was in the reassuring sounds of the wind and sea. For now they were my only companions.

* * *

The next morning I found my location on the map to be in a shallow bay, outside the town of Guásimas. The water around was not as clear as it had been, and the scenery was beginning to change. The barren slopes of the windswept mountains and the vast deserts that covered the land to the north were gradually giving way to more vegetated soil. Half dried swamps and lagoons began to appear, and the few palm trees that came close to the shore gave good sturdy anchorage for tying my line to at night.

I paddled all day, still with the waves choppy and rough. Every hour or so I would stop, and pull out the pump, ridding the cockpit of extra water. My muscles were still cramped from their lack of use, and I took more breaks than usual. The PowerBars and dried oatmeal tasted like sand.

That night, I camped beside a clump of mangroves. Their roots, half out of the sand, came down just a few yards shy of the water. There was no problem finding a tree to tie the safety line to, and for once I didn't have to endure the nuisance of tying the rope to my ankle.

On October 21 I set out early, with the wind, for once, at my back. The swells rose to seven feet, and I felt the power of the ocean rise with the sun to give me my daily workout. I welcomed and accepted her power, but wondered if one day she would grow too strong for me to handle.

More thunderclouds appeared to the west and the wind increased in intensity. Something was wrong. I couldn't quite put a finger on it, but I'd sensed the weather changing for the worse.

I paddled for as long as I could that day, with my muscles struggling to keep to my previous pace. The coast was long and flat now, and I angled toward the shore until I was close enough to surf the waves to the sand. By six o'clock the gusts of wind were so strong I could barely stand upright. I prayed that a hurricane was not in the making.

I tried to pitch the tent, but the wind caught it like a parachute and pulled me all over the beach. Finally, I tied the bottom straps of the tent, to the outrigger poles of the kayak. Only then I was able to climb inside.

The wind by then was incredibly strong. Black clouds surrounded me on all sides. I huddled in my tent, listening to the sounds of the ocean pounding against the shore with incredible might.

The tent flapped wildly above me, adding to the noise. The waves were pounding with such force that I worried they'd come to shore and sweep me away. I opened the flap and peered out. All was black. I retreated to my skimpy shelter.

At midnight, with the wind still howling overhead like a pack of wolves, the rods that held the tent together snapped in half. I crawled out of the tent and wrapped several strips of duct tape around the broken metal. But the wind caught the tent and it wasn't long before the poles broke again.

I stood helpless on the shore. The wind was making the air cold, and I wrapped my arms around myself in an attempt to keep warm.

The tiny strip of sand that I stood on was a pitiful hiding place. As far out as I could see, the water foamed and curled in an angry snarl, white streaks extending themselves and flinging their contents in my directions. The air was heavy with salt as the wind picked up the water and blew it in all directions.

I was terrified of the power that lay before me, so in keeping with the fears I'd had only recently. The howling, haunting, dance between the wind and sea was deafening. I turned quickly and crawled back inside the tent, which still stood halfway on its side, flapping wildly in the gale.

The sea continued to wreak havoc around me for the next hour. Once, when I opened the flap of the tent to peek out, the metal end of the zipper flew back and lashed out at me, leaving a gash above my eyebrow.

I removed the broken poles and threw them aside, then turned my attention to the tent. Taking a piece of rope and tying it to the top of the tent, I wrapped it around the outrigger. There was only a foot of space now inside the tent, and I burrowed as close to the kayak as possible.

For the rest of the night the wind continued to roar. Sleep was impossible. I didn't know it at the time, but the eye of Hurricane Hernan was only two hundred miles south, and heading rapidly into my path. There was nothing I could do but pray.

EIGHTEEN

I AM THE SEA
I AM POWERFUL AND MIGHTY
NOTHING CAN COMPARE TO MY STRENGTH

MY ARMS STRETCH OUT
TO DISTANT SHORES
WHEN MY WILL IS STRONG
NOTHING DARES DEFY ME

WITH ONE HAND OUTSTRETCHED
I CAN WIPE OUT ENTIRE CITIES
THOSE WHO DISHONOR ME
WILL CRY OUT FOR MERCY

I WARN YOU, WHO SO CARELESSLY TRED
UPON MY BROW
WITH BUT ONE FLICK OF MY WRIST
I SEND YOU CRAWLING
BACK TO YOUR HOVELS
UPON THE DRY LAND, THINKING
THAT SAFETY HAS COME UPON YOU AT LAST

FOOL, PITIFUL MAN
KNOW NOT THOU MY FORCE
OR HATH THOU FORGOTTEN THY FOE?
DOTH THY OWN FEEBLE MIND FORGET
THE WHIPPING I GAVE THEE LAST
WHEN THOU CAME UPON THE MIGHTY SEA

IT CANNOT BE TRUE
THAT THY LIFE WILL CONTINUE

FOR I KNOW ALL
AND CONTROL THY DESTINY
TEMPT ME NOT
TREAT ME WELL
FOR I AM THE SEA
ALMIGHTY AND POWERFUL

BUT NOW I TURN TO ONE
THOU TREAD UPON MY SHORES
AND LOOK TO ME FOR CHALLENGE
THOU PILLAGES NOT MY TREASURES
NOR RAPE ME OF MY CONTENTS

YET, THOU ART THERE
FOR MANY A DAY
LOOKING TO CONQUER MY POWER
CAN I HAVE THAT HERE?
CERTAINLY THOU THINKEST WRONG

LITTLE MAN
COME INTO MY DEATH CHAMBERS
AND WELCOME TO THOUGHTS OF DESPAIR
THOU WILL NOT PASS THESE WATERS UNMOLESTED
NOR WILL YOU SEE ANOTHER DAY

AT FIRST I COULD NOT REACH YOU
FOR MY FINGER ALONG THAT COAST WANES THIN
BUT NOW YOU ENTER
WHERE MY STRENGTH RETURNS
AND MUST KNOW THOU CANNOT WIN
YOU FEEL MY POWER GROWING EACH DAY
AND SEE MY STRENGTH PREVAIL

COME CLOSE NOW I BECKON THEE
TODAY WILL BE YOUR LAST
YOU CANNOT HOPE TO ESCAPE ME
I COME TO BRING FULL WRATH

YOU SIT ON TOP THY LITTLE BOAT
ACROSS MY MIGHTY CHEST
AND THINK YOU CAN CHALLENGE MY MIGHT

THEN SLEEP SAFELY AT NIGHT ON LAND

BUT THOU KNOW NOT OF MY POWERS
OR OF THE OLD LAW TO WHICH I BELONG
I LIVE BY THE RULES OF NATURE
AND ANSWER TO ONLY ONE

HERE, NOW IS MY RIGHT HAND
LIFTING HIGH ABOVE THE SEA
DO YOU LIKE THE HEIGHT I HAVE PUT YOU TO?
FOR MILES AROUND YOU CAN SEE
NOW PLUNGE DOWNWARD INTO MY TROUGH
AND FEEL THE RUSH OF DEATH

I CAN SENSE YOUR FEAR NOW LITTLE MAN
I CAN FEEL THY FEEBLE HEART
POUNDING WITH THE RHYTHM OF MY OWN
YOUR LIFE YOU SOON WILL PART

THIS WAVE WILL SURELY BE THY DEATH
MY FINGER STRETCHES TOWARD THE SKY
TWENTY FATHOMS HAVE I TOSSED YOU NOW
AND STILL YOU RIDE ON HIGH

LIKE A MAD MAN ON THE MIDNIGHT WIND
YOU GIVE ME MORE THAN I BARGAINED FOR
BUT SO MUCH MORE THE PLEASURE THEN
OF BRINGING YOU TO DEATH'S DOOR
AYE, NOW COMES THE POINT OF TIME
I WILL BRING THY SPIRIT TO THY KNEES
AND SEE WHAT ERE THOU ART MADE OF

ONE HAND HITHER AND THE OTHER YON
CONVERGING TOGETHER IN ONE GREAT FEAT
AND CRASHING UPON THY SOUL AT ONCE
I FEEL THY LITTLE HEART BEAT
AND TASTE YOUR BOAT BENEATH
SUBMERED WITHIN MY BREAST
YOU CANNOT HOPE TO RIDE THIS OUT
I NOW HAVE GAINED CONTROL
YOU ARE ON MY SHOULDER NOW FOR ONE LAST RIDE

APPROACHING MY MAWS OF DEATH
YOU TRY TO SHOUT

SEE HOW BLACK THEY ARE
SENSE ME
SMELL MY POWER
FEEL THY FEAR

HARK, WHAT DISTANT RUMBLING HEARETH ME
YET LOUDER THAN MY OWN
TELL ME, NO, IT IS THE MAN
WHO FORMED ME FROM THE BONE
TIS TRUE, THE VOICE OF MY CREATOR
THE LORD THE GOD ABVOVE
WHO TELLS ME NOW TO STOP THY PLIGHT
AND CALMS ME LIKE A DOVE

'THOU OH MIGHTY SEAS'
'WHICH I CREATED WITH MY HANDS'
'QUELL THY SPIRIT OF DESTRUCTION NOW'
'AND QUICKEN NOT MY CHILD'S DEATH'
'TAKE BACK THY HARMFUL THOUGHTS AND PRIDE'
'I WILL MAKE YOU STILL AND MILD'
'YOU KNOW I HAVE THE POWER TO DO'
'SO REQUIRE ME NOT TO ASK THEE TWICE'
'YOU WILL NOT TRY AGAIN THIS YEAR'
'TO TAKE THIS YOUNG MAN'S LIFE'

I HEAR THE WORDS OF GOD HIMSELF
I DARE NOT DISOBEY

I NOW AM GROWING CALM AGAIN
THOUGH NOT BY MY OWN WILL
TWAS THE GOD ABOVE WHO MADE ME NOW
TO QUIET MY HEART AND SET ME STILL

I AM THE SEA
HEAR ME ROAR

NINETEEN
"Lord, this is a really bad time."

The date was October 22, a Tuesday. I'd begun to doubt I would live to see the next day.

Overnight the ocean level had risen fifteen feet. Breakers, some more than twelve feet high, crashed on the shore, licking hungrily at the edges of my tent, soaking my sleeping bag.

After wringing out the excess salt water, I placed my belongings into the kayak compartments. The powerful waves posed a continued threat, possibly even preventing me from going out into the Gulf.

As far as I could see, from my vantage point on the little dune of sand, there were white walls of foam. Fear crept down my spine. The morning drizzle filled the air with an unusual chill, adding to my sense of doom. My instincts warned of danger, and my senses told me to wait. The wind, however, was blowing from the north, and I thought if I could just force my kayak past the dangerous surf, the wind would be at my back and I might make some substantial progress.

Progress was not my only thought that morning as I pushed my kayak to the ocean's violent edge. I knew I could not sit idle for an entire day. No matter what the conditions, I was prepared to face the ocean, regardless of her fury.

Foolish man.

After a few deep breaths, I set the paddle firmly in place beside my seat, lowered the rudder into the sand, and pushed off. I leaped into the cockpit and braced myself as the first wave smacked against the right side of the boat. I turned to meet the next wave and gasped. It was huge. Closing my eyes and taking a quick gulp of air, I felt the second wave, more than ten feet high, slam into me.

Once upright and on top of the water again, I watched the other waves crash around and in front of me. On all sides, it seemed, the ocean had risen up to rid herself of this hapless invader. The cockpit was already half full of water from the last wave. I was waiting for an opportunity, a temporary lull in the ocean's activity, to put on my spray skirt.

A wave broke in front of me, crashing against the bow, sending saltwater and seaweed into my face. My eyes shut tight, I was temporarily blinded, but I thrust my paddle instinctively into the water. After a few moments, I forced my eyelids open despite the stinging pain.

The cockpit was now full to the rim with water, and I could feel its great weight seeking to sink my craft. I was not yet halfway across the field of white, with the surf still thundering all around.

It was later, several weeks after that day, when I learned that the eye of Hurricane Hernan was a scant two hundred miles to the south, its fingers stretching out toward me. Oblivious to its power and course, I paddled like a mad man possessed by demons.

Taking a deep breath to remain calm, I called out for God to calm the winds. The howling didn't cease. I looked ahead, searching for a smoother path, but found only white snarling teeth and a wind that tore at my skin.

I was rapidly becoming fatigued. The dark waters had begun to seep into my soul, creating both frustration and despair. This was no longer a challenge—this was a fight for survival.

"God, please give me strength now," I prayed.

At that moment two smaller waves broke ahead, and there was the momentary lull in the ocean's fury that I had been looking for. I quickly bailed out a few gallons of water from the inside of the cockpit. I had just enough time to put on the spray skirt before the waves increased again.

My strength was drained. I thought that I should head for shore, but when I turned and looked over my shoulder, I was stunned to find the shore nowhere in sight.

I realized that I must be at least five miles out. I turned to face southeast and slowly set into a decisive rhythm. My face was grim-set, hard against the wind, not willing to give up. Not yet, at least.

The ocean continued to churn beneath. After another hour of backbreaking paddling, I saw the outline of the distant shore. The sight lasted only about a second, as I plunged down the face of the ocean's swells. For now, I thought wistfully, despite the turmoil in the walls of water that rose sharply and thundered on all sides, I might be safe.

I could not have been more wrong.

That's when the rain started. Softly at first, but then thundering down, soaking everything on the kayak. I blocked out renewed feelings of despair, set my teeth, and continued forward. Despite the heavy rain and strong gusts of wind, I could see for miles around. In the few seconds that I rode atop one of the waves, I could see the entire ocean spread below. I clearly saw the shoreline and the mountains that rose behind it.

The wind rose to a howl. The water around me foamed and boiled. The wind gusted forcefully, and the rain poured down as if the floodgates of heaven had opened. I lost sight of the shore.

On the back of the next wave I perched unsteadily. Time seemed to slow down. I looked down into the cavernous mouth of the trough that was about to swallow me. The water seemed darker there, waiting for me.

I believed then that I was looking at my last few seconds of life. Thirty feet below, rumbling with discontent, was my final destiny.

Time stopped. Everything around me hesitated, as if the ocean was unsure of its next move. Distant memories floated by. Better times, better places. I thought of my family and other loved ones. My sorrow was not for myself, but for the ones I would leave behind.

As I floated on top of this huge mountain of water, I braced myself. I closed my eyes and waited for the impact.

It was then that I heard the voice:

"My son, what have you done for me lately?"

"Lord," I said, "this is really a bad time."

"There is always time. What have you done for me lately?"

I looked around. The trough of the wave still yawned thirty feet below. But the wave still hesitated, suspended in time.

"I will protect you," God continued. "As a result, the name of my Son Jesus Christ will be on your lips for the rest of the journey. Everyone you meet will hear His name."

I looked up to the heavens in awe, and a smile broke across my face. Then I began to pray in earnest. A feeling of lightness and the sensation of falling overwhelmed my senses as I crashed down the face of the wave. The water rushed by in a blur of motion, my speed terrifying.

The kayak bottomed out several feet in front of the crashing white water. I continued to paddle as the foaming water thrust me toward the bay. After its power was spent, I sat still for a moment in the dead wake. Then, with a wrenching of power, I felt the next wave pick me up and pitch me forward.

The night before, while listening to the violence of the wind and waves, I had spent a good hour studying my maps. I'd noticed a lighthouse that marked the entrance to a small bay. There was an island to the west of that bay, and I knew that if I got into trouble, that island would be the place to head.

Now, as I gathered my senses and realized that I was still alive, I looked around to get my bearings. If I could make it to the bay, I would survive. Figuring that the bay was about three miles away, I turned my bow and headed for safety. Again, ignoring the pain in my weakened muscles, I paddled for my life.

About three hours later I saw the welcoming beacon of the lighthouse, this time it was much closer. Hope arose within me.

The waves were now headed in the direction of the lighthouse, but the wind was blowing the other way. As a result, smaller waves formed, rolling in the opposite direction of the existing breakers. This created a pocket of air between the waves. When the waves collided, the compressed air, which broke through the surface, sounded like a shotgun.

On one such occasion, I became a part of this phenomenon. A ten-foot wave, coming from the front, rose up to meet the smaller one. The two waves came together and met with stunning force.

The ocean swirled about, first pulling me one way and then another. I felt the icy fingers of water reach around my throat to squeeze out my last breath. My paddle was wrenched from my hands. The weight of the ocean ripped the spray skirt from around my waist.

I felt like a small rabbit being hunted down by a wolf.

Finally, the front of the kayak surged upwards. I bore my full weight onto the rails, refusing to be thrown off the boat.

The kayak, with me clinging to it, was pulled beneath the waves. When I thought I could hold my breath no longer, we shot to the surface.

* * *

It took a moment for me to clear my head. I no longer felt the reassuring foam rubber of the cockpit seat. It seemed as though I was floating in the water. Sure enough, as my senses returned, I saw that my lower half was dangling in the ocean, my arms still clutching the outrigger's poles.

To my dismay, my supplies floated everywhere, bobbing up and down, just out of reach. A three-gallon container of water rapidly passed by my outstretched fingers. I dragged myself back into the cockpit. The percussive effect from the colliding waves had left me with a high-pitched ringing in my ears.

Without the spray skirt, the kayak was sinking. I had just enough energy to pump out some of the excess water. I was weak with exhaustion and fright. There were several cuts on my arms and fingers, and my blood trickled into the water. The rain continued its downpour.

Without my paddle, the kayak would be powerless against the stronger swells. I looked to where the Emergency Locating Beacon had been strapped down. With a start, I realized that the ELB was not there. It had been swept overboard, along with my radio and other things too numerous to count.

Something in the water caught my attention. It was the blade of my paddle. It was coming my way, so I reached out and grasped it just as it went by. Several feet to my right I saw the orange head of the beacon, floating in the water. I quickly paddled over and placed it firmly between my legs. The waves had died down for a period of time, but now they were beginning to grow restless again. I was able to retrieve some of my supplies before the rest was swept away by the breakers.

Reluctantly, I turned again for the backside of the island. The waves were breaking directly toward the island, and I stopped my paddling to let their momentum carry me. I felt strangely detached from what was going on around me. My shoulders ached, and I could barely keep my head up. With one last, futile push, the ocean calmed itself as I floated into the shallow bay. I only wanted one thing—to stand again on solid ground.

Thoroughly exhausted, my mind shut down for a few minutes. The current slowly pushed me through the serene waters.

I prayed for the next several moments, thanking God for His protection. I would never forget what He told me on top of that wave. As I felt the kayak nudge the soft sand of the island, tears rushed to my eyes. I rolled out of the cockpit and on to the beach. Shaking, I pushed up on my hands and knees and vomited.

* * *

For the next several weeks, nightmares of that day continued to haunt me. That day I had survived what turned out to be the remnant of a hurricane, the last of the season. It was truly a miracle that I was able to survive four hours in that dangerous, pounding ocean.

In the months that followed, I never encountered another storm with half the intensity of the one that day. I was fortunate to have been saved, and I would not forget the promise I made to my Lord.

Leaving San Felipe, 1996

Leaving San Felipe; No Turning Back

Baja, California,
to Mexico

Photo from Bill Ronstadt's
Boat, San Carlos

The author
and Bill Ronstadt

Shark bite from paddle

Coming to port in
Mazátlan

Setting out from
Mazátlan

Landing on Colombian Shores

Triumphant Return:
March '97
Nogales, Mexico
Allan Perry, the Author,
Aaron Booth

Celebrating in
Nogales, Mexico

TWENTY
Where Were My Rights?

Isla Lobos, or Wolf Island, where I had found refuge from the storm, was divided into three regions. To the south is desert. Giant sand dunes stretch out, rolling like the ocean below. No vegetation of any type grew in this area.

It was over these hot dunes that I walked to get to the second region. In the middle of the island, right beside the desert, the forest begins. I found myself surrounded by trees, the shade welcoming and cool. It was the first time I'd seen vegetation so dense since I'd begun my journey. Palm trees towered overhead. Tall grass grew on either side of the path.

At one point I stepped across a tiny stream. There were animal tracks in the soil but no human inhabitants on this island. I felt comfortable among the trees, blending in with nature. I inhaled deeply.

Once out of the forest, the trail led me to a swamp. More tracks in the mud, larger ones than the prints in the forest, told me that they might have been left by the animal for which the island had been named—wolves. Indeed, after I'd returned to the kayak, I heard a rustling in the nearby bushes. Looking up, I was surprised to see a pair of wild, fearless eyes staring at me. The wolf's body was covered with a fur thicker than any dog I'd ever seen. She was crouched there, content to watch me. But when I took a step toward her, she turned and strode majestically into the forest.

That night the wind picked up again, battering my tent from all sides. But my mind and my body, both weary and bruised, gave way to sleep, despite the noise.

* * *

The next day the sea remained calm. I got in my kayak and paddled away with my diminished supplies. As I neared the mainland I noticed that a half dozen steel 60-foot fishing boats had been tossed about on the shore. I waved to one of the captains standing on the deck of his stranded vessel. He shook his head and waved back tentatively, not sure what to make of the tiny kayak that had survived the storm better than he.

The water remained tranquil, so I decided to continue paddling through the day and into the night. There were several lighthouses on the map, marking various inlets and towns-so navigation was not a problem. I stopped and slept several hours in the kayak, and the night gradually turned to day.

When the sun rose I saw the town of Yavaros to my left. The salt and shrimp boats were busily working in the harbor. I stayed clear of the bay and cut straight across to Agiabampo, another small fishing town. I was beginning to make good progress, nearly thirty-five miles a day. My muscles were recuperating from the storm, and I could paddle on a normal day for six hours without stopping for a break.

I pulled into the town after passing the estuary that marked the boundary between the states of Sinaloa and Sonora. As soon as I pulled the kayak onto the shore, I saw that police were everywhere. They were searching for something, asking questions of the locals. I'd heard rumors that the police in Mexico were corrupt, and I sensed trouble around the corner. As I pitched my tent on the beach, several of the officers looked my way.

I ignored them and set about eating my meager meal of beef jerky, trail mix, and water. I tried not to imagine what I must look like to the police. An eerie silence settled over Agiabampo. No one came to talk to me, and the lights all went out shortly after dark. Something wasn't right. I had an uncomfortable feeling, so I told myself that I'd leave first thing in the morning. I curled into my sleeping bag, away from the chill of the night air, and slept.

* * *

Early the next morning I packed my gear into the kayak and untied the safety line. I was nosing the bow toward the waves when I heard voices yelling for me to stop. I looked around, and to my surprise saw one of the men from the Mexican Army running toward me. His rifle flopped up and down, making him look a little silly as he tried to tuck it to one side. His uniform was dark blue with a long-sleeved shirt and pants. I waited patiently for him to approach. When we were face-to-face, he asked me for my papers.

I opened up the front compartment in the kayak and pulled out my passport. Unwrapping it from the plastic bag that kept it dry, I opened it to my picture and handed it to the officer. Then I looked for the photocopy of one of the newspaper articles, which would explain my unusual mode of transportation. After glancing at them with disinterest, he handed them back to me. He pointed to the storage area. By the gleam in his eye, I could tell that the various items within had piqued his curiosity.

By this time two more officers had come over, their rifles grasped firmly in both hands. They waved them menacingly in my face so I stepped away from my kayak. Both rifles remained pointed at me.

I tried to show them the newspaper article, but the first man, who seemed to be in charge, was uninterested. He motioned for one of the other men to come over, and without another word they began to yank everything out of the compartment. Outraged, I stood with my arms folded. I had to remind myself that I was in a foreign country.

After they'd finished, my clothes, food and rope were strewn across the sand. The first guard motioned for me to open the other compartment. Disgusted, I threw my hands in the air. While I was putting my supplies back into the front of the kayak, I heard one of soldiers swear. All three began to speak rapidly in Spanish. They talked excitedly in low voices, as though they'd just stumbled upon a hidden treasure. In a way, they had.

I glanced over and saw them holding my 10-pound box of vanilla flavored weight-gainer, the powdered dietary supplement that one of my sponsors had given me to help me maintain my body weight. Nothing incriminating about that.

Unless . . . hold on. A white powder substance . . . oh no!

They were looking for drugs, and regardless of the truth, I knew I was in trouble. I began to explain as best I could that the powder was a dietary supplement. They weren't listening. One of the officers made an abrupt about-face in the sand and stalked off. The box of powdered weight-gainer was tucked under his arm, confiscated as evidence.

One of the remaining officers lowered his rifle. He pointed it directly at my stomach.

"*Dinero ahora,*" he said, and the other officer brought out his handcuffs.

He took a few menacing steps in my direction. In disgust, I spat on the ground and went over to the kayak. I knew the only way out of this predicament was to give them money. I pulled out my wallet.

Heather's arrival in San Carlos had prompted a bit of spending, and I only had a little over $300 dollars left. I pulled some money out, trying to conceal the amount and hoping to get out of the situation with only a couple of twenties lost. I was not so lucky. The officer was suddenly beside me. Lowering his gun, he wrenched my free arm behind my back. As I winced in pain, the other officer, his gun still pointed at my belly, grabbed the entire sum of money from my hand.

I was speechless with fury. Where were my rights?

The officer folded the money, tucked it into his shirt pocket, and slung his rifle over his shoulder. The other man released me. Without another word, they turned and walked away.

I wanted to yell out, to run after them. But there was nothing I could do. A few people had gathered at a safe distance, watching to see what would happen to the *gringo*. Now, that the show was over, they slowly began to walk away. I felt empty and depleted as I was left alone on the beach. Never before had I felt so humiliated.

I looked in my wallet and counted the bills that remained. Seven dollars. What was I supposed to do with that? Seven dollars wouldn't go far, even in Mexico. I shook the sand off my strewn supplies and returned them to the back compartment.

I paddled that day with little energy. I felt sapped of motivation.

That night, I pulled in and camped on a remote, uninhabited stretch of beach. I sat alone on the sand, contemplating my next move. I hated to worry about finances but now I had no choice. If I didn't locate more money, somehow, I could not go any farther. The trip would be over.

Feelings of despair and loneliness overwhelmed me. It's only fitting that I give you a sample of the raw emotions that coursed through me during that lonely night. Here is an excerpt from my journal:

> *Thursday, October 24*
>
> *I have no money now, thanks to the Mexican government. I was ripped off blind today because the army thought I was carrying cocaine. I tried to tell them that it was vanilla powder, but they were too stupid to listen. I hardly have any money left,*

only seven dollars. Seven worthless dollars! That won't go far! I have never felt so wronged in my whole life. What did I do to deserve that? What am I going to do now? I feel so lost. So lonely. So helpless.

No direction of where to go from here. Why should I continue on such a miserable journey? Why did I take on such a challenge in the first place? Pride, yes pride. They couldn't take that away from me today, could they? I have been humbled, humiliated, and reduced to tears by this Ocean and her country, but I will not quit! I have too much pride to give up now. But, I do want to go home, to my friends and family. I feel so lonely now. But I know that I can't go home. Everyone would say, "Its okay, we know you did your best." I would think differently, though. Inside, I would know I was a quitter. Sometimes I hate this trip. A challenge? You better believe it. Next time I want to do something extreme, I'll think twice about it. One thing is for sure, I'll never do this alone, again.

If I had a companion, at least right now, we could sit here and talk about it. Draw strength from each other. Now I can only talk to myself. My only solace is to get these words out as quick as I can, on paper, and then move on. Being alone really stinks. I feel so down, like everything has gone wrong and everyone has deserted me. I feel out on a limb. The solitude has crept into my mind. The branch is now being cut. Falling now, in this dark, forsaken area. Nowhere to turn, no one to help. Except God. I know He will deliver me from these perils. Is that enough?

It should be. I know it is enough, but then why do I still feel so empty?

After writing, I lay back down to sleep.

By the next morning my misery had abated somewhat. The cheerful rays of the morning sun always seemed to put me in a better mood.

I was thinking about the good old USA when I paddled out that morning. I missed a roof over my head, a home to sleep in, and the companionship of friends. But thinking about my goal, and the promise of strength that went along with it, gave me hope that morning as I continued to paddle south with new vigor.

On the outskirts of Topolobampo, near a protected stretch of beach, I rode the kayak to shore and picked up five more gallons of purified water. The store was like all the rest of the places along the way where I'd bought water. Small, dusty, and full of little children and dogs, playing in harmony. The five gallons cost me twenty-five *pesos*—about three dollars in American money.

I always enjoyed talking to the people I met when I came into these towns, telling them of my journey. Now, I added comments about the protection God had given me.

With my new supply of water, I soon returned to the sea. It began to rain, and though I put on a windbreaker, it was impossible to stay completely dry. The cool night air, along with the rain, sent chills down my spine.

Though my body was cold, I found that it was becoming easier to travel at night. The demons that had haunted me earlier in the trip disappeared altogether as my familiarity with the ocean and my own inner peace increased. The water was calmer at night than in the day, and I was always surprised at the distance I gained by the additional hours of paddling in the dark.

Sleeping for only fifteen minutes at a time had, at first, been incredibly exhausting. Now, it almost seemed natural. Analogous to taking a short afternoon nap, I always woke up refreshed and alert. The night air worked as an alarm clock. When I stopped paddling to sleep, my body temperature would drop slowly. After twenty minutes or so, I would be cold enough to involuntarily awake. I welcomed the warming sensation of the blood circulating through exercise and was almost eager to resume my rhythm.

For the next three days, it continued to rain. The monsoon season, I presumed, was finishing up in the southern latitudes. This was probably just the tail end of that season, so I didn't complain. It was, to me, a sign of progress.

The tailwind continued, and I saw the outlines of a few cities as I passed by. To prevent my entire supply of food from getting wet, I placed a few days' rations in the cockpit behind my seat.

The surf was noticeably larger than before. I could see, off in the distance, the backs of the breakers, blue turning to white, as they curled over and broke against the sand. I knew, by looking at the maps that I kept in see-through plastic bags, that the Pacific Ocean was beginning to push around the Baja Peninsula. I was now in the open sea.

When the rain finally stopped, I saw the distant lights of Mazátlan. Tomorrow, I thought, I would be able to rest, dry off, and concentrate on raising enough money to continue.

But I was rapidly tiring. The night air, rain, and lack of sleep were beginning to take their toll. How long had it been since I'd rested a full night? Three days? I couldn't remember.

I now carried only three dollars and some change. I wasn't going any farther along the coast with that kind of money. A thought came to mind. Allan Perry was my partner in a business we owned in the States called Sports Leagues of America. He'd thrown the going-away party at his house. Allan and I had talked a few times over the phone. He'd wanted to come down and visit farther south, and we had agreed on the city of Mazátlan. When he arrived, we would put our heads together and come up with a plan.

As I paddled closer to the beckoning lights, I thought about calling my mom and dad. They could easily wire me a couple hundred dollars. But as I remembered their disapproval of my expedition, I knew I didn't want to ask them for help.

I came up with no real solution that night and decided I would just have to wait and see what would happen.

* * *

On October 30, I paddled into the city of Mazátlan. The long stretch of hotels lining the main street seemed to welcome me back into society. I headed for shore in the wide mouth of the bay. The waves rose eight feet high to crash on the shore, but there was only one set of breakers curling at a time, and I rode between the swells. Timing their surge just right, I landed on shore with ease.

I knew I would be in Mazátlan for a while. I needed to raise money and wait for Alan's visit. My first order of business would be to find a storage area for my kayak. I'd always been careful not to leave my belongings for too long. In the big city a few moments unattended could bring disaster.

It was just past 6:00 AM when I stepped out of my kayak and onto the beach. My legs felt a bit shaky, and I realized that it had been three days since I'd set foot on land. I leaned back, stretching my back and other tired, cramped muscles.

Just past the edge of the sand I saw a road with a few cars already whizzing past. I climbed up the stairs from the sand and looked up at the hotels that towered above. I felt a little awkward and out of place, surrounded by buildings and other modern structures. The smell of exhaust made my nose twitch and the pavement under my feet felt hard and cold compared to the sand I'd gotten used to.

After I recovered from the culture shock of seeing these signs of civilization, I looked down the street. A cab was slowly approaching. I waved. The driver gave a friendly honk and then pulled over to the curb. He didn't seem to be in a hurry, so we chatted. He parked his cab and walked down to the kayak with me, where I showed him a few articles about my trip. I explained to him that I needed a place to store my boat for a few weeks. He smiled and said he had a brother who worked in a warehouse next to the train station only a few blocks away.

"*No tengo mucho denero,*" I said in Spanish.

"*No problema,*" he responded, smiling again. "*Tu eres famosa.*"

Together we hauled the kayak up the beach, took off the outrigger, and secured it to the top of the taxi. The kayak was now considerably lighter than when I'd first started. I had done a lot of rearranging in the last several weeks. Everything that was more of a luxury than a necessity, I had thrown out. The ocean too, had done its part to lighten my load.

Back in September, when we'd first loaded the kayak onto Heather's truck in Fullerton, it had taken three men to lift it. Now, the taxi driver and I handled it with ease. After securing it with rope, we drove through the central part of Mazátlan. Sure enough, after a few stoplights, the warehouse loomed in sight. We placed the kayak in the warehouse, and the taxi driver's brother, for some reason awake at such an early hour, shook my hand warmly.

The storage area was actually part of the train station, and I wondered about the legality of the situation. But I was too tired to ask any questions. After chaining the kayak to a steel pole, I closed the lock and stretched my tired limbs. I shook hands with both men and gave my last three dollars to the cab driver for fare. I told the men I would be back tomorrow to get some of the supplies. I walked away relieved that my first problem had been solved.

I was blissfully oblivious to the new problem I had just created.

TWENTY-ONE
She Smiled, Taking Pity On My Situation

I immediately fell in love with the city of Mazátlan. The tourist season had not yet started, and the population of more than 300,000 was relaxing in the foreigners' absence. Although there were many people living in the city, the urban clusters were spread over an area of ten miles. Some parts of the city felt like isolated villages, set apart from the shopping malls and traffic-laden boulevards. There were several different sections that I was able to discover on my own as I explored the city and its surrounding vicinity during the next three weeks.

The same morning that I dropped the kayak off in the warehouse, I found myself walking through a section called El Centro, on the south side of the city. This was the old part of town, where the city first began. I could smell fresh baked bread on the corner, and saw two older ladies patting their own homemade tortillas from soft dough. I reveled in the sights and sounds of this old-world civilization, and my feet took me past many narrow streets and meandering alleys. Most of the shops, small restaurants and kiosks had apartments above them, and they towered over the small streets. In some sections, the sun had little chance to shine, but the closeness only added to the quaint setting.

People walked on every street, but still, I didn't feel rushed or crowded. The air seemed to blow lazily through the avenues with a gentle, easy pace. Once out of the downtown area, I followed the curve of the ocean and the avenue that ran parallel to the beach. From there I could see the entire bay and the islands that dotted the horizon.

The city changed rapidly, once past the older section. There was another section, newer than the downtown area, yet still weathered with age. I learned later that this had been the popular area for vacationers from Hollywood during the fifties and sixties. The buildings reached to the sky, but the once-white concrete towers were now yellowed and worn.

Finally this area gave way to the gold zone, or *zona dorado*. Here the city changed to a glittering series of newly built hotels, restaurants, and shops. The tourist section of the city unfolded, and I blinked in astonishment. Nightclubs, resorts and fancy restaurants beckoned. The sleek, modern architectural designs, and the ever-present bustle of *gringos*, revealed this as the next big resort city along the Pacific. It was different, though, from some of the more popular places, like Acapulco or Cabo San Lucas, as Mazátlan's center was neither oppressive nor hectic.

Everywhere I looked, I found hidden jewels: a private restaurant tucked in one corner, with a balcony that overlooked the city, on another street a tiny shop, tucked behind a larger building. Waterfalls poured into stone fountains, lined with miniature palm trees. The streets were clean, and I found a new haven in this busy, tropical port.

That evening, as the darkness set in, I realized I had no place to sleep and nothing to eat. During the last few months my tent had provided adequate shelter. The food in my kayak, though unexciting, had satisfied my hunger. Now, I had neither. This was the first time I had been separated from my kayak and its bounty of provisions and supplies. I felt naked, and the happiness and energy of the people that passed by on the street only heightened my feeling of alienation.

With my tent and sleeping bag, I could sleep anywhere, but now, with my kayak in storage five miles away, with only the clothes on my back, I realized how isolated I'd become.

Up ahead was a brightly lit sign for the local marina. A big, blue sailfish was perched on top of the kiosk, and the man that stood at the table was attempting to sell resort tours and time-shares to Americans that walked by.

I walked up and said hello. "Do you know if it's safe to camp on the beach around here?" I tried not to sound too desperate.

He looked at me strangely, and replied, "I'm not sure. Maybe down near the marina." He spoke in accented, but clear, English.

I told him my story, and my reason for needing a place to stay. Upon hearing what I'd been through, his personality changed and he was immediately friendly and talkative.

"My name is Juan," he said.

"I'm Ben. My kayak is up in the old city, now. I left my tent in there and everything!"

"Well," Juan said, "now that I think about it, it might not be a good idea to camp on the beach. Usually the city is safe, but you never know."

"Do you have any suggestions?" I asked.

"You could always sleep here. The floor is hard, but you'll be out of the weather and no one will bother you."

With relief, I readily accepted. I thanked him for his help, knowing that God again was providing for my needs. Later on, his wife came by, and he closed the steel gate. He locked it and said goodnight.

The small kiosk had a fan overhead, two stools, and a wooden counter. I chose the wooden counter as my bed, curled up and used my shirt as a pillow. I was used to the soft sand on the beach. In comparison, the counter was hard and cold. The cars that passed in the busy intersection outside reverberated in my head.

I was in for the night—with no bathroom. My sleep was uneasy.

* * *

I woke up early to the sound of rain spattering on the metal roof. Juan came to work early and opened the metal door. After we talked and I again thanked him for letting me sleep in the shop, I spent the morning looking for work. The best job I could find paid thirty *pesos* a day, the equivalent to three U.S. dollars. That wouldn't work. I needed to find something better.

I walked back by the shop and found Juan. When I asked him if he knew of a place to stay that didn't cost a lot of money, he took me to a nearby hotel, away from the main strip, called La Mission. The rooms were old but clean, and the woman at the front desk told me I could stay there for three weeks for sixty dollars. I had no money, and told her so. I would have it in a week, I said, which I didn't know for sure, but it sounded good at the time.

She smiled, taking pity on my situation. She agreed to let me stay if I promised I would have the money by the following week. Once we settled on the price, I picked out a room that was upstairs and in the back of the hotel. My window looked out on a small courtyard that was filled with blooming flowers.

After I'd settled in, I went to the train station warehouse to retrieve some food from my kayak. I hadn't eaten in more than thirty-six hours, and my rumbling stomach made sure that I knew it.

Juan went with me, to act as my interpreter. Once at the storage area, I packed as many PowerBars and bags of oatmeal as I could into a plastic bag. I had a place to stay and food to eat. Things were beginning to look up, and I hoped that my financial woes would soon be resolved.

There was a different manager on the day shift, and I told him, through Juan, that I would need at least three weeks of rental space.

"*Quanto questa*?" I asked. How much?

"Two thousand *pesos*," the man said without smiling.

"What?" I asked incredulously, thinking I must not have heard him correctly.

He said it again, and I felt my stomach tighten.

Now I would have to raise an additional three hundred dollars, on top of what the rest of the trip would cost. I vowed I would move the kayak to another place as soon as I had the funds.

Waiting tables for three dollars a day wouldn't bring what I needed. I was left with only two choices—find a decent paying job, or call my parents and ask them for a loan. I still couldn't bring myself to do the latter.

Juan and I went back to the booth and sat down. He knew I had to get some money quick and was doing everything in his power to help.

"Do you want to sell tours?" he asked. He kept his eyes on the people passing by, ready to snag a quick sale.

"I don't know," I said. "Doesn't seem like anybody is buying anything."

"It's a little slow right now, but you can make a lot of money here," he said. "Commission only, but if you push the tourists, you can really rake in the bucks."

I sat back and watched. He didn't make one sale in the next three hours. The tourists that walked by were all dressed in fancy tropical garb. There were bright flowered shirts and neatly pressed khaki shorts. All were well groomed.

I looked down at my clothes and realized that I had been wearing the same pair of shorts and shirt for the last three weeks. The once white T-shirt was caked with mud, sand and sweat. It had been a while since I'd considered my appearance. My isolation from civilization had changed the way I thought of myself. Now, with people staring at my shoddy appearance, I felt self-conscious and dirtier than ever.

Another fellow came into the booth to work. He seemed friendly, with a broad smile on his face, so I told him a little about my trip. This interested him.

"You're kayaking the entire coast?" he asked.

"I sure am."

"That's like rowing, right?"

"Yep. I use a paddle with two oars, though," I said, demonstrating the forward motion with my hands.

"Have you ever done any crew, like with a team?" he asked.

"No, not really. Why?"

"I used to coach a national team, a long time ago. We competed in Mexico City." He spoke with confidence, remembering those days with pride.

"What happened?" I asked.

"Not enough jobs to go around," he shrugged. "My name is Alonso Gutierrez."

We shook hands. That night, over dinner, I listened as Alonso spoke about his coaching days. He was disappointed at what he was doing now, and his future seemed to be without hopes or dreams.

"Alonso," I said, "The only thing that's standing in your way is you. If you want something badly enough, focus your mind on getting it."

"It's different here in Mexico," Alonso replied. "There are no coaching jobs anywhere right now. I've looked!"

We walked in silence for a while, then found some plastic chairs to sit on, just outside a small taco stand.

"Everyone who tries to do something great in life runs into obstacles," I said, picking up on our earlier conversation. "Take this trip of mine. My kayak is locked up tighter than a drum down there at the train station. I'm almost out of money. What would be the easiest thing for me to do right now?"

I had his full attention.

"The easiest thing would be to quit. But that word," I continued, "has ceased to be part of my vocabulary. What about you? Are you really satisfied to stay here in Mazátlan and sell time shares and tours to the tourists?"

"But what other options do I have?" Alonso asked, somewhat taken aback.

"The world is at your fingertips, Alonso. Before I even started college, my dad told me that I should figure out what it was that I would do for free. In other words, find something I truly loved. Well, at the time I thought it was just talk, so I majored in business. But I soon learned that I was miserable at work, and even hated getting up in the morning. Finally, I decided I was not going to live my life that way anymore. I started thinking about what I really love to do, and look where that got me—in the middle of the Pacific Ocean."

There was a moment of silence. Alonso was looking at the ground.

"What job would you do for free?" I asked him.

"I want to coach rowing!" he said emphatically. "I have done it for no money in the past, and would not hesitate to do it again, if I had the opportunity.

"Then get to Cabo, if that's where you think the money is. Save up for a while, and then go to the United States."

After a moment of thought, Alonso said, "I could do it."

"Well, then, I guess it's settled."

We continued to talk like old friends, and eventually our conversation turned back to my financial difficulties. When he learned that I had no other clothes with me, Alonso took me to his house, where his mother, father and two sisters lived. It was a small place, made of stone, without carpets. I knew they didn't have much, but he gave me two pairs of pants, a belt, and a couple of shirts. I was incredibly grateful to him for helping me feel like a new man.

"Listen," Alonso said before I left. "I've been thinking about your situation. The newspaper stays open late. Why don't we go down there and tell them your story. I bet they'd love to write an article about your trip. Maybe they could even help you raise some money."

"That sounds great," I said, "but it's almost 9:00. Maybe we should try it tomorrow morning."

"No," Alonso insisted, "we'll go right now. I'm telling you, they're open until midnight."

We went down to the newspaper, where, with Alonso acting as interpreter, we talked for two hours. The editor of the newspaper, J. Roberto Rivers, was extremely helpful and receptive to my story. He promised that the article, accompanied by three photographs, would appear in the morning newspaper. Good to his word, it did.

I was hoping that the phone in the hotel lobby would start ringing the next morning, with a barrage of phone calls from businesses that wanted to sponsor my trip. In that, I was disappointed. Not one company called the next morning.

Discouraged, I went back down to the kiosk to find Alonso. I asked Alonso to call the editor back.

Thanking him for the article, we asked Roberto to keep his ears open for further news and assistance. Then we telephoned the train station to set up a meeting. That also led to a dead end. Though they agreed to reduce the fee to a flat rate of $200 dollars for the duration of my stay, I still could not get the kayak out of storage until I paid in full. The manager insisted that was the best he could do.

With a heavy heart, I left the warehouse and returned to the hotel. I sat on the tiny bed in my room that night and stared up at the ceiling fan as it slowly whirled around. On the stone wall, a few lizards crawled along the smooth surface.

A refreshing night breeze blew through the open window and over my bed. I relaxed and began to think.

I remembered the last words of my friend, Edward Guzman, as we parted in San Carlos: "If you ever need help while you are in my country, don't hesitate to call."

He'd given me his business card just before stepping into the cab, and now I got up to see if it was still in my wallet. I smiled as I found the white card with his name on it.

The next morning, I walked down to the pay phone in the lobby of the hotel. I picked the card out of my wallet and dialed the number, collect.

"*Agre de Mexico*," the lady answered as she picked up the phone.

"Edwardo Guzman, *por favor*," I said.

"*Une momento.*"

After a few seconds, I heard Edward's cheerful voice.

"Edward!" I said excitedly. "This is Ben Wade, do you remember me?"

"Ben, my friend! How are you?" His response was welcoming. "Where are you?"

"I'm in Mazátlan now."

"Really! You are making good progress."

"Yes, I am. By the way, do you remember when you said to call if I needed help?"

"Yes, yes. Of course. You, know you are going to be in Manzanillo soon. Don't forget, I have a boat there in the harbor. You can stop and spend the night on my boat."

"Thanks for the offer. I'll definitely take you up on that. Right now, though, I have a favor to ask."

"Anything," Edward responded.

"Well, my kayak is locked up, and I can't get it without paying some money. Could you call the owner of the company and ask if they can drop the charges?"

I figured he was a man of stature and financial prowess in this country. Maybe he could pull some strings.

"Sure, Ben. Give me his name and number, and I'll call you back."

I did, and Edward said it should only take about thirty minutes. I gave him the number of my hotel and hung up. Exactly a half an hour later, the phone rang. The lady behind the desk handed me the phone.

"Ben?" Edward asked.

"Yes, it's me. Any luck?"

"No, sorry. The man I talked to said the Federal Office in Mexico City sets those rates. We can't do anything about it."

"That figures," I said, disappointed.

"But look," Edward said. "If you need for me to, I'll wire the money directly to you, and we'll get your kayak out."

I couldn't believe what he was saying. Half of my problems would be over. But after a few seconds of thought, I told him no.

"Edward, I really appreciate you offering that, but I can't take your money. I'd rather earn it."

"I understand," he replied. "But if you change your mind, or need anything else, let me know. Don't forget, call me when you get to Manzanillo."

"I will," I said. "Talk to you then." I hung up, feeling a little better just knowing that someone else was on my side.

A couple of days later, I took the job as a host at the restaurant outside the hotel. I'd no other offers and agreed to work for three meals a day, instead of the thirty *pesos*. At least I wouldn't go hungry and I had a roof over my head and friends on my side.

Now all I needed was some money and my kayak.

Sooner or later, I told myself, I would get the money I needed. I continued to make contacts throughout the city.

As each day passed, instead of becoming more discouraged, I felt a confidence that all would soon be resolved. During those two weeks my friendship with Alonso grew stronger. Almost every day, after work, we would meet on the corner near the kiosk and travel to town. Sometimes, he would pay for a movie or a bite to eat. Mostly, though, we talked of the future.

I called home every week, collect, to keep my parents from worrying. They were always glad to hear I was still alive. Finally, early in the second week, I broke down and told Dad that, as a last resort, I might need him to wire me some money.

"I'll send you a plane ticket instead," he said sternly. "Maybe it's time to come home."

Perhaps I shouldn't have told him of my circumstances after all.

I also talked to Heather a few times. We talked fondly of her visit to San Carlos, and of the future times to come. I wondered if the next few months would change our attitudes. I hoped not.

Christian, at the same time, was rallying for support back home. He'd already gone to several people asking for donations. For those who could not send money, he asked for cards and gifts.

"I need some money pretty badly," I said one time. "I'm working on some sponsors down here but haven't had any real luck. The landlady at the hotel keeps asking when I'll pay the rent."

"I'll see what I can do," he said.

Two days later, I got a call back from Christian.

"Is there a Western Union office near you?" he asked.

"I think so."

"Well, you need to get to it by two o'clock this afternoon. Can you do that?"

"I guess I'd better," I said enthusiastically.

I called Alonso, and we went down to collect eighty dollars from the local teller. I was elated. Finally, I had some real money, and though it wasn't enough, it was definitely a start. The first thing I did was go back to the apartment and pay half of the rent. After taking Alonso out to eat for all the help he'd given me, I put the rest of the money back in my room.

I learned later that Dave McShane, the same person who'd given me my knives before the start of the trip, had been the one responsible for the wire. I was truly grateful.

* * *

There is one thing I've learned in life: True friendship is not based on good times and hanging out. The metal of character is tested not when times are smooth, but when everything seems to have fallen to pieces. If a friend is then willing to sacrifice their own personal wealth, emotions, and time, to benefit the person in turmoil—that is a bond worth keeping. All other relationships are meaningless.

TWENTY-TWO
"You're one crazy guy, you know that?"

On November 14, I picked up a copy of *The Pacific Pearl*, a monthly publication for American residents and tourists. On the back page, where the classifieds were listed, I saw a small column, written by the editor, asking for articles. I flipped to the front page and found that the editor's name was Mike Veslik. There was an address below his name. I certainly had a story to tell. I decided to pay him a visit.

When I reached his address he was in the process of moving to a different office. When I approached, his wife, who was standing outside, she greeted me. I showed her some of the articles about the expedition.

"Is Mike going to be back any time soon?" I asked.

"He's at the other office right now," she told me. "He should be back any time."

True to her prediction, a few minutes later Mike came walking through the door, took a look at me and in a booming voice said, "Who are you?"

I looked up, a little intimidated by the huge man standing before me. I had no idea at the time that this man would be the one who would really get things moving in Mazátlan.

Things began to get better in a hurry.

Mike Veslik was a big man, forty-six years old, six-foot-three and about 240 pounds. He had played a lot of football in college and even tried out for the Green Bay Packers. He didn't qualify for the team, and after many years of work in the United States he married, moved to Mazátlan and started an English-language newspaper.

Besides being big, Mike was a fun loving, down-to-earth farm boy. Everyone in town knew who Mike was. He owned *The Pacific Pearl*, along with his wife, and had two beautiful daughters, ages four and eight. When he heard my story, I saw the wheels turning in his head.

"You know," he said chuckling. "A couple of buddies and I went on a canoe trip for seven days about thirty years ago. It was the best time I ever had. Problem was, we'd go down the rapids too fast and tip over. Most of our supplies ended up in the river. Of course when that happened, I'd always go for the beer first."

I liked him already, and told of my shortage of funds. He agreed to publish the article and also said he would talk to some local business executives. He knew several of them personally and thought that would be a place to begin in looking for sponsors to raise the extra money.

"I know a way to start you off with a little cash," he said. "What are you doin' right now?"

"Nothing really," I said.

"Well, come on and help me take my furniture to the other office," he said, slapping me on the back. "I'll pay you for helping me move."

I did, and he ended up giving me twenty dollars for an hour's work. It seemed like a fortune compared to three dollars a day.

Later that night he took me to a local sports grill, where we watched NFL football and talked about other adventures. Mike had plenty of stories to tell, and several came up during the night.

While telling me about his canoe trip through the state of Minnesota, he said, "You know, Ben, if I didn't have a wife and kids, I'd set myself on the back of your kayak, grab an extra paddle, and go with you."

"I'm sure you would," I said laughing. "You're crazy enough!"

Over the course of the next four days, Mike and I traveled around to several companies. We were asking for donations of fifty dollars from each company. In return, we told them we would give them publicity, either in the form of mentioning the company name on the local television, or a space on my kayak for their logo. It worked like magic. Every company we talked to agreed. Casa Country (a restaurant), Iguanamo's (a bar), Anglers Inn (a fish and game specialist), Boyas de Mexicana (a buoy manufacturer), Ray Demeral (author of *Mazátlan, Inside Out*), and BV Marine contributed. Mike also gave me, via The Pacific Pearl, fifty dollars and much time and effort. On my own I set up an interview with Señor Frog's clothing store and succeeded there as well.

It was a great week. We collected more than $350. I was extremely excited when Mike drove me down to the warehouse and we took my kayak and placed it on top of his station wagon. I felt as though a missing body part had just been reattached. If Mike hadn't been there, I might have kissed that kayak.

"I couldn't have done this without your help, you know that Mike?" I told him after we finished loading the kayak and tying it down with rope.

"You know," he said with a big grin on his face. "I only ask one thing from you in return for all my help."

"You got it. Just name the price."

"When you get done with this thing, you're going to be famous. You'll be the biggest thing to happen since sliced bread."

"I don't think that's going to happen," I said cautiously.

"Trust me, you are. The press is gonna jump on this story like a duck on a June bug. Hell, they already have. Look at me! Anyway, when you get big and famous, and they offer you a big contract in some movie, don't you forget old Mike."

"I won't, don't worry about that."

* * *

Over the next few weeks, everyone in Mazátlan heard about the film that Mike would be in one day. I must have listened to him tell that story a dozen times and laughed every time he did. Mike was quite a character, and I owed a lot to him. I just hoped I hadn't promised him something I couldn't do. Only time would tell.

The wonders and support never seemed to cease in the city of Mazátlan, where residents and visitors alike embraced me with much love. Even a few families who came to the city for vacation took me under their wing. One family in particular I remember fondly.

I was sitting at the restaurant where I worked, relaxing after the day's work was done and, as so often happened in the afternoon, had joined Mike and Alonso for dinner. We were all eating and talking when three people walked in and sat down adjacent to our table. It was a man, his wife, and a young woman, whom I presumed to be their daughter. The husband looked like a rough character, the kind of guy you wouldn't want on the opposite side in a brawl. He had tattoos up one arm and down the other.

His wife was just the opposite, with dark skin and bleached-blonde hair. She had a wide grin that she seemed to wear most of the time. When she sat down she began to laugh at something. She teased her husband playfully as they both ordered margaritas.

Best of all, however, was their daughter.

She looked to be about my age, with long blonde hair. Her figure was slim. I looked over several times, trying to make eye contact. Mike caught my stare and poked at my arm.

"Go on over there and talk to her," he said with a wink.

"Yeah," Alonso chimed in. "Let's see you work some magic."

"She's with her parents," I said reluctantly. "If she were alone, you know I wouldn't hesitate."

"Yeah, right," Mike said. "If you won't, I will."

"I'd like to see that, big man," I said, and we all laughed.

Of course, neither of us did anything. A short while later, the family left.

"There goes your chance!" Mike said, loud enough for everyone in the restaurant, including the girl and her family to hear.

"Whatever," I said, a little embarrassed but smiling anyway, showing him it didn't matter one way or the other.

The next day, though, while I was working in the restaurant, the same man came back during lunch. He made his way over to the bar and sat. I was just getting off work, so I went over and sat on the stool next to him.

I learned that he was from Seattle, was in Mazátlan for a short vacation with his wife and stepdaughter, Rainee.

"Call me D.W.," he said, and I shook his hand. He had a grip like a steel vice. After he heard parts of my story, he was interested in the possibility of me writing a book and said so several times. After a while, his wife, Sharon, joined us. She invited me to go with them to the Mexican fiesta that night. When I heard that the price to attend the fiesta was twenty dollars, I hesitated, but D.W. insisted that it was well worth the money.

It was. I piled my plate high with chicken tacos, enchiladas, tamales and other foods too numerous to mention. The hotel put on a stage show to display the native culture, and by the end of the night I felt as though I'd been adopted into the family.

Over the next week, D.W. would come by work after I finished, and we would sit and talk while the women were either shopping or sunning on the beach.

I knew the city pretty well by then, so one day I took them to the outdoor market downtown. There we looked at everything from Mazátlan T-shirts to an entire beef carcass.

Mazátlan was beginning to feel like home to me. It was going to be hard to leave.

I had it in mind that, before I left, I would get another tattoo, this one portraying the perils of my expedition. I already had a crown of thorns banded around my right arm. It was a symbol of the Lord Jesus Christ. I wanted to put something on my left shoulder.

D.W. encouraged me to do it, showing me his own new tattoo.

"I'd like to," I said, "but I don't know exactly what I want to get. Something about the expedition, but I might not have enough money."

"Don't worry about that," D.W. replied. "I'll slip you a couple of bucks when my wife's not looking. We'll come up with an idea too, shouldn't be that difficult."

I got a pen from the bar and began to scribble on the paper placemat. "I want it to represent how God has helped me through this trip. Maybe a shark, my kayak and a cross."

"Let me see that piece of paper," he said, taking the pen from my hand.

After a minute, he showed me a crude drawing. I liked the depiction immediately. D.W. took me to a tattoo place he'd found, and with the tattoo artist's help I decided exactly what I wanted.

I was definitely satisfied with the end result. My new tattoo showed my kayak, around which curled a big shark. Waves rose on either side, as though about to engulf my tiny craft. Above the cockpit, where I normally sat, was a cross, made up of two oars.

"Just think," D.W. exclaimed excitedly, after he saw the new artwork. "Every time you look at that tattoo, you'll think of me."

Shortly after that, D.W., Sharon, and Rainee prepared to leave. On the day of their departure I gave both women a hug, and got another firm handshake from D.W., and promised to call them when I finished my trip. We waved goodbye, closing another chapter in my adventures.

* * *

During my last week in Mazátlan, I found it difficult to cope with the emotions I was experiencing. I hated the thought of leaving, so instead focused on getting back into shape. Early each morning I took my kayak out into the ocean, and began the slow, painful torture of preparing for the rest of my journey. I wasn't in as bad of shape as I thought I would be and felt the old strength returning after only a few workouts.

I did face two small disappointments before I left. I had stayed in Mazátlan an extra week, awaiting the arrival of Allan Perry. But a few days before he was supposed to leave the States, he telephoned to say he couldn't make the trip. Some personal problems had come up. At first I was a little angry at his decision, but I reminded myself that situations often come up that are out of our control. No matter what good intention people have, God was the only one I'd found who would uphold his end of the bargain every time.

To make up for his absence, Allan told me he would send down a care package.

The Mexican Post Office took two weeks to deliver the package. I had expected it to come in only a week and was incredibly anxious to leave the city when it finally arrived. If it had not come that day, I would have left the following morning without it.

It was well worth the wait. Several of my close friends had pitched in, and when I opened the package I found several cigars, some clothes, good luck cards, cassette tapes and a new radio.

The other disappointment came on Thanksgiving Day. I walked down to the marina, hoping to visit my friends Stuart and Dee. If you remember, they were the couple, along with their baby daughter Coral, with whom I had spent a good week and a half, traveling across the Gulf of California. We had planned to meet in Mazátlan for turkey dinner, but I couldn't find their boat registered in any of the sloops. By asking around, I learned that the *Running Shoe* had run into some problems on the other side of the coast and Stuart and Dee had decided to stay in La Paz for Thanksgiving.

On a positive note, the Mazátlan newspaper, *The Noroeste*, ran another article the day before I left. It seemed everyone in town wanted to say goodbye. On the eve of my departure, I agreed to a small get-together. One of my sponsors suggested we hold the festivities at his restaurant and said he would pick up the bill.

It was nice to see all my friends one last time. I gave a toast, promising my return in early to mid March. Mike and Alonso, who sat at my table, said, "Here, here," and we clinked our glasses together.

Alonso motioned me to the side of the table before leaving. "You're leaving tomorrow early, aren't you?" he asked.

I placed my hand on his shoulder. "I don't like goodbyes. That's why I haven't told anyone exactly when I'm leaving. You've been a great friend these last few weeks. I'll never forget all of your help. Remember, I can help you when you make it to the United States."

"Thanks," Alonso said. "You know, I've decided to save up the money, either here or in Cabo, and then go to America and coach, just like you said. So I just might take you up on that offer."

"Good for you. Remember, follow your heart."

"Make sure you call me when you complete your voyage. I know you said you'll come back to Mazátlan for a few days, so be sure to give me a call before you do."

"I will, Alonso." We hugged and parted sadly.

* * *

The next morning I went to see Mike Veslik one last time. He was in the newspaper office. When I knocked on the door lightly, he looked up, saw me, and waved me inside.

"Well," he said, standing up and smiling. "Guess this is it."

"Yeah, I guess so."

"You're one crazy guy, you know that?"

"You better believe it! Seriously, though, Mike, I can't thank you enough for all of the help and support you've given me. I couldn't have done it without you."

"Don't mention it," he said. "Just remember me in that movie. Guy with the tobacco, right?"

"I know, I know. I won't forget."

"One more thing," he continued. "Call me collect any time. I want to hear how you're doin'. When you get done and come back up to Mazátlan, we're gonna throw you a big party, so you better make it back in one piece."

"Don't worry," I replied, "I will."

"I wish I could go with you. Just to be safe, let's check the weather out." Mike walked over to his computer screen, got online, and brought up the National Weather Channel.

"It feels good out there to me," I said, while I looked over his shoulder, waiting for the screen to print the images. "Cloud cover and all, but I think the weather will hold."

"Uh, oh. Look here." Mike pointed at the blue and red streaks dotting the screen. "Big storm there. You can tell by the big swirling clouds. By the looks of the air currents, it's comin' our way. You gonna hang out here and see what she does?" he asked.

"No, probably not. Time to go."

"Yeah, I don't blame you." We shook hands and patted each other on the back the way two tough guys do to be affectionate.

An hour later, at 11:00 AM on Monday, December 2nd, after spending more than three weeks in that beautiful city, I left Mazátlan. Upon cresting over the first wave, I dug into the water with my paddle. The sun beat down on my back. I pulled my hat down over my brow and adjusted the sunglasses.

After a few minutes I turned around to allow myself one last look at the city. There was a knot in the pit of my stomach. I would miss the people there. But now that I was back on the water, my senses burst to renewed life, and I knew I was exactly where I was meant to be.

Everything around me seemed new, and yet familiar. I heard the slap of the waves against the hull and felt my muscles as they bore my kayak onward. The ocean moved beneath, rising and falling in her gentle rhythm, as though welcoming my return. I was back, traveling again over the water, and I was alive.

More than ever before.

TWENTY-THREE
Times Like These Would Not Last Forever

Once past the busy port of Mazátlan, the coastline stretched out in a long straight line. I avoided all of the late morning traffic in and out of the harbor and waved a final farewell to my second home.

By nightfall I was tired and decided to stop, eat dinner, and stay in my kayak on the ocean for the night. I knew that now, with more than half of my trip still ahead, I would have to face it with a new attitude. I welcomed the time alone. The ocean charged little for her quarters, and the beaches never asked for rent. That night, I took courage in the miles I had conquered and hope in those yet to come.

Early the next morning I was awake when the sun began to rise. Sometime during the night I noticed that I had drifted two or three miles south. For once, the current was working in my favor. I had been away from home a little less than three months. My entire focus and experience in life now seemed to revolve around the waters I so boldly passed. Life in the United States seemed a different time, a different place, almost like a dream. This was my new reality.

At noon I spotted the town of Las Cabanas. The coast was a pleasing sight of lush, tropical hills.

I had four gallons of drinking water left. To be safe, I paddled in and pulled to shore. At a Pemex gas station just beyond the beach I bought three more gallons of purified water, which I carried back to the kayak. I managed to get past the mid day swells with a minimum of salt water getting inside the cockpit. My spray skirt had been lost in the last storm, but there was nothing I could do about that now.

Once past the inlet, the shore ran straight as an arrow for as far as I could see. I checked the map of that area. Isla Isabelle appeared on the horizon, rising like an ancient serpent. There were several beaches on which to camp, with no rocks in sight.

A mile or so past the huts I pulled in past a small inlet near the town of Los Corchos. I set up my dilapidated tent, with its duct-taped poles and torn bottom. There was only a slight breeze coming down from the hills behind, so the wobbly frame was held throughout the night. I wondered how much more abuse the tent would take before it collapsed entirely.

I was again in the middle of nowhere, but now, unlike before, I felt a calm settle over my being. I closed my eyes and listened to the music of the waves. My attitude had changed since the beginning of the expedition. No longer did I feel the need to rush through each day, to finish the trip at the earliest possible moment. I drank in deeply of each day, each hour. Times like these would not last forever, I knew, and I wanted to enjoy them while I could.

* * *

The next morning, December 4, I felt refreshed and more alive than ever. I stretched, rested from a good night's sleep on land. I felt as though a weight had been lifted from my soul, and it was definitely a change for the better. I was free from the burdens of the world. Out here, I answered only to God.

* * *

On Friday, December 6, I pulled into the marina in Manzanillo. With the hope of seeing Edward, I found the public phone and dialed Guadalajara, Mexico. Maybe he would come down for the weekend and take me fishing in his boat. I was ready for a break.

It was not to be. The phone rang several times, until finally I hung up.

My kayak was secured tightly on one of the docks, and I knew, with the much larger boats around, that no one would even notice my tiny craft. I walked around the city, which was considerably busier than I'd expected. I decided to rent a hotel room for the night, and found a plain building with a faded sign in front.

The room cost sixty *pesos* for the night—about eight dollars. The room was bare but relatively clean, and I immediately jumped in the shower. The pure water felt heavenly, and I stayed there for almost half an hour. Yes, there was something to be said for life in the city. That night I slept on a real bed.

I tried to phone Edward the next morning before leaving. But again I couldn't reach him.

Back again in my kayak, I crossed the bay to Punta Compos with ease. The coast south of Manzanillo was bare, with little greenery. Gray sandbanks offered little room to camp, and the cliffs behind rose sharply. The surf along this stretch was extremely dangerous and rough.

Before I'd started my trip, people had asked all kinds of questions. I'd thought of the idea to kayak to South America long before I knew there was a previous record. I was asked how I would be able to verify the longest solo kayak trip as a world's record. The current unofficial record for a solo kayak expedition on the ocean was said to have been 3,600 miles. It was, however, an undocumented event. How would I substantiate mine?

"Will the record count if you stay in a hotel one night?" asked one radio station DJ.

At a television station, the interviewer inquired, "What if you take a week off and go inland?"

"What if someone else goes with you part of the way?" someone else asked.

I didn't know the answer to any of those questions, then or now. When I left San Felipe, going for the record had seemed important. Now, two thousand miles later, it didn't matter if I set the record or not. All that mattered to me was my personal safety, my happiness, and my relationship with God.

I'd said I would make it to South America. Now, regardless of who liked it or not, I was going to go back home for Christmas.

Several changes had taken place in my mind over the past months. I'd found a peace within myself. I had spent my birthday and Thanksgiving alone, and I spent another holiday away from my family.

I had asked my dad, one time when we were talking on the phone, if he would mind buying me a plane ticket to Knoxville, Tennessee for the holidays. My family was excited about the prospect of seeing the son they'd feared would never come home.

A week later, my dad would give me the confirmation number for my flight home. Who cared what anyone else thought?

TWENTY-FOUR
Signed, Benjamin Wade, Kayak Extremist

Even after my decision to go home for Christmas, I still dreamed about world records. What can I say? I couldn't help myself.

I had paddled seven days without stopping. My muscles were to showing signs of fatigue. The tendons in my arms would quiver, then spasm.

I worried that if I continued at this pace I would do real damage to my muscles. I forced myself to rest. I sat back, stretched, and let my body relax. After a few hours and a meal, I felt stronger.

I promised myself that in a day or so, I would stop in Ixtapa and rest some more.

I paddled past a large bluff called Bufadero. The reddish cliffs of the point were steep, and the surf broke wildly at its base. I pushed on, looking for a spot to take shelter. The coast, however, had other plans, and I watched in dismay as the relentless surf pounded on the shore. The sun quickly dropped below the horizon, and still I found no place to pull in safely.

I paddled for as long as my muscles would allow that night and then let my kayak drift away from shore. I stretched out, tying myself down, looping rope around my waist and then around the hull of the kayak. My eyes closed.

When I woke up, it was very dark. It took nearly a minute for my eyesight to adjust. I couldn't see anything, even my compass, with which to navigate, and at first I panicked, fearing the current might have taken me out several miles.

Then I realized that I was only using one of my inadequate senses. I strained my ears, and in the distance I heard the ever-accompanying rumble of the waves breaking on a beach. Relieved, I paddled for a while toward the sound.

When I was satisfied that I was in a safe location, I crawled back up to the front of the boat and again strapped myself down. By listening carefully, I found I could tell my approximate distance from the shore.

The coast was still void of substantial landmarks, and it wasn't until nearly noon the next day before I found my bearings and located my position on the map. By identifying the topographical features of the coast, I eventually was able to pinpoint my location. It was a skill Stuart had taught me during those few days on his sailboat.

"Take that point over there and look at the compass," he had said.

"Got it," I replied.

"Good. Write that number down on the chart. Take that island's bearing there. You got it? Now write that number down too."

"Now what?" I had asked, puzzled and completely unable to read the various other numbers on the map.

"Simple, mate. Just draw two lines, at their given angles, and where they intersect, that's where you are."

It never ceased to amaze me how much I'd learned from all the people I met on this trip.

* * *

By the next day I was closing in on the Ixtapa-Zihuatanejo area. Instead of the lethargic twenty to thirty miles a day I had been covering at the start of my journey, I was now flying at almost forty. My tired muscles and weary mind were encouraged by my progress.

After rounding Punta Mangrove, and the lighthouse that stood at its end, I passed the mouth of another river. The ocean went wild. Breakers crested in all directions, and I headed farther out to sea.

Once clear of the breakers, I bailed out a few pints of water that had collected between my legs. I then cut straight across the Bay of Petacalco, a large, angled bay, five miles wide and fifteen miles long. Late that evening I saw the impressive hotels and structures of Ixtapa.

The breakers still looked impressive, and I waited until I saw a small break in the coastline before I paddled to shore. The name of the beach was Playa San Juan.

After securing my kayak to a *palapa*, I stared in awe at the glitter and glamour of the city. There were new hotels and shops everywhere. The city looked as though it had been built yesterday. The streets had been swept clean, there was fresh paint on the buildings, and the hotels rose far above my head.

The city itself began a few blocks north of where I had landed on the beach, and my pace quickened as I neared civilization. Though I felt out of place, it still drew me in. My clothes were ragged, there were too many people, and things seemed to be going at a much faster pace than I was used to. I checked the prices of a nearby hotel, and found it to be almost three times more than the one I'd stayed at in Mazátlan.

For me, it was another night on the beach.

The next morning I allowed myself several hours to browse the shops around the town. This port of Mexico was unlike any city I had been to. It was a stark contrast to the more laid-back cities in northern Mexico.

I spent part of day in the lobby of one of the hotels, dozing on one of the over-stuffed couches. It was also interesting to watch the people walk by. They were all in such a hurry and dressed as though they were going to a parade. I'd the decency to put on a shirt before walking inside, but I still looked like a beach bum.

Refreshed, I left the city shortly after 5:00 PM. I decided not to spend another night on the beach because I wanted to arrive in Acapulco as soon as possible. The thought of being with my family for Christmas made me eager to get going. After buying three more gallons of drinking water, I departed from the city of Ixtapa.

I set the compass on the bow to a steady one hundred and twenty degrees, southeast. Settling into a decisive rhythm, I paddled forward, waiting for the moon to rise.

By midnight, though my muscles were only beginning to tire, my eyes were heavy. I stopped my stroke, strapped my paddle to the outrigger, and dozed. Again I was restless, for fear of drifting away from the coast. By morning I was more tired than I thought I should be, and relished my upcoming vacation all the more. The rising sun chased away the flickering beam cast by the lighthouse at Punta Japuntica.

On Friday afternoon, December 13, I finally reached the outskirts of Acapulco. Already, after rounding the point of Lorenz, passing between the mainland and Isla La Roqueta, I saw a mass of skyscrapers reaching toward the sky. It was an assault to my eyes to see such a swarm of people concentrated in one area. I was intimidated by the size and mass of this city. I was beginning to have second thoughts about immersing myself in the States for a week, but the arrangements had already been made.

I pulled into shore on a beach I later found to be Playa Calea. Once ashore, I walked up the sand, past some trees, and found the nearest house. There was a great iron gate that protected the entrance; it appeared no one was home. I needed a place to store my kayak for the next week and a half, and didn't want to waste time hunting. I took a closer look through the dense underbrush to the side of the house. No cars were in the driveway, and the grass had not been mowed for several weeks.

I went down to the beach, where a couple of tourists were already looking at my kayak. One of the men spoke English, and I asked him if he had seen anyone in the big, two-story house up the street. He told me that he'd been coming to this beach for two weeks and hadn't seen anyone there.

"I figured the owners are on vacation," he said. Tall and thin, his face was red, probably from being in the sun too much during this vacation. "Can you imagine that? Livin' in Acapulco and goin' somewhere else to get away."

I could believe it.

I asked him for a hand, and after a few minutes we set the kayak down inside the fence, on the lawn. It was incredibly light. I had consumed over two hundred pounds of food since the beginning of the trip.

He hung around for a little bit, watching me as I wrote a note in case the owners of the house returned before I did.

> *To the owner of this house:*
>
> *This kayak is only here for a short time. I am in the process of taking a long distance trip to South America and needed a place to store it during Christmas. I hope it is not an inconvenience. When I get back, I will compensate you with what I can. Thanks in advance.*
>
> *Signed, Benjamin Wade, Kayak Extremist*

I placed the letter in a plastic bag and tied it to the chain with a small piece of rope. I prayed it would be safe until my return.

My dad, as I said earlier, had purchased my tickets from Mexico City to Tennessee a month before. The dates on the ticket were from the December 21 to the 29. Since I was ahead of schedule, I decided to change the flight to one leaving a few days earlier. One small problem—I still had to get from Acapulco to Mexico City.

I spotted a taxicab, and asked the driver to take me to the airport just outside of Acapulco.

The cab wove in and out of the afternoon traffic, and after what seemed like hours we arrived at the airport. Palm trees rose from the far side of the landing strip. There were only a few people walking in and out of the airport entrance, and I found myself relaxing. I rolled my shoulders and neck from side to side, shaking off the tension that had built up from the ride through the city.

The cab ride cost 140 *pesos*, a little under twenty dollars. I hadn't spent that much money at one time since I'd entered Mexico! I shook my head and handed him the money. Welcome to the city, I thought as I went inside the airport terminal.

Suddenly I had an idea. I found the nearest pay phone and picked up the receiver, then asked the national operator to make a collect call to Guadalajara. Edward picked up on the other end.

"Edward, this is Ben!" I said with enthusiasm.

"Ben, my friend, how are you?" Edward asked. "I have been worried about you. You haven't called in a long time."

"I know. I tried to call you when I got to Manzanillo, but you weren't at home."

"I'm sorry. Did you stay on my boat?"

"No," I said a little sheepishly. "I forgot the name of it."

"That's too bad," he said with a laugh. "You know, I told Carlos, my friend, about you, and we were going to come down and meet you when you got there."

"Well, that stinks," I said. "I guess I messed up."

"No problem. We can always do that when you come back up this way. Where are you now?"

"Acapulco," I said. "I've been making good time. Listen, I was wondering if we could get together over the next couple of days."

"What? I guess I don't understand."

"I'm flying home to Tennessee to be with my family over Christmas. The plane leaves from Mexico City on the 21st, so I have a few days to spare. If it's okay with you, I thought I'd take a bus to Guadalajara. What do you think?"

"You got the time, I got the place. I am happy for you that you get to see your family," he said. "I have to go to Mexico City on business in the next few days. One of my customers, Quaker Oats, wants to have a meeting with me. Tell you what, I'll meet you at the airport in Mexico City."

"Really?" I asked, surprised.

"In fact, I'm going to make some phone calls. In thirty minutes, go to the Aero Mexico ticket counter and pick up your ticket."

I said, "Edward, I can't let you do that."

"I insist!" he said, and there was no further arguing. "Ben, you are my friend, you are in Mexico. You are my special guest, and I wouldn't have it any other way."

I couldn't believe what I was hearing. Edward, as I would learn in the next few days, was the most generous man I'd ever met.

"I'll meet you in front of the ticket counter at 10:00 tonight," he finished decisively.

"I don't know what to say," I muttered feebly. "Edward, you are the man. See you in a couple of hours."

Indeed, when I asked the Aero Mexico ticket agent if there was a ticket for me, she smiled and handed me my boarding pass. I boarded the plane and arrived an hour later in Mexico City. Acapulco had been just a warm-up for my introduction into Mexican society. Mexico City, one of the most densely populated cities in the world, with over twenty million people, was an absolute zoo.

Stepping off the plane, I was met by thousands of people, pushing and shoving to get to their respective departures. It was wall-to-wall chaos. I fought my way, carrying two bulging bags, down the runway and into the terminal. It was even more crowded there.

I sat down and took a moment to collect my thoughts. I felt claustrophobic sitting there with everyone swarming around me like bees in a colony.

Instinctively I tried to visualize where the ocean was. I realized that I was a hundred miles from the nearest beach. That thought filled me with a deep longing to be near the ocean again, to feel the waves beneath my kayak. I yearned to hear the breakers crashing, and to taste salt water. I understood then that I could never again live without the ocean nearby. It was now as much a part of me as anything had ever been.

TWENTY-FIVE
Christmas Came And Went

Edward met me at the Aero Mexico ticket counter at 10:15 PM. His hand was outstretched in greeting, and the broad smile on his face told me he was as happy to see me as I was to see him. The crowd at the airport had died down, and Edward quickly led me outside and hailed a taxi. At the hotel, right in the middle of downtown Mexico City, we checked in. The reservations for the room had been made an hour before. I was amazed at Edward's resourcefulness and planning.

The room was plush, with a living room, two queen size beds and a Jacuzzi. The standards far exceeded anything I had stayed in recently. It was a luxury I could not have afforded on my own.

That night we went to eat at an Italian restaurant just a few blocks from the hotel. Over dinner we talked about Edward's business, and his wife and kids.

I told him of the adventures that had befallen me since we'd first met. We agreed that when I returned to Mexico I would stop in Manzanillo. He promised, again, to set aside a few days to meet me there. After dinner, though it was very late, we walked back to the hotel and watched a movie before drifting off to sleep.

The next day Edward met with the executives from Quaker Oats. I took the rare opportunity to sleep late. I needed the rest. For nearly three months I'd spent my nights on the water, on the sand, or at cheap hotels. This morning, with the fresh clean sheets surrounding my body and the soft pillow cushioning my head, I slept until noon.

After I woke up, Edward called and said to meet him downstairs. We had lunch, then we went through the crowded streets of Mexico City, where I looked for gifts to take home to my family. I purchased a handmade doll for my mother, an Aztec stone calendar for my Father, and an Indian onyx necklace for my brother,

Peter. Our family had lived all over the world, and I knew they'd appreciate the culturally diverse gifts.

After dinner that night we went to one of the largest dance clubs in the city, La Boom. There was a long line of people waiting to get in, but we were dressed in nice suits, both from Edward's wardrobe. Within a few minutes, we were ushered inside. In Mexico, money talks. Edward made arrangements with a waiter to reserve an entire section for us.

Edward introduced me around, and soon there was a crowd of people in our reserved section. He loved to tell them about my adventures. Since everyone was genuinely interested, I talked about the various storms, sharks, and gunmen I had met along the way. I also made sure to tell them the reason I was still alive. The memory of that storm, when God had spoken to me, still weighed heavily on my mind. I was eager to share with them my faith and the miracle I'd experienced.

* * *

The next morning we got up early and went to the airport. Edward would fly back to his home, and I to mine. I put my arm around him and told him how much I appreciated his generosity. Not once since I'd met him had Edward asked me to pay for anything. Mexico City had been no exception, and I felt honored to be with such a big-hearted man.

Soon I was boarding my plane, headed for the states. At one point, halfway through the flight, I looked out the window and saw the waters of the Gulf of Mexico. The bright blue water stretched out for miles. In the distance I could saw the white sandy shores. I smiled at the memories this image brought, and of a life where I had been reborn.

Soon, I thought. *Very soon. I will return to you.*

I had called my dad from the hotel the night before and let him know the new time and date for my arrival. Our family has always been very close, and I was looking forward to our reunion. I tried to imagine their reaction when I stepped off the plane. Shaved head, dark skin, and a long goatee. The hair on my chin had been growing out for three months. Also, I had a long shark's tooth hanging from the earring of my left ear.

My excitement mounted as I walked down the terminal at the airport in Knoxville, Tennessee. I rushed to where my mom stood and hugged her for several minutes. After I picked up my luggage, which consisted of two backpacks, we headed to the car, where my dad was waiting. He raised his eyebrows, no doubt surprised at his changed son, then smiled.

Contrary to my conservative roots, I had always gone my separate way. My family was as different from me as night and day. They were professors and teachers, content in their way of life. But with the ever-loving arms that only a family can provide, they welcomed me, no matter how I looked.

On the trip home we talked about the journey I'd been on for the past three months.

"Your father and I have been very worried about you," my mom said from the back seat.

"Yes, we have," my Dad chimed in. "You know, I'm fifty-three now. A little too old to be going through something like this."

"Now, Dad," I said, placing my hand on his shoulder. "My whole outlook has changed. For instance, if at the end of this trip of mine I'm closer to God than I've ever been, then in my mind it's all been worth it. Or if this opens up new doors for me, like a career, or even a new ministry, then it's been time well spent. I feel that these things have happened, and will continue to."

I looked over at Dad, then back at Mom, to see their expressions. They seemed receptive, so I continued.

"I feel so at peace with myself, and with God. It's awesome. To be out there, one with the environment, is incredible. I feel myself in this slow kind of dance with the ocean and her Creator—I can't describe it. God is really changing my life, getting me ready for something even better."

I talked for the rest of the trip home. At the end, I took a deep breath and felt a great weight lifting off my chest. They could see now, I hoped, that I wasn't completely insane, and after awhile, everyone relaxed.

A few days later, Peter arrived. It felt just like old times. With him, I could discuss, in more detail, the many harrowing situations I'd found myself in recently. I'd been reluctant to tell my parents about all of the dangers of the journey. During the previous phone calls from Mexico, I had told them little of the storms, sharks and other mishaps. I hadn't wanted them to be more concerned than they already were. But at my brother's prodding, I told them some of the more exciting stories. Fortunately, they seemed to take it well.

Christmas came and went, as did the rest of my time at home. Before I could really settle in, it was time to repack and head back to Mexico.

My parents had one last surprise for me before I left. It did, however, come at an inopportune time.

"Make sure you leave Friday night open," my mom said to me one night before dinner.

"Why?" I asked.

"Just because we said so," my dad interjected. "There's going to be a surprise for you."

"That's going to be kind of difficult," I said. "My friends are planning a going-away party for me that night. Can we make it Thursday or Saturday?"

"I'm afraid not, Benjamin," my mom said, shaking her head.

"Well, why not?" I asked stubbornly.

"We are not at liberty to say," she said. "Someone else is in charge."

We went back and forth for nearly an hour. My parents requesting that I move the party to another day; I insisting they tell me why it had to be Friday. None of us would budge.

Later that evening I called my friend Rick, who was in charge of the party, and asked if we could move it to Saturday. Rick and I had gone to high school and college together. I knew well his moods. He wasn't going to like this one.

"Nope," was his simple but firm reply.

"Why not?" I seemed to be asking that question a lot lately.

"Dude," Rick said impatiently, "we've already sent out the invitations. It's your party, man. What's the problem?"

"Some kind of surprise my parents are planning," I said. "They won't tell me what it is."

We finally agreed that I would go to the going-away party until 10:30 PM. After that I promised my parents I would come back to the house.

* * *

The party was a blast. I continued to be touched by the number of caring friends on my side. When it came time for me to leave, though, everybody began to groan and complain.

"This is the last time we'll see you," I heard.

And, "Why're you running off so early?"

And, "The fun's just getting started!"

Touched by their words, I asked everyone to come over to the house in two hours. Whatever surprise was going on at home, these friends would just have to be included. Ray, another close friend from the University of Tennessee, drove me back to my parent's house.

I walked in the door at exactly 10:30. Only my parents were there. I hid my disappointment.

A few minutes later a car pulled in the driveway. I got up and looked out the window. The last person I expected to see stepped out of the car—my cousin, Brad Jordan. Brad and I were like brothers, and I was thrilled that he'd come up from Atlanta to see me. I opened the door to greet him with a hug.

Coincidentally, Brad was going to be in Puerto Escondido, Mexico on January 9, for a business meeting. Since it was along my path, on the Pacific coast of Mexico, we made tentative plans to rendezvous there. I couldn't believe my good fortune as consistently, every week, someone was brought into my life that helped me proceed to the next step. I couldn't imagine surviving the long, grueling months on the open ocean had it not been for the sacrifice of others.

I had been somewhat embittered towards humanity in the months preceding my journey to South America. My faith since then had been restored. I'd seen so much of the good in others, good that far outweighed the occasional glimpses of the bad. I was ready to continue, not just my travels in a kayak, but the more important journey of my soul.

TWENTY-SIX
I Greeted The New Year With Neither Flair Nor Festivity

Heather and I spoke twice while I was in Tennessee. Though we had wanted to spend a few days together, time did not permit it. I left Knoxville on December 29. I had plenty of time to reflect on my relationship with Heather during the seven-hour flight to Mexico City.

Something was wrong. I couldn't quite place my finger on it. We'd been so passionate at first, and if I had asked, she would have flown to every major city I passed through to be with me.

Looking back, I don't believe that there was anything we could have done. There was a pull, so powerful and magnetic, that neither of us could see nor fight it. It was the power the ocean had over me. I could not devote myself to anyone else while I was in this spell. Heather had come in second to my first love. Few women would tolerate that.

* * *

Though it was hard to leave my family, I was eagerly looking forward to the rest of the trip. My heart beat faster as I once again smelled the salt air.

That night, as I lay down to sleep in a darkened hotel room, my mind raced with anticipation. Was my kayak still there near the beach, where I'd hidden it? I had given it little thought until now, but if it wasn't, what would I do then? I sat up in bed, sweating a little, and wondered if I should get dressed, call a cab, and go down to the house where I had left it. But I lay back down, knowing that at this point I could do nothing about it. If my kayak was there now, it would still be there in the morning.

At sunrise I took a taxi back to the hill where I hoped my kayak still rested. I walked back through the winding roads to the point of Bolsa Chica. When I saw the corner of the street where the house stood, I broke into a run. Several yards from the gate I saw the turquoise stripe along the gray, fiberglass hull of my kayak. I cried out in relief when I saw it was still there, protruding a few feet from the iron bars. I opened the side gate and stepped up to my old friend. The note I had written was gone, but everything else was in good shape.

Relieved, I took another taxi back to the edge of town. The Super Mercado was already open. I needed to restock my supplies, which were nearly depleted. Of the food I'd started out with, I had only a dozen PowerBars, ten bags of oatmeal, and a few bags of dried mashed potatoes.

I bought sixty-eight bags of oatmeal, six boxes of *Zucharitas* (Mexican Frosted Flakes), ten pounds of beef jerky, and six loaves of bread. After the meals I'd feasted on over Christmas, I looked bleakly at my groceries. Though a part of me was still annoyed at the confines of society and the hassles it brought, another part would miss the comforts I had enjoyed recently.

In addition to the food, I also bought three bottles of Aloe Vera gel. Being constantly in the sun had severely dried my skin.

I took the four bags of groceries, plus six gallons of water, back to the kayak. By the time I hauled the kayak down to the beach, Playa Caleya, it was almost noon.

I secured my new supplies in the front and back storage compartments, being careful to rearrange them according to frequency of use.

Before pushing off, I paused a moment in prayer. I had much to be thankful for. I was still alive, of course, but God had also blessed me with great health. With the exception of drinking contaminated water, some serious bruises and a few scrapes and cuts, I'd done remarkably well. The many people I'd encountered along the way had, for the most part, been welcoming, supportive and generous. A wave of confidence swept over my being. With God on my side, I would successfully complete the rest of the expedition and would return home safely in both mind and body. I was sure of it.

I put my craft's nose in the water, let the small waves break over the bow, and felt the cool water splash around my feet. I smiled and jumped quickly into the cockpit, ignoring the few people who had gathered on the shore. There was only one thing that mattered to me now.

As soon as my paddle broke through the swirling water, I felt a peace of mind return. Pelicans soared overhead, the waves crashed behind, and the breeze gently stirred. All was exactly as I had left it.

* * *

The humidity was oppressive by midday, and my energy was sapped after paddling only a couple of hours. I had expected to tire easily this time, and I took several breaks. Sometimes I paddled for only an hour before my muscles begged for rest. Obviously I was not traveling a great distance that day, but the lack of mileage didn't bother me. I knew my old form would return.

When I reached the beaches of Playa Caletilla, I headed straight across the bay.

Once out in the deeper waters, I felt surprisingly vulnerable. There was an excessive amount of traffic from motorized boats. Again I felt the helplessness of being the slowest, smallest vessel in the water. I forced myself to quicken my pace, avoiding the other boats.

Soon enough, the hotels, houses, crowded streets and stench of Acapulco were a distant memory. That evening, muscles aching, a deep, throbbing pain in my right shoulder, I headed for shore. Near San Macros, I decided I'd exerted myself enough for one day. I surfed the smaller waves to the sand, leaning back in the cockpit and enjoying the helping hand and power of nature pushing me to shore. It was easy to ride the smaller waves, and I watched the water rush by as I steered the kayak safely to the beach. I looked around and saw that it was deserted, and I was once again alone.

Surprisingly, as I ate and later set up my dilapidated tent, I didn't feel the depressing walls of solitude close in as they'd done so frequently before. I missed my family and home, but felt at peace again with my surroundings. The loneliness I had endured earlier in the trip was long gone, and I could look ahead and focus on other issues.

* * *

The next day was December 31, New Year's Eve. I woke to the familiar voice of the ocean, crashing against the shore. I rose eagerly, stretched my cramped muscles and ate a small breakfast of oatmeal and cereal. It was about 5:30 AM, when I headed out to sea. I wondered what my friends would be doing back home, this last day of the year.

The ocean ahead grew restless. The waves that rolled in to shore near Punta Acamama were starting to form more than a mile out. The white tips broke in perfect rhythm with my own stroke. I couldn't afford to be pulled closer to shore, so I headed farther away from the beach.

My muscles, after several hours of constant work, loosened. I didn't quite feel like my old self, but I was getting there. The night was closing in fast. I looked for a place to camp. Nearing Punta Maldonado, the breakers were still forming far from the shore, seven to ten feet in height. As tempting as the white sand of the beach looked from my vantage point, I dared not pursue it.

The night air was hot and humid, so I stayed in my kayak on the open water. As I leaned back in my seat and looked up at the stars, I greeted the New Year with neither flair nor festivity. There were a few shooting stars, my only fireworks. Midnight passed. I was either dozing or too tired to notice.

* * *

The next day I estimated I was gaining ground on my *per diem* goal. Eventually I wanted to travel fifty miles a day. I was doing about forty-three.

Brad Jordan would be flying into Puerto Escondido on the 9th, and I wondered if I should wait for his arrival. We had agreed to meet for the weekend, but by the looks of my recent progress, I would have traveled far past that city by the 9th. I would have to take a bus back up the coast to Puerto Escondido. I was beginning to doubt the practicality of such a move.

A glance at my watch told me it was almost 4:00 PM. The heat was beginning to slow me down, and I set my paddle across the outrigger to rest. To cool off, I decided to take a quick swim around the kayak. I crawled out of the cockpit, swung my legs over the edge and into the cool water. I was just about to jump in when I saw a shadow only a few feet beneath the surface of the water, inches from my dangling legs. The oddly shaped head and side-to-side movement told me that it was a bull shark, twelve to fourteen feet in length. Almost as long as my boat, its powerful movements sent ripples to the surface of the water.

I slowly brought my feet from the water, trying not to draw attention to myself. I held my breath. The shark glided slowly by. I eased the paddle from the side of the outrigger. As I brought the oar parallel to the water's surface, I spotted another shadow, a few feet behind the first.

My arms jerked. The paddle clunked against the side of the kayak, the sound echoing across the still water. I saw the head of the second shark jump in response, looking for whatever had made the sound. Both sharks drew closer to investigate. They were less than a foot from my midsection. I saw their eyes, flat and cold, staring up into mine.

After a few intense minutes in which I held my breath, they swam slowly away. I breathed a sigh of relief and immediately gave thanks to God for my safety.

I was still shaking a bit when I paddled away from the site. I made up my mind that no matter how powerful the breakers were tonight, I was going to sleep on land—far from any sharks!

TWENTY-SEVEN
Beneath Some Overhanging Trees, We Made Camp

On January 3, a Friday, I paddled to the northern tip of Puerto Escondido and landed on Bacocho Beach. The sun sparkled off the blue water like a thousand diamonds. The few rocks that stood alone at various distances from the soft sand easily withstood the pounding breakers. Palm trees, a hundred feet tall and in groves a mile deep, seemed to stand guard over this sacred property.

Children ran around on the beaches, jumping in and out of the surf. A few fishermen waded into deeper water, casting their nets and hooks. They stayed well away from the people as they did their work, so as not to disturb anyone's fun. Older tourists lounged about under cabanas, sipping their soft drinks and soaking up the sun. A small restaurant, beneath a thatched roof, served fresh fish and shrimp.

This was the morning I was to call Brad and confirm our rendezvous for the following week. Though we might possibly meet at this very spot, I decided that in a day or two I would push further on, in hopes of completing the expedition by early March.

When in Acapulco, I had checked the bus fares and schedules from the small cities south of Puerto Escondido and found the rates to be reasonable. On the one hand it seemed counterproductive to paddle south, only to bus north again, but I was eager to see my cousin again.

South of the cabanas, fishermen and tourists, I spotted a small stretch of sand, where the waves were less powerful. Protected by the curving upper arm of land and rocks that thrust out into the sea, I guided my kayak through the tranquil waters and onto the beach. I locked my kayak to a nearby palm tree. At a nearby pay phone I dialed the international operator, gave her the phone number for Hussman Corporation in Atlanta, and in a few moments was talking to Brad.

"Where are you Ben?" he asked.

"Puerto Escondido, dude!" I said proudly.

"No way! You made it there quick."

"I sure did. Incentives, you know?"

"We're still meeting there, right?" he asked.

"You bet!"

Brad gave me the name and address of the hotel where he would be staying. I wrote the information in my journal.

That night, instead of going back to the kayak, I walked to the outskirts of the city, looking for a room for the night. There were a few hotels along the beach where I'd landed, but they were too expensive for me. In the city, it was the peak season for vacationing tourists, and I couldn't find one available room. At every hotel I was told that there would be nothing available until after the weekend. I was about to head back to the beach when I saw a man waving me over.

He asked if I needed a room for the night, and I said I did. He showed me his place, which consisted of four small *cabanas*. There was one vacant, and I said I'd take it.

The outside of the cabin was made of wood slats, which barely met in spots. Cockroaches clung to the walls, and the bathroom, damp and rank, looked like a prime breeding ground for mosquitoes. Later I found bat droppings on the bed sheets, apparently coming from the rafters above the bed. The shower was cold water only. But a roof over my head, a mattress to sleep on and running water was all I needed at the moment.

I took my first shower since leaving Acapulco and put on a clean pair of shorts. The sun had set, but there was enough light yet to see the ocean in the bay, a hundred feet below. The cabanas had nice, wide front porches, looking out over the water. Bamboo chairs were spread along the verandah. I sat on one.

There was a couple from the Czech Republic next door, and we struck up a conversation. Jakob, at about six-foot six inches, towered over me. He also had a shaved head and goatee. His wife, Lucia, was medium height and build, with shoulder-length blonde hair. Both were tanned by the sun, even more so than me. They had been in the cabana next to mine for over a month, they told me, but were soon heading up the coast. Jakob and I looked at a map of Mexico. I told him the best places to visit and the ones to avoid. By the time I went to bed, I decided I would spend one more night in the little town of Puerto Escondido.

* * *

The sun shone brightly the next morning, coming through the cracks in the walls. I walked onto the front porch and after a few minutes was joined by Jakob. He was drinking hot tea from a gourd of some sort, and Lucia brought out an additional one for me. We stood in silence for a few moments, sipping our tea and looking out over the dazzling blue water.

After awhile, Jakob looked over to me and asked, "What are your plans today?"

"I'm not sure. What are you guys doing?"

"We're going to a river nearby to fish. You're not going to continue on your kayak?"

"No, I don't think so. Not today," I said. "I need a break from the action."

"Why don't you come with us, then." So with that, we were off.

Lucia and Jakob were a very easy-going couple. They talked about their lives. They had been married for five years, but still displayed the affection and playfulness of newlyweds.

After an hour of winding through the foothills we reached our stop. A dirt road meandered off from the paved road. An old metal sign with the word "*La Cieba*" printed on it, told us we were in the right place.

As we walked to the river, we passed several small farmhouses. Birds chirped in the trees overhead, and a few cows grunted contentedly from the tall grass on the side of the road. We heard the lazy flow of the river around a bend in the road before we actually came upon it. The road ended in a long spit of gravel, and soon we were standing at the water's edge.

We had picked up a guide along the way, and he pointed upstream. "More fish, up there," he said.

After a few minutes of walking upstream, we could tell by the increase of vegetation that the banks of the river would soon disappear. It was time to cross to the other side. The river was only about twenty feet wide but clearly deep enough to require swimming. We each stripped down to our swimsuits and holding our dry clothes above the water, did a one-handed stroke across to the other side.

We stopped at a place where the water spread out to form a small lake about five feet deep. There was a small waterfall leading out of this area, marking the first surge of power to the river below. Beneath some overhanging trees, we made camp.

The day was spent relaxing. Lucia collected rocks and sunned herself on a spit of sand. Jakob and the guide first caught crayfish, used them for bait, then cast their lines. They put some of the bigger crustaceans in a plastic bag filled with water, to eat later. They each caught a fish.

I was content to sit and meditate. It was nice to be around people, but I needed time to myself, as well. At about 2:00 PM, we jumped back into the river. The current carried us swiftly to the road, our clothes still held above our heads in triumph. We walked up the hill, and were soon back in the city.

* * *

On the morning of January 5, after a shared breakfast of sweet bread and hot tea, I said goodbye to the couple from the Czech Republic, promising them I would be back in a few days.

As I paddled off toward the horizon, I thought about Brad, whom I would see soon. Before I had been surprised by Brad's visit after Christmas in Knoxville, it had been more than three years since we'd last been together. It was interesting to see how our different paths in life sometimes lead us back to each other.

The sun was high in the sky. The ocean swells were large but not threatening. I let my mind wander to the past . . .

* * *

It was 1990. I had moved to Whittier, California, for the summer. The University of Tennessee was out for the summer semester, and my Uncle Deryl had agreed to put me to work sweeping floors at his company. The work itself wasn't important. What I had really looked forward to was being on my own. Though I was going to stay with my grandparents, I had the guesthouse in the back to myself. The world was at my fingertips; my future a bright certainty.

One Saturday morning, my mom called. By the tone of her voice I knew it was serious. She told me my cousin Rod had been killed in a motorcycle accident two days earlier. The funeral was that very day, and Mom urged me to go.

I showered quickly, dressed, and headed to the cemetery. Though my brother and I had grown up with Brad and Rod, I hadn't called either of them since my arrival in California. I was uncomfortable seeing Brad like this for the first time. How should I act? What could I say? I knew the loss of his brother would be devastating.

I stepped out of my car and squinted in the bright sun. There was a crowd of people at Rose Hills Cemetery, heading toward the chairs that had been set out. At first I was unsure if I would even recognize my cousin, Brad. Then I heard my name being called. Turning around, I saw my cousin coming toward me. I saw the hurt on his face, but he managed a weak smile as we locked together in a strong hug.

After the burial, Brad and I had a chance to go back to his house and talk. There I learned the details of Rod's death. Through frustrated tears we talked of our future and our dreams, trying to escape the depressing present.

The next summer, 1991, I flew to California again to work for my uncle. This time I had only been inside my grandparents' house for a few hours when the phone rang.

"Dude!" came the familiar voice. "What are you doing out here so soon?" Brad sounded excited, and I knew already that it was going to be a great summer.

"We need to get together and really spend some time," I said. "When are we getting hooked up?"

"What are you doing this weekend?" Brad asked.

"Nothin', of course. What's up?"

"You and me are gonna do some dirt bike riding in the dessert."

I knew I couldn't say no.

Brad, at that time, was one crazy young man. He lived for the thrill of danger, and every weekend he had some new scheme for us. Back then I was less than adventurous. I was in college, making good grades, and I had plans. I did a little partying, but always kept on the safe side. Looking back, I think I was a little uptight. Spending time with Brad opened my eyes. After that summer, I looked at life with an entirely new attitude.

* * *

When I saw Brad again, during this most recent Christmas, it wasn't a surprise to find that he'd moved to another city, locked into a better job, and had started a family. He had come to Knoxville that Christmas with his wife, Nina, and son Ridge. The feeling of brotherhood between us had not changed. I was impressed with the way he'd turned his life around. From a wandering kid, haunted by memories of death, he'd become a top sales representative for

Hussman Corporation, in charge of the South American market zone.

Brad and I had several hours to talk, laying down strong foundations and making our plans to meet in Mexico.

"You know, Ben," he said as we sat in my dad's office looking out over the mountains, "if I didn't have a wife and kid, I'd drop everything and go with you."

"I know you would," I said. "There's nothing more I'd rather experience than you with me on the ocean."

"Man, sometimes I feel so trapped. You don't know how it feels."

I looked over and saw the frustration in his eyes.

"Wait a minute," I said cautiously, sensing his despair. "Don't talk like that. I'm really proud of where you've gone in life."

He looked surprised, but pleased.

"Look at you!" I continued. "Everyone wants what you have. A great job, a beautiful wife and a healthy son. You have a lot to be thankful for."

"I know," Brad said, nodding. "But I miss the crazy adventures."

"Well, the grass is always greener on the other side of the fence. You've had your fair share of excitement, now I'm having mine. That doesn't mean we can't do something together in the future."

"You're right. Maybe next year we can go to Brazil and hike in the jungles." He grinned his old grin.

"Exactly!" I said. "In the meantime, let's enjoy Mexico."

"You bet we will."

Later that afternoon, we drove around for a while, when Brad stopped at a sporting goods store and bought me a hammock to take with me. I thanked him, not knowing there was more to come. Next Brad stopped by the bank. He withdrew two hundred dollars, then looked over at me and said, "You need some money, don't you?"

"Well, I don't have much, and I'm nearly out of food for the rest of my trip."

"Take this, then." Brad smiled as he held the entire sum out to me.

Astonished, I told him I couldn't take the money.

"Yes, you can," he said.

Slowly, I accepted the money. "On one condition. We get together once a year and do some trip like the one I'm taking."

"It's a done deal."

* * *

I smiled at the recollection. With my head held high, facing the southern horizon, I continued paddling on into the evening. What a turn of events, I thought to myself. And I would have missed it had I not gone home for the holidays.

Circumstances, I have found, do not just happen in life. Everything happens for a purpose, and if we are following God's plan, these things benefit us. I knew then, at Christmas time, that Brad's re-entrance into my life was not a coincidence. I smiled as I heard him talk about his upcoming sales conference in Mexico, just 200 miles south of Acapulco. I knew no matter what the cost, delay, or hassle, that I should be in the city at that time too. Already, I had been looking forward to the one-on-one time we would spend. Just like the old days.

TWENTY-EIGHT
"Life, and living it to the fullest."

A few days later, after parking my kayak at the Bay of Conejo, part of the city of Salina Cruz, and paying a local 100 *pesos* to watch it for a few days, I made my way to the nearest bus terminal.

The fare was only eight dollars. I was amazed at how short a time it took to travel the distance between the two cities. What had taken me five days on the ocean was only a few hours by land.

The bus station in Puerto Escondido was a few blocks from the cabanas where I'd stayed the week before. Sure enough, Lucia and Jakob were sitting in the old wicker chairs, enjoying the beginnings of a fine sunset. I called out as I walked down the path to the cabins. They looked up, smiled, and came out to meet me.

They would be leaving for Acapulco the next morning and had planned a going away party. The owner of the rooms fixed several pounds of fish and lobster. Jakob opened a bottle of wine, and we all talked well into the night, enjoying the food and friendship. Jakob would be coming to the States in a few months, and I made him promise to call me if he ever got to California.

* * *

The next morning we exchanged addresses and said goodbye. I went back to the cabana I'd rented and set about putting my few supplies of clothes, papers, and toiletries into my backpack. Brad wouldn't be arriving until later in the day, so I killed time for a few hours. Then I walked to the address Brad had given me the week before. In the lobby of the hotel, I sat down, pulled out my Bible and waited. After an hour, several taxis pull into the carport.

"There he is!" I heard Brad shout.

I looked up to see my cousin's smiling face. Soon I was being introduced to several of the top executives from the company, all of whom had questions about my trip. After I'd told and re-told some stories, the vice president, Mark Shaffer, asked if I wanted to join them for dinner. I looked at Brad, who winked his approval, and accepted with a smile.

For the next two days I lived and dined amidst the finest Puerto Escondido had to offer. Brad's associates had welcomed me with open arms, and I joined their entourage wherever they went. During the day we sat under umbrellas in wood lounge chairs, looked out over the blue water and sipped coconut drinks.

For dinner we ate lobster, fish, shrimp and octopus. Then more entrees and drinks were produced. I felt like a pig being fattened for the roast, but didn't mind one bit. Soon enough, I would be out on my own again, working off all the fat I'd stored.

After another elaborate meal, Brad, his boss Jay Mathis, and I went to the disco. We danced for a while, but later, while outside, we had a serious conversation.

"So, Ben," Jay said. "I don't know if Hussman is going to sponsor you. Might as well tell it to you straight."

Brad had mentioned this possibility, but I hadn't wanted to get my hopes up.

"I'll tell you what we're going to do, though," Jay continued. "Before we leave tomorrow, I'm going to go to the ATM in town and take out a hundred dollars. Brad, you're going to do the same, okay?"

"No problem," Brad said. He was grinning at me like a monkey.

"You should be able to get most of the way to South America with two hundred dollars, right?" Jay asked.

"Absolutely!" I said.

"I ask only one thing," Jay said. "When you get to Atlanta again to see Brad, we're all going to go out and have a good time. My wife would like to hear some of your stories, I'm sure."

True to their word, the next day they handed me the money in *pesos*. I thanked Brad and Jay in turn.

When Jay left, and Brad and I were alone, he turned to me.

"I miss Nina," he said.

"That's what I want to hear," I said. "She's a good wife for you. Come on, let's walk back to my place. I need to get my stuff so I can spend the night at your hotel.

Soon we were sitting on the front porch of the cabana, looking again over the dark water of the bay.

"Funny how things change," I said after a few minutes of comfortable silence. "You've settled down, and I'm the wild one. Who would have thought it?"

"I know," Brad said. "Hard to believe"

"Being out there on the water really changed my perceptions on life," I said. "Things that used to matter a year ago don't now."

"What do you mean?"

"Like when I moved to California. All I wanted was to make money. Now I couldn't care less if I'm ever rich."

"Then what *is* important to you?"

"Life, and living it to the fullest. God is number one, no doubt. Then comes my family and those who love me. Last is my career and how I make ends meet."

"Sounds like you got it all figured out," Brad said with a laugh.

"Not really. I just know that when I die, God won't care how many cars I drove, or how much money I made. He won't want to hear about how many books I've written. All that will matter is whether or not I brought glory to Him while I was alive on earth, and that I knew and loved Him."

We continued our deep conversation that night, one that lasted for several hours. I knew that the renewed sense of brotherhood between us would endure through the years.

* * *

I left early Sunday morning, January 12, and caught the 7:00 AM bus back to Salina Cruz. My kayak was where I had left it. I unlocked the chain and put it in the front storage compartment.

After several minutes of huffing and puffing, I set the kayak in the water and set off.

The water and shoreline were filthy; I picked my way with care through the broken bottles and garbage. It infuriated me that people could treat something so beautiful with such contempt. I paddled out of those waters as quickly as I could.

I wouldn't make much progress that day. It was already 1:30 PM, but I wanted to get out of there. It was an ugly, dirty city. The man made harbor had giant barges cluttering its entrance, many abandoned and left to rust. The only relief in the scenery was the lighthouse at Moro de Salinas. There I saw the white brown bluff, some two hundred feet tall. The ocean lapped lightly at its base, sheltered by the point I had just passed, the light shining in the midday sun.

Soon I passed the jetty and found myself in the calm Bay of Salina Cruz, so different from the city it was named for. But the ocean was restless, and strong gusts of wind sporadically blew across my bow. I braced myself in the cockpit, gripping the paddle tighter, and set my jaw.

Salt water lifted off the waves, smacking my face. I bobbed up and down in the choppy waters.

Past Cerro Moro I fell into a steady rhythm, despite the angry waters surrounding me. I was entering an area of water known to be some of the most dangerous in the world. I would have to be alert and ready at all times. Rest was no longer an option.

By sunset I had reached the entrance to Lake Inferior, a small lagoon on the outskirts of the peninsula. The waves that broke toward the shore started their white frothy foam a good four miles out. Fortunately, they remained only a few feet high as they reached land. The added thrust of motion sped my kayak to shore.

On the beach I set up camp and crawled into my tent. Before going to sleep, I read, by the light of a candle, a guidebook on Central America that Brad had given me. Adding to the ever-present dangers of the sea, I would also have to worry about the different political situations. Guatemala had just ended some type of civil war a week earlier. El Salvador and Nicaragua were not friends to Americans.

On top of that, I also read that malaria in Central America was on the rise. Every page in the book seemed to detail some new danger: parasites, yellow fever and malaria.

Tired of all this negative news I blew out the candle and closed the book. Most of the time, I told myself, these stories were exaggerated. Look at all of the dangers people had warned me about Mexico, yet I'd had only one major problem in that country. Besides, I had more urgent things to worry about at the present. The future would work itself out, like always.

TWENTY-NINE
"Dangerous buggers, they are."

A Tehuantepecer is a northeasterly gale that strikes with little or no warning. Many times, cloudless skies will be seen overhead, and the barometric pressure seldom drops. They occur year round but most often in the months of October through April. In January, which is the worst month, the storms occur nearly once every four days. The wind speeds can reach over forty knots, with eighteen to twenty-five foot waves in all directions. In a matter of minutes, such a gale can capsize a boat and push it twenty miles out to sea.

The area I was approaching was so treacherous that few boats risked even entering the Gulf of Tehuantepec. Most stay well out to sea, two or three hundred miles away.

On the morning of January 13, I cautiously headed out into the calm waters. The breakers I had ridden to shore the night before were now little more than ripples. An eerie calm had settled over the water, and the air smelled stagnant. I was in the middle of the Gulf of Tehuantepec, at the worst time of year. I knew it was only a matter of time before I ran into one of the infamous gales, and I was nervous. Like prey, if I let my guard down, the beast would pounce.

I remembered the advice Stuart and Dee, of the *Running Shoe*, had given me three months back. "Stay twenty yards from shore, mate, just outside the pull of the breakers," Stuart had said. "If you feel the wind start to gust, get on shore as fast as you can."

"What happens if I can't make it to shore?" I'd asked tentatively.

"I wouldn't give you much of a chance to survive it, that's for sure," he said, grimly. "The Tehuantepecers are nothing to fool around with. Dangerous buggers, they are."

With those haunting words in my head, I continued to paddle close to shore. By noon the waves were becoming restless. A stiff wind came from the north, and I struggled to maintain a steady course. As the wind continued to build, I looked over to the shore,

181

fifty yards to my left. There was enough beach to land on, should it get worse.

Shortly after 2:00 PM, I heard a noise that made my heart jump. The distant sound increased. A low groaning in the distance made its way to me, sounding like the wailing of the dead.

I sat motionless, listening to the wind. I took a deep breath and began to pray, at the same time turning the rudder sharply to my port side, toward the shore. The moaning of the wind rose to a violent shriek. In a matter of seconds, the wind had traveled down the mountains and ripped into the ocean. The Tehuantepecer was coming, and I hoped I could make it to shore in time.

I was only a few yards from the shore when the full force of the Tehuantepecer hit. The sand on the beach kicked up violently, blinding me, and I lowered my head to avoid the stinging pellets. The water beneath me surged and boiled. The wind smacked me in the face, nearly ripping me from the cockpit, and before the kayak's front end had even scraped onto the sand, I leaped out of it.

Fortunately, the water was only a few feet deep. Shielding my face from the pelting sand, I grabbed the front rope on the bow with my left hand. My Oakley sunglasses, which covered the entire area around my eyes, held firm. Even with their protection, I could still barely see in front of me.

I half stumbled, half crawled onto the sandy shore. Thankful to be on solid ground, I hauled the kayak a few feet from the water's edge. A seashell, or rock—I couldn't tell which—was hurled through the air. Its sharp edge cut into my legs, and I looked down. A small stream of blood was already trickling down onto my foot, and I yelled out in pain.

Grunting with the strain, I could no longer stand because of the force of the wind. I turned my kayak over and crawled underneath. The sand continued to blast the frame, gusting everywhere as I tried to shelter as much of my body as I could. Closing my eyes and gritting my teeth against the sting of sand on my exposed legs, I prayed to God for safety.

Thankful I was not out on the water, I peeked out. The ocean looked as though a giant hid just beneath the surface, tossing the water high into the air. The waves seemed to grow arms, stretching well over thirty feet in height.

At one point the wind gusted so powerfully that my kayak began to lift off the ground. I grabbed the inside hooks of the cockpit and tried to hold it down. I was lifted off the sand, and after a moment skidded down the beach to the water. The craft slammed back into the ground, and again, I ducked beneath it to hide from the winds.

After an hour and a half of continued struggle, the winds subsided. I crawled out from under my shelter. I washed the cut in my leg and placed a bandage over the damaged skin.

It took another hour before I could get up the nerve to place the kayak back into the water. By then the water had calmed. It was as though the great wind had rolled over the ocean, flattening the surface. I knew I'd better act fast, and though I didn't really want to travel, I knew I'd better get out of the Gulf as quickly as possible. Another gale could happen in a day or so.

With that in mind, I put my head down and paddled like mad. By late afternoon I saw the lighthouse at Puerto Arista. Several sailboats were there, anchored in safety.

I left my kayak on the sand and walked over to the nearest store. After buying some water and a loaf of bread, I went back down to the beach. The captain of one of the nearest sailboats lowered his dinghy and headed my way. When he reached shore he waved. A skinny old man, he looked barely fit for the harsh torments of the ocean.

"What the hell are you doin', son? You get stuck out in that gale?" he asked in a gruff voice. On closer inspection, he looked wiry and tough.

"Thank goodness, no," I said. "Were you anchored here?"

"Yep. We heard the report on the radio just a few minutes 'fore it hit. Had time to throw out another anchor. Sea got awfully rough, eh? We were holdin' on for dear life. Almost went completely under one time. Where'd you hole up?"

"Up the coast on a stretch of sand. Wasn't much room for me to hide under the kayak but there wasn't much else I could do."

We talked, and he asked if I needed anything. I said I could use a bite to eat. He nodded, and after going back over to his sailboat in the dinghy, returned with several ham sandwiches.

"Wife just made 'em," he said gruffly.

I thanked him. He wished me luck and shoved off.

* * *

On Tuesday, January 19, I got an early start. The next forty miles to Santa Cruz seemed to take forever, and it was past nightfall when I spotted the lighthouse on the small point. The ocean was relatively calm, and the breakers were practically nonexistent. I paddled my way to shore and found a good stretch of beach on which to camp.

I laid out my sleeping bag, crawled in, and fell asleep. The night air was still hot, and most of the time, I slept with half of my body out of the sleeping bag. By morning I'd sustained a few mosquito bites.

My books on Central America continued to warn about malaria, especially in Guatemala and Panama. I promised myself that when I reached the next town with a pharmacy I'd get some chloroquine, the medicine used to prevent 75% of all types of malaria, which was sold throughout Mexico without prescription.

* * *

Two days later, just past the lighthouse at Barra San Juan, I noticed large waves crashing to the shore. These breakers officially signaled the exit point of the Gulf of Tehuantepec. I sighed with relief, grateful to be back on the open ocean.

The weather continued to be hot and humid, the sky clear. I reached the point where the Huixtla River poured into the ocean, and paddled past it.

At the small city of Puerto Madero, a little past 11:00 AM, I spotted some fishermen taking the morning's catch out of their nets. Walking a few yards to the boats, I pointed at my kayak and asked them if they could keep an eye on it, explaining I would only be gone for an hour or so. They smiled, showing their brown teeth, and one of the older men extended his hand. I handed him a few *pesos* and hiked up the small beach to the main road.

Everyone I had met over the past few months had warned about the political situations in Guatemala, El Salvador, and Nicaragua. I didn't want any red tape tying up my expedition.

Since the coast of Guatemala was about two hundred miles in length, I deemed it best to obtain a visa and any other necessary papers at the border before entering international waters. Cuidad Hidalgo, the closest border town, was only a forty-five minute bus ride. The fare was less than one American dollar

The bus ride took us down a long, dusty road. There were several little villages along the way, and as we continued more people came on board, making the narrow seats even more crowded and hot. At the border I saw a large bridge that connected Mexico and Guatemala. People milled about, looking for handouts.

The stench of burning trash filled the air, and I breathed in as little as possible. Everything looked unclean, including the people, with their bare feet, matted hair, and dirty clothes. I got in line to obtain the necessary paperwork.

A few children came up to me and tugged at my shirt. They raised their tiny palms, hoping that I had something to give. I shook my head sadly. But they must have thought that the *gringo* had money, and for the next thirty minutes I moved with a growing escort of children.

Finally I found myself standing at the window of the immigration office. I handed over my passport, thankful that my visa was intact and grateful to Edward for his assistance long ago. The officer asked a few questions, then stamped a thirty-day clearance into his country. I walked quickly back to the bus, gently avoiding the children that now swarmed on all sides. There were several buses running, and I took the one that went through Tapachula, to Puerto Madero.

I thought I would shout with relief when I saw the crystal-blue waters of the Pacific Ocean again. It lay like a beautiful painting, sparkling and winking at me in the hot afternoon sun.

I got off the bus, waved to the driver, and walked down to the beach. I breathed in deeply of the clean air. The fishermen were still there. I smiled at them, brought my kayak to the water's edge, and shoved off into the narrow islet of water.

Four hours later, helped by the surging current, I landed in Champerico. Long before I surfed the waves to shore, I saw the black sandy beaches.

I timed the break of the waves, paddled as quickly as I could, then jumped out of the kayak into the shallow waters. Even though it was late in the afternoon and the sun had sunk low in the horizon, I felt the heat coming off the black sand. I was standing on what felt like a furnace. I jumped back into the water and retrieved my sandals from the kayak. I tied up my kayak and walked to the town.

Sinister looks were cast my way by the locals. Shacks and dilapidated old buildings were in a state of decay, most beyond restoration. Garbage littered the streets, which contained pigs, chickens, and flies. The air was stifling. Before I reached the main street, I was drenched in sweat.

The locals' attitudes seemed to reflect the ugly side of humanity, as if the black beach had darkened their souls. I tried to talk to a few people but was met with only rudeness, or just plain silence. After only a half hour I gave up and walked back to my kayak.

Pulling my kayak behind me, I walked down the shore until I was out of sight of the town and, hopefully, out of mind.

The heat continued to radiate from the sand long after the sunset.

No one disturbed me that night, and I woke early the next morning with a new vigor, ready to overcome any obstacle this new continent might throw my way.

* * *

The next town I came to, Semillero, was even less friendly than Champerico had been. After buying three gallons of purified water, I passed three middle-aged men.

"Hey, *gringo*," one of them said loudly.

I looked over in time to see one of the men unsheathe his machete and run his thumb over the blade. I continued to walk, ignoring their rude comments. With my heart beating fast, I looked over my shoulder to see if I was being followed and was relieved to see I was not. I felt unnerved and a bit like a coward but headed, in haste, back to the beach. After replacing my tent and sleeping bag into the storage compartments, I shoved off into the ocean and headed south.

As the blackness of night enshrouded me, I contemplated my next move. Obviously, it would be foolish to visit any more towns in Guatemala. Maybe El Salvador would be a more hospitable place, but I doubted it.

It had been more than a week since I'd spent the night on the water. The breakers in this new country seemed to save their energy until the last few feet, then they would surge upward, crashing down onto the beach. The sand rose sharply away from the ocean, leaving only a few feet of shore. Its steep ascent caused a powerful undercurrent, further discouraging me, and I decided to remain on the water for the night.

The air was very warm. I lay still in the cockpit, letting the ocean rock me to sleep.

* * *

The sun's reappearance on the horizon the next morning, after a long cold night, was a welcome sight. A quick check of my charts indicated that I was closing in on the city of San Jose. Sure enough, by noon on Friday, January 17, I saw the tall hotels and other buildings in what I had heard was one of the nicer coastal cities of Guatemala. I chose, however, to continue on.

I paddled toward the smaller town to the south, by the name of Montecito. I was hesitant to visit another Guatemalan village, but by 3:00 PM, my muscles would take me no farther.

As I neared the shore, the rumblings of the waves faded, then ceased entirely. I found myself navigating through a small waterway that led into a lagoon. The water there was crystal clear, and as I entered the channel the tropical vegetation rose up on both sides. Birds of all kinds seemed to be moving about in the tall bushes, and their cries filled the air with raucous chatter. The air was extremely humid; a stillness settled over the water and into my own body, and I felt at peace in this giant sanctuary

Once inside the lagoon I paddled over to a long stretch of shore. Large turtles poked their heads above the water, startled by my human presence. After a few seconds they swam away, leaving only a few small ripples in the still water.

The tropical landscape thrived. There were water lilies just around the bend, floating almost to the bank. Mangroves, leafy trees covered with vines, and other large-leafed bushes crowded the sand.

Nature was alive, and bringing me into a deep state of relaxation.

I breathed in the fresh air, and for the first time in several days felt safe and at peace. I pitched my tent beneath a giant palm tree. After eating the last of my beef jerky, along with some oatmeal, I crawled into my sleeping bag.

The sun was setting behind the rim of trees that stood guard over the entrance to the lagoon, and I was relieved to be off the water, sheltered in this haven.

THIRTY
Aaarrgh!

The next morning, in my kayak, I explored the swamp, which was so densely vegetated in some places that I had to duck in order to pass beneath overhanging branches. Few boats, I was sure, had ever navigated these waters. The channel I paddled through was only a few feet wide in places. Above, only a little patch of sky peeked through, hidden by the tall trunks and leaves of the thick growth of trees. Vines grew in abundance on every branch, hanging down like monkeys, knotted together. The trees provided extra shade for the reptiles, birds and amphibians that chose to call this paradise home.

More than once I heard the shriek of a waterfowl, probably a heron. Flowers of all shape, size and color draped themselves over trees and water. Brilliant red petals, looking like drops of blood, brushed my bow at every turn. The greenery around me seemed to pulse with life, and in the bushes I heard the rustlings of small animals. They seemed to be monitoring my progress.

I was in another world that morning, and I paddled as far as I could go. The little river eventually ended in a tiny trickle. It was too shallow for me to continue. The landscape in front of my kayak took a turn uphill, toward the original source of the stream.

I sat in the cockpit for a minute, motionless, almost afraid to breathe as I looked across the swamp. I felt drawn to the silence, a part of this wild, steamy jungle. There were few sounds: water running down the hill, an occasional rustling among the trees, and the steady beating of my heart, a rhythm that joined with the powerful dance of nature and beast.

I could have stayed all day in that sanctuary, but the mosquitoes had another agenda. Despite the repellant I'd smeared on my arms, legs and face before leaving in the morning, I heard the whine of the tiny insects, impatient for a meal. I swatted furiously at them.

Despite my precautions, several were able to penetrate my defenses and attack with a vigor I could not withstand.

Reluctantly, I turned around and headed out of the jungle the way I'd come. Pretending to be one of the early explorers, I looked to both sides, imagining jaguars and other big game peering at me from their hideouts. The minute I lowered my guard, I imagined they would be at my throat.

Where would man be, I wondered, had it not been for the pioneers who'd ignored the threat of death and pressed on to greater achievements? Hadn't everyone thought Christopher Columbus was sailing to his death back in the 1400s? Yes, I knew that was different from my contemporary circumstances, but the thought of our similarities nonetheless made me smile that morning. This wasn't such a crazy idea after all.

I stopped back at my campsite for a few minutes to rest and eat. I looked again at my navigational charts and saw there were no convenient cities where I could obtain my visa for the next country. The only cities along the border, according to my map, were too far inland to reach in a day. El Salvador was only twenty miles away, so there was no turning back to another city for information. I decided to press forward, especially since the next country's coastline was only a hundred and fifty miles long, short enough to paddle through in a week.

I hoped I would not get stopped.

Past the channel and again on the ocean, I headed southeast. My water supply made me nervous. I had three gallons left and didn't want to stop before I reached Honduras. After my encounter with Mexican Officials, I didn't want trouble with any other governments. Since I wouldn't have the correct papers for El Salvador, it would be risky to stop there.

The weather that day continued to be sunny and cloudless, the temperature in the 90s. I decided not to head for shore as night approached, but to spend the night on the water for the second time in three days. I turned the bow of the kayak around to face the setting sun and took a deep breath. In the final moments of the sun's fiery glory, I leaned back and took in the sights and sounds of this part of the Pacific Ocean.

My feet dangled lazily in the water as I looked up at the sky. I lifted my hand and thanked God for His majesty. As the sun disappeared completely, a stillness fell on the water as it did every night. Even the breakers ceased their loud crashing and lapsed into a more peaceful rumble.

I loved the ocean and its surroundings, especially at the end of the day. I stretched out over the bow and closed my eyes, letting the stillness and solitude envelope me.

Resting my body and soul, I waited for the next day and the challenges it would hold.

* * *

I awoke just before the sun rose and ate a quick breakfast of dried oatmeal. I was headed due east, according to the compass heading, which was still mounted to the front of my kayak. I was at a point on the ocean where the sun would rise over the water directly in front of me and set at night to my back.

With the beginning and end of each new day I was able to feast my eyes on the sun's imminent climb. There was truly nothing so beautifully satisfying as the sun reflecting across the water.

By midday I saw what I presumed to be the city of Acajutla. I had only one gallon of water left. By tomorrow I would have to stop and obtain more.

The swells here rose with enormous power. Some I estimated were more than twenty-five feet high. I would ride up to the top of one, then plunge into its trough, the dark blue waters rolling up around me. All day I rode those huge swells, never in danger but constantly aware of the power around me.

I reached the outskirts of La Libertad, El Salvador, just before sunset. The western part of the city, where the beach curved around to form a point, was where I surfed one large wave to shore.

I set up my tent, not much more than a fluttering rag, next to several palm trees. Remembering that it was Sunday January 19, I read my Bible. The only audience I had was the gently swaying branches overhead, but it felt good to read the Bible out loud. The occasional crab came over to investigate, but must have decided that my sermon was not exciting enough and scrambled off.

Afterwards I lay down to rest. I no longer slept in my sleeping bag, for it was too hot. Comfortable and stretched out, I let my mind drift away to other times.

* * *

A loud thud, only inches from my tent, jolted me from sleep. Somebody was outside! Remembering the poor reception I'd received during the last few weeks, I jumped up. With my heart beating wildly, I grabbed the Bowie knife that I kept close to my side and leapt from the tent.

With a loud cry that startled even the birds that roosted nearby, I ran outside, brandishing the 12-inch blade. I felt like a pirate—wild and brash and bold. *Aaarrgh!*

I was greeted by silence. Thinking the culprit had crawled to the other side of the tent, I ran there, stabbing the air futilely with my knife, until I finally realized that there was no one on that long stretch of sand except myself.

Wondering what had made the sound that had awakened me, I walked to the front of the tent. There I saw a small, dark shape in the black sand. A coconut. I picked it up. Milk trickled out and down the smooth outer shell.

It was rotten and not fresh enough to eat, but it did give me an idea. I wondered why I'd not thought of it sooner. For the last four hundred miles, the shore had been covered with palm trees, and almost every tree bore dozens of coconuts. If I could just reach a few each night, I'd have coconut milk to drink for dinner. I might even find a way to pour the excess liquid into my empty water jugs.

I put my knife away, a little sheepishly, and climbed back into the tent. I felt a little foolish for the way I'd reacted, but at least something good had come of it.

The next morning I went outside and looked up at the tree that had caused me such alarm the night before. There were more coconuts on the limbs, just out of reach. After piling a few rocks to form a sort of stepladder, I twisted the fruit until they fell from the limbs.

I picked four coconuts that I thought would be to my liking. I set the first one on the ground and took out my knife. Slicing away the soft outer surface with a few hacks, I soon found the hard brown shell beneath. I raised my knife, keeping my other hand well out of the way, and struck the fruit with great force. With a second blow I saw the soft white meat inside. I placed the hole to my lips and tilted my head back, letting the cool liquid run down my throat. The coconut milk was delicious and sweet, its tastiness no doubt enhanced by the fact that I'd obtained it from the wild myself.

After I poured the contents of the remaining three coconuts into an empty gallon jug, I walked down the beach, to the outskirts of La Libertad. The small fishing village was much cleaner and nicer than the last few I had visited. I walked down the main street to the market, where I purchased four gallons of water. The townspeople were pleasant. I went back to the hot black sand, and untied my kayak.

I was out on the water before 10:00 AM, refreshed. Perhaps El Salvador wouldn't be so bad after all.

I could see the pier from where I paddled; the restaurants that dotted the shore seemed as plentiful as the black sands of the beach. I had seen no dolphins, whales, nor sharks during the last week, and their presence was sorely missed. Clouds on the horizon meant the possibility of a storm by nightfall, so late in the day I looked for appropriate cover. Shelter was in a deep lagoon, fifty miles southeast from where I'd started that morning. I was amazed at the number of miles I covered each day now, sometimes almost effortlessly.

I camped just inside a lagoon, about two miles from the ocean, just in sight of a city my map identified as Jiquilisco. I set up my tent and placed a sheet of plastic over the mesh top so that if rain fell later, I wouldn't get soaked. The wind was coming from the south. By 7:30 PM, the first few droplets began to fall. The storm brought a chill to the air that I'd not felt for several weeks. I drew my body close inside the sleeping bag and watched as a few raindrops seeped into the tent.

* * *

There were no coconuts to forage for in the marsh soil, so I left early the next morning. The rain had stopped sometime during the night.

The water that morning was as smooth as glass, and I paddled into the ocean feeling positive about the turn the trip had taken. The rain had cooled the air down several degrees, and the new day and good night's rest gave me additional strength.

That strength, however, did not last. The day passed by slowly. At times, I felt weak.

By 5:30 PM I calculated that I was nearing the Gulf of Fonseca. I was exhausted. My hands shook slightly as I hauled the kayak onto the sand. A chill crept over my body, and I shivered despite the warm air.

I pitched my tent and took out several articles of clothing, food, and medicine. I knew I would be too weak to paddle the next day, so I settled into my temporary home. In addition to my flu-like symptoms, I had developed a slight case of dysentery during the night. The intestinal cramps continued well through the next day, where I spent most of my time either doubled over in pain, or squatting in the thick brush behind my tent. It felt, at times, like my intestines were going to fall out along with the rest of my organs.

I won't go into the gory details, but let me just stay that for the next week everything I ate seemed to turn to water. My bowels rid themselves of waste in a pistol-like, rapid-fire motion.

My flu subsided and my weakened muscles recovered from the dull, throbbing pain. In a few days I felt better. I rested those days, making sure to take vitamin C pills every few hours, as I was anxious to resume my travels. Most of the time I slept, which my body no doubt needed, making up for the last few weeks of abuse.

* * *

On Thursday, January 23, I felt like a new man. My stomach had settled, and my strength returned. I turned my sights to the Gulf of Fonseca, where I would be entering Honduran waters.

The Gulf, as I rounded the point I had marked a few days prior, was calm. The water rolled by rapidly, and I made good time. A school of dolphins passed by, several yards to my right side. I felt welcomed to these new waters by my old friends and rejoiced at the return of marine life.

Heading to the mainland to spend the evening, I saw the deep inlet of water to the Bay of San Lorenzo, and made my way to the city there. As I passed several handmade wooden canoes and other small vessels, I waved at the friendly people with every stroke. In return, I was greeted with similar gestures, smiles, and words of *hola* and *bueno*.

I felt relieved to have passed by two unfriendly Central American countries unscathed. Relieved also by this warm Honduran welcome, I decided I would stay in Honduras for a couple of days.

Soon I was pushing my kayak up the small beach that sat on the outskirts of San Lorenzo.

There were many people in the area. Some sat on a concrete wall near the beach where I had landed, while others strolled down the streets on foot and on bicycles. No one seemed in a hurry.

I tied the kayak to a wooden post, perhaps a part of an old pier, and walked a few blocks to the immigration office. Inside the small building I handed the officer, who looked a little surprised to see me, my passport. He raised his eyes when I told him my mode of transpiration, but he stamped the page anyway. I paid him thirty *limperas* for his service, about $2.50, and smiled as he handed me back my passport, along with a thirty-day visa.

I went back down to the beach, relieved as always to see my kayak still resting near the water's edge. I still had ten feet of chain, a lock, and a steel eye loop screwed into the hull of the kayak. I locked the kayak up securely.

I walked through the small city, looking for a place to spend the night. It had been a long time since I'd slept in a bed or taken a fresh shower. Though I didn't yearn for those comforts as I had in the beginning, it would be a nice change from the usual accommodations.

At a small hotel I paid for a room and followed the proprietress to my quarters. It was indeed small, with a bed in the center, on which was an old blanket, and a stand-up shower in the corner. After setting my bag on the bed, I practically jumped into the shower. The water was cold—there is rarely hot water in lower-end hotels in Central America—but I felt revived nonetheless. Soon, the salt was washed away from my skin.

I went back down to the lobby and noticed a large deck overlooking the water. I went outside, sat down at one of the tables and ordered dinner. I closed my eyes, enjoying the moment.

When the meal of rice, beans, tortillas and fried plantains arrived, I attacked it with the same vigor as I had the shower. I enjoyed every bite of it, whereas in the States a year prior I would have complained because there was no steak.

The next morning I showered again, checked out of the room and shoved off from the small beach.

I spotted El Tigre Island shortly after 11:00 AM. It was a small island, shaped like a tiny volcano. Its conic shape stood out from the water, lush and green and tropical. A few beaches dotted the western shores, and that was where I headed.

I went to shore on the island and climbed out of the cockpit to stretch my muscles.

It appeared that I was definitely in the tropics now. Banana trees, palm trees, and other types of vegetation densely covered the entire island, leaving little room for the sun to shine once off the beach. I slung my hammock—the one that Brad had bought for me—between two palm trees. The giant branches leaned far out over the water's edge and provided perfect shade for me to get out of the hot sun.

Being out in the sun all the time had negative effects on my skin, eyes, and stamina. I was constantly applying lotion, and though my skin had gotten somewhat used to the abuse, I still didn't want to take chances with skin cancer. In shade from its rays, my body relished the comfort and cool protection of the trees overhead.

Lying in the hammock, I closed my eyes and listened to the sounds of the jungle. Parrots and macaws squawked in the branches all around. The waves brushed up against the shore, soft and reassuring. The wind blew the leaves of other trees, their rustling joining with the water's hypnotic rhythm. A symphony of life and motion surrounded me.

El Tigre Island put its soothing arms around me, lulling me to sleep. I stayed there for several days, losing track of the hour, the day and the week.

Occasionally I would walk to the other side of the island, to a small town that was built into the sides of the hills. There were a few tourists there, looking in the shops and eating in the restaurants.

A quaint town, really, and most of the visitors must have thought it fairly isolated, but I was changing into a person who needed space, time to think, and few distractions. Each time I visited the village, I would look forward to getting back to my side of the island, away from human contact.

It wasn't that I disliked other people's company—I was just learning to live on my own. Whether I was on my side of the island, void of civilization, or out in the Pacific Ocean, I was filled with a sense of peace. Something, certainly, had changed inside of me. I felt at home, and I was becoming aware that I might not ever want to go back. I felt little need for companionship.

With all of nature's beauty at my fingertips, what more could I want?

I understood, at last, what it meant to survive on my own. Time seemed to have a different tempo on the water. Days seemed like weeks, weeks like months, and months like years. Indeed, it was as if my existence on the water was all I had ever known.

Lying in my hammock beneath the palm trees, looking out over the blue ocean, I thought of the many struggles, triumphs, and joys I had experienced during this expedition. The memories of my former world grew dimmer, receding into the recesses of my mind. I let them go, not wishing to hold onto them any longer. I was perfectly happy to live in this new world, and did not need anyone or anything to tell me differently.

THIRTY-ONE
"Do you have any drugs?"

I'd thought of Heather occasionally, even after leaving Acapulco. Her beautiful face and the scent of her hair lingered, comforting me in the darker hours of the night.

I called her from the phone in one of the shops in El Tigre. I wasn't looking forward to the call, but it was one I had to make.

"Hey, Heather, I'm still alive," I said after hearing her voice.

"It's been a long time since you've called," was all she said.

I heard the disappointment in her voice. We both knew the relationship was over.

"I don't know when I'll call again," I said slowly. "Things are changing. I don't spend time thinking about my old world any more. I don't even know if I want to come back when this is all over."

"I can't believe you'd say that," she replied. Then, more softly, "But I knew something was happing to you. I've noticed it for a while. But what could I do about it?"

"Nothing. I still miss you. But I don't think you should wait for me to come back. If you find somebody else, don't think about me. Take care of yourself, and keep praying for me." I sighed deeply. This was difficult, but it felt right. "If I ever get back, I promise I'll call you. Okay?"

"Okay," she said softy.

And then we hung up. That would be the last time I'd talk to Heather while on my journey.

I swallowed hard, trying not to let my emotions get the better of me. I resolutely looked ahead, eager to resume my solitude—clutching at it like a climber to a mountain, gripping tighter, seeking a foothold on which to inch forward.

The romance with Heather no doubt had been ill fated from the beginning. Plagued by bad timing. I thought of it now as closing another chapter in the book of my life. The home I had left behind seemed like another world, dissolving into distant memories I could scarcely recall. As I sat under the palm trees, near the end of January 1997, I felt the refreshing breeze blow against my face. I looked back over the past few months and could hardly believe I'd ever lived elsewhere. The birds, the waves, the trees and the beaches were my friends. The creatures that swam beneath the surface of the waters took the place of romance.

Work. The word seemed to mean something, but I couldn't quite place it. Glimpses of the past occasionally surfaced, but my mind refused them entrance. The ocean herself told me what I should and should not do, and I readily embraced my new freedom.

I was a free man, and I felt that I could float away . . . down this new current of life, forever.

My relationship with God strengthened. I tried to imagine what it would have been like in the Garden of Eden. This had to be the next best thing to that paradise.

Again, I wished my journey would never end. The only reason to go back, I thought, was to see again my mother, my father and my brother. I felt those ties strongly at times, even in this place of solitude, and knew that my days here were numbered. This time, however, my eyes would be truly open and my soul newly alive. I didn't know how I would fit in, or even if I would remain in that society, but one thing was for certain, I would never again live life with my head down, oblivious to the wonders life could give.

* * *

I left El Tigre Island, Honduras, on Saturday, February 1st. After my days of inactivity on the quiet shores, I felt invigorated by the rhythm of the morning's paddling. There were a few smaller islands that I made my way around, before moving out onto the Pacific Ocean.

Although I had stayed in Honduras for nearly a week, I didn't apply for a visa into Nicaragua. I admit that this was due, in part, to my own laziness. The nearest border town to the island had been a good two and a half hours away.

Now, as I looked out across the long coast of Nicaragua, more than 200 miles in all, I wondered if that had been such a good idea.

The humidity was stifling. Afternoon showers came and went. The coast was long and grueling, without much diversion or points of interest. The long beaches stretched for miles, as far as they eye could see across the water to the horizon. I saw no coves or bays inviting me in for the night, and I became bored by the monotony of paddling.

Two days after leaving the island, I landed on my first beach in Nicaragua. The surf thundered to shore, and I had a hard time riding the waves in. At one point the wave I was riding turned suddenly, breaking to my left. I jammed the rudder to that same side, trying to pick up the curve of the water. The white foaming mass behind me snarled at my misfortune, and I thought I would turn end-over-end. But I regained my balance, keeping a step ahead of the giant, crashing white water, and surfing sideways down the wave until I reached the beach in one piece.

I felt the strength of the undertow as I leaped into the receding water. Holding the safety rope in one hand, I crawled up the sand, safely away from reach of the surf.

Poneloya, the name of the city near where I had landed, was small, somewhat dirty, and void of tourists. The broad beach where I stood stretched out as far as I could see. Several locals were surfing. Some had stopped and turned their attention on me, probably wondering what kind of crazy *gringo* would attempt to kayak through the monstrous waves.

At dusk, a little after 8:00 PM, I ate a small dinner in town; two tortillas with beans and cheese, with some type of lumpy meat. I didn't ask what it was, and, frankly, I didn't care.

Soon, I was back at my little campsite. When I sat down to write in my journal, I realized that it was Monday again. I stood up, went over to the kayak, and found the small bottle of pills I had purchased in Honduras. I swallowed a chloroquine pill. I had enough to last two more months, ample time to get through the rest of Central America. I'd paid only two dollars for the bottle of pills, a small price for a drug that could prevent most strains of malaria.

* * *

The next few days on the water seemed to drag by. The coast remained flat and the weather hot. The ocean grew still. The moon was telling me that the tides had receded.

Looking back at the first months of my journey, I realized how much I had been through to get to this point

On Tuesday, February 4, I landed on shore close to a fishing village named El Astillero. A few men stood around as I paddled to shore.

I soon learned that there was only one dirt road that led out of town. No longer concerned about the need for a visa, I tied my kayak down and sauntered into town. As usual, the locals gawked at me, this strange white man wearing only a pair of shorts, walking calmly through their streets. I wondered if they'd ever seen a *gringo* in these parts.

The town only had one avenue, which cut down the middle. I walked along this small street, scattering chickens and dogs wherever I stepped. I seemed to be the only one moving in the hot, sleepy little town. With the afternoon sun beating down mercilessly, the people had wisely sought refuge under shaded awnings and wooden platforms that lined the street.

There was a small abandoned taco stand sitting on one of the corners. The fire still burned beneath an iron skillet. There was no such thing as propane down here. I figured the owner was taking a siesta, so I sat on one of the stools and waited there by myself, figuring somebody would show up eventually. After a while an old, rather large Spanish woman came out of the shadows and asked if I wanted something to eat.

I ordered several pieces of what looked like fried pork, and a Coke to drink, which came in a glass bottle. Coca-Cola in Mexico and Central America is made with more sugar than that in the U.S., and it was delicious.

Soon, after I finished my meal, the sun dipped down over the horizon. In the cooler evening air, the people of the town stirred. Carts appeared out of nowhere, pushed by their owners down the narrow street, attempting to sell their wares. More taco stands appeared on the opposite corners, and two cowboys, on their horses, showed off their animals with obvious pride.

I was a little relieved that I had not walked into a ghost town. it was nice to know people were still going about their lives. I sat back on the small wooden stool, ordered another soda and wondered if these people had ever left their small corner of the world. Would they live, breed, and die within this small village? Looking around at the people, I guessed that to be true. They had remained unchanged for decades, unaffected by the evolving world. I saw running water, no cars, and no electricity. I could have gone back in time fifty years and not seen any difference.

At the beginning of my expedition, the ignorance of a country whose people had never traveled to a "civilized" community of prosperous, industrial citizens would have galled me. But now, after months of being exposed to the realities of another world and the freedom one possessed after ridding themselves of these burdens, I admired the small village for resisting the change of outside forces. I was almost envious, sensing that though they lacked knowledge of other places and the larger scope of the world's unresolved problems, they were completely at ease with their current lifestyle. Something other parts of the world might have overlooked on the road to becoming rich.

I was so lost in my thoughts that I didn't notice at first when an old man came over and sat beside me. His small, frail hand tugged gently at my arm, until I turned and looked him in the eye. With his white beard flowing past his neck, he seemed older than the village itself. The wrinkles on his face were deeper than the scar that ran along the side of his right cheek. His body, too, was gaunt, and his frame was stooped from many years of living. His eyes, though, were clear and alert, and they seemed to see right into my mind.

"*Que pasa?*" I said after a few seconds.

"I speak English a little," he said, which surprised me. Then, "Do you have any drugs?" he asked, in almost a whisper.

Disgusted by his question, I pushed his hand off my arm and quickly got up to leave.

"Wait a minute, please," he said, clutching at my arm again.

No one around us took notice, so whether by choice or habit, I didn't know, I reluctantly sat back down.

What he told me then probably saved my life.

"I don't want any, *tapatho*," he said angrily. Then, more quietly, he added, "People come here from the States to buy drugs. Cocaine. Sometimes Colombia, too. No good to get involved."

"Okay," I said shortly. "So, why are you telling me this? I don't have any drugs."

"Maybe," he said, eyeing me again. I wondered, was he some kind of *policia*? "I saw you come in on boat. Gringos don't come here too much. They stick out, and that is no good."

"Well, okay, that's true. So why are you talking to me? And how do you speak such good English?"

"I live in Florida for a while. Parents got deported. It's no important. You look like you could get in trouble."

"That's crazy, old man," I said, losing my patience. "I'm leaving first thing tomorrow." Again I thought about getting up to leave, but something told me not to. Not just yet.

"Look at you," he said. "*Pelón*. Beard, earring. Anybody saw you, they think you were crazy on drugs. Here alone in Nicaragua? Hah!" He spat.

"I don't care. I'll be out of this country in a few days."

* * *

"I hope so," the old man said slowly. "If police catch you, they make you pay. If someone else find you, they think you trying to get in on their trade. Then, you dead."

His words cut into me. Suddenly I was afraid, knowing that what the old man said was most likely true.

"You better get out of this country as soon as you can. Don't even look back," he said.

I needed no further urging.

One of the cowboy's horses strutted by, and I looked up. I looked over to the other vendors who had come out from the shadows, and they now seemed to be eyeing me more closely than before. I was uncomfortable with their sidelong glances. My earlier ease had vanished like mist in the desert.

I turned back to ask a question, but when I looked over to the seat next to me, the old man was nowhere in sight.

* * *

The next morning, February 5, I left the small town of El Astillero. Still worried about my meeting with the old man and his sudden disappearance, I paddled quickly, eager to be out of sight of the town.

I should be close to Costa Rica in two days, I thought, and decided to take no more chances and head straight there without going ashore again. If the police questioned me in the next town, I would probably be deported.

But, if I ran into any drug traffickers . . . I tried to put it out of my mind.

By five that evening I had traveled a good forty-five miles. The sun had not yet dipped into the horizon, and though I knew I would have to spend the night on the water, my spirits rose. Tomorrow I would be in Costa Rica. Everything I had heard about the country was positive. Good relations with tourists, beautiful beaches, clean cities, and friendly people. I was ready for a change.

As I passed by a small point, I looked into the cove that housed what I presumed to be the city of San Juan del Sur. The half moon bay that curved around to the other side was pretty and quiet in the stillness of the late twilight. It looked inviting. I was tempted to stop and spend the night, but, heeding the warnings of the old man, decided to keep pressing on.

The bright lights of the town came on, one by one, winking across the water. Then, on the other side of the bay, where the hills behind the beach seemed ominously dark in the last rays of the sun, I spotted a boat. Thinking it to be a pleasure cruiser, I was going to turn in and pull alongside. But as I drew closer to the boat, my guard came up.

The large yacht sat still in the water. It was well over fifty feet in length. Another smaller motorboat was tied to the side of the yacht by a long rope. While I paddled, I saw there were two men on the deck of the yacht and two more in the other motorboat. They were busy unloading cargo from one to the other.

I decided I'd seen enough. And I hoped the bundles were not what I thought they were.

I moved slowly, in a wide circle, heading out to sea. Quietly but quickly, I thrust my paddle into the water. My heart was beating fast and hard, loud in my ears, as I glided out of the bay.

Soon I saw the hills on the other side, and sighed in relief.

The sun had set, and the last lingering light of the day was giving way to the night. I sat back in the cockpit and stopped paddling, reached for a drink of water. It was then that I heard a shout from behind, faint but distinct across the water.

Looking around, I could barely make out the two men on the deck of the larger boat, but one of them seemed to be pointing in my direction. I sat very still, hoping I could shrink back into the shadows of the shore. Then I heard the engine of one of the smaller boats spring to life, shattering the evening's stillness.

I picked up my paddle.

My mind raced as I heard more shouts from behind. The low rumbling of the engine increased, and I prayed that they were not coming after me. I paddled like crazy, my arms burning with the power of each stroke. My heart pounded fiercely in my chest.

Not now, I prayed. Not like this.

The engine behind me grew louder, and I knew it would be only moments before the boat rounded the point. Soon there would be no place for me to hide. With only seconds to react, I headed for the shore. I looked around once and saw the spotlight of the boat dancing over the dark waves, flitting back and forth. The evening shadows were hiding me for now. But would it be enough?

Were they looking for me, or just heading back home?

Heedless of the waves and without time to wait for the surf, I leaped into the foaming white water. Dragging my kayak behind me, I finally felt the sand beneath my feet and heaved myself to the shore. I fell a few times as the surf crashed into me from behind, hitting my back and pushing me over. The kayak, being more buoyant, raced ahead, and it was pulling me closer to the shore.

Finally in shallow water, I plowed through the receding surf and then up the beach. I pulled my kayak onto the sand, then left it and ran into the jungle, beyond the beach, into the dense growth of trees. My limbs weakened, either from shock or exertion or fear, and I collapsed to the ground.

I hoped that the men on the boat would not see my kayak, abandoned there on the beach. I lay flat on my stomach and peered out to the ocean. The noise of the boat's engine was now fairly loud, and I saw its light again as it swept the shore, briefly blinding my vision. I heard the engine roar, mixed with shouts from the men on board. They were close to the shore.

I kept as still as possible, hiding in the undergrowth.

After a few seconds, which seemed like forever, the boat passed by. Eventually it faded from sight, the light still flickering across the water.

I let out my breath in a rush of air. Slowly I stood, and walked cautiously back to the kayak.

There I laughed softly, trying to relieve the tension. Had I reacted without thinking? Were the words of the old man haunting me still, causing me to panic? I would never know.

Though I had not planned to spend the night ashore, I figured I might as well, now that I was on it. Still shaken by what had just happened, I secured my safety line to one of the trees under which I had just taken cover. The kayak was safe for the night, and hopefully so was I.

I was too tired to pitch my tent, such as it was. Rolling out my sleeping bag near a palm tree, I lay down.

Sleep was a long time coming. As I lay there, tossing and turning from one side to the other, I couldn't help but wonder if I'd just had another brush with death.

THIRTY-TWO
Some Of The Biggest Turtles I Had Ever Seen

A glorious coast stretched out before my eyes. This was a land of streams, monkeys, tapers, sloth, boa constrictors and pristine, tropical beaches with brilliant white sand. Never before had I seen such beauty. Never before had I seen such lush vegetation, teeming with life and abounding in spirit. Even the name brought about a certain degree of adventure and wonder: Costa Rica.

I entered that beautiful country on February 7, a Friday morning.

A mysterious mist hung along the shore, and I strained my eyes to take in the outline of this wonder before me. The mist rose shortly after dawn and the sun emerged, casting forth its cheerful rays. What struck me the most, as the coast emerged slowly into view, was the lush, tropical rain forest that sloped down to the ocean, stopping only a few feet from the water's edge. The trees there were so thick I could only see a dark mass of vines and branches that seemed to have no beginning and no end.

In stark contrast to the long, straight cost of Nicaragua, here there were too many coves and hidden beaches to count. Islands emerged on the horizon, inviting me to their beaches. The coast itself jutted wildly out into the ocean, confusing my sense of direction.

It was a costly mistake as far as my daily progress was concerned, but it was one I was glad to make. The humidity was gone from the air, and although the temperature still flirted with ninety degrees, I felt dry and comfortable. Because I had miscalculated the peninsula's length, and mistaken it for another island, I had lost several hours and miles.

By 5:30 in the afternoon, I had still not gone ashore. I looked with the greatest of interest at the varying hills and mountains-darkish green in color-and could not hold back my curiosity any longer. I skirted around what I thought to be the Parque Nacional Santa Rosa, making sure that I was far enough away from the ocean's currents that broke against the mainland with great fury. At times, riding above the noise of the surf, I imagined the cries of monkeys and the roar of a jaguar. The first accessible cove, I told myself, and I would head for shore.

Sure enough, just as the sun was descending low over the horizon, I saw two jagged rocks rising out of the water. The ocean surged mightily against these two enormous structures, but they failed to give way to the surf.

The beach was only about fifty yards wide, curving in a perfect half moon. The forest, although not as dense as I had thought from the water, came down in some places to just a few yards from the crashing waves. I saw no monkeys, no snakes, and no big cats. Maybe, I thought, they were waiting for me to go to sleep.

I pulled my kayak up the beach and tied it to a nearby tree. There were many different types of vegetation. There looked to be a small trail that cut through the wilderness, and whether animals or humans, had made it, I could not tell. There was, however, no trace of civilization, and I relished the peaceful, quiet air. No cars, no traffic, no people, no hassles.

After awhile, I untied an empty gallon of water from my outrigger and sat down with my back against the kayak. The sun had set, and in the twilight, I took out one of my charts to see if I could tell where I had landed. There were so many inlets, coves and rocks, that it was impossible to find my exact whereabouts. There was one beach on the map called Nancite, but I doubted that I was there.

Sometimes, after a long day, I would sit back on some strange beach and wonder about my life. Nobody in the world knew where I would be sleeping on any given night. Being totally independent, the solitude was almost overwhelming. At first it had terrified me to think that if I got into trouble, no one would be there to help. But now I reveled in the secrecy and simplicity of it all.

I put the map away and looked at my watch. I felt silly sometimes, keeping track of the time. It had ceased to become a habit long ago, and now I was just wondering if I should go to sleep or not. At the mercy of nature, so unlike the security of civilization, with its electric lamps, stone walls, and stable living quarters, I did as it told me, when it told me. When it was dark I slept, when it was light I awoke, and when I was hungry I ate. The rules of society no longer governed my life or daily habits.

I pitched the tent, hoping that the rods, all of which were taped together, would hold for a few more weeks. Soon I would have to leave it behind, which worried me less and less each day.

As I climbed inside the tent and lay down, the jungle behind me came alive with sounds that I had been too busy to hear until now. I heard the whining of some type of insect. I didn't know if they had tropical crickets down here, the size of footballs, but that's sure what it sounded like. Also, a few raucous birds bickered long into the night. I listened to all of this as it blended with the other more familiar sounds that I knew well. The ocean was calm, too, and I fell asleep to this jungle chorus.

* * *

The next morning I discovered that mosquitoes had found a way into my tent, which wasn't surprising, considering that there were many holes and tears in the outer structure. Though my exposed skin was covered in bites, I shrugged it off as just another part of nature, and went outside.

I sat for a while that morning, looking out across the cove and onto the other side of the bay. I didn't know if there would be more spots as pristine as this in the days to come and wanted to enjoy this one as long as possible. Before shoving off into the surf, I checked my supplies to see if I had enough to make it the rest of the way.

Perhaps. I had two weeks left in my travels, maybe three. There was plenty of oatmeal, and I had a few multigrain bars left, but knew that at the next big city I would have to buy more food.

I walked knee deep into the water, and slipped under the gentle surf. Though I had no soap, I scrubbed vigorously at my skin. Next, I took out my mirror, about the size of my palm, and peered intently into it. The face that stared back at me didn't look familiar. The gradual transformation my harsh surroundings had on my visual appearance was astonishing. Strange that I hadn't noticed it before.

The tough, weathered face that peered from the mirror looked haggard. My beard, unshaven in a week, partially hid a face that was a dark tan, with wrinkles I had not seen before creasing the skin around my eyes. My hair, unkempt and uncut, fanned out like a rooster's feathers.

I shook my head slowly, marveling at the change to my once-handsome face. I took out my razor, lathered the shaving cream across the long whiskers—keeping only my goatee—and began to shave. It was a slow, painful process, but after a few nicks and cuts, I finished. The salt water burned the new skin, so I spread lotion on my face.

I hopped into my kayak.

Once out past the two large rocks, I turned to head south again. By midday I had entered a calmer stretch of water. I paddled that day and the next, resting in my kayak when weariness got the best of me.

Time seemed to blend into itself, the days losing meaning. When I grew tired of being on the water, I set up camp on whatever beach welcomed me.

* * *

The sun was beginning to emerge from behind the hills of Costa Rica when I heard a rustling in the waves that caused me to sit up. I looked at the surf through bleary eyes, wondering what it was that had made a sound. A Seal? I heard it again. Turning, I stared at the incredible sight before me.

In the sand, a few yards to my left and then farther on down the beach, were some of the biggest turtles I had ever seen. I watched in amazement as they pushed the sand with their legs, creating large mounds across the beach. Several were already heading back to the ocean, and as their large frames—some with shells more than two feet in length—hit the surf, they parted the waters with ease. Thrusting into the swirling breakers, they were soon out into the open waters. One by one, the turtles finished what they were doing on the beach and slid into the water.

I wondered if perhaps they'd just laid their eggs. The ecosystem here was fragile. I didn't want to disturb whatever they'd done with the mounds of sands, but I couldn't resist taking a closer look.

I walked carefully up and down the beach. There were dozens of little mounds. Back at my camp I looked at my charts. There was a beach by the name of Playa Grande, within the boundaries of the Parque Nacional Marino las Baulas de Guanacaste, which was a frequent location for large turtles to lay their eggs. What great luck that I had witnessed at least part of this miracle!

My food supply was almost exhausted. I had only a few bags of oatmeal left, along with two nutritional bars and a bag of dried mash potatoes. I checked the map. Puntarenas was only a few days away. I would stop there. It wouldn't be long after that before I reached South America.

This expedition would soon be over, and then what would I do? There was a woman from home who flitted past the outer reaches of my memory. What was her name? I couldn't recall.

Where would I go once I had finished? Surely, I had a home, but where was it? I only knew of the sand for a bed and the open sky for my roof.

Maybe it did not have to end. I was a free man. I could just continue to paddle around South America and live off the ocean. She would provide for me.

That thought gave me an idea for dinner that night. Fish swam in abundance around my kayak, day and night—and I was worried about how many bags of oatmeal I had left? What was I thinking?

I was paddling off the Nicoya Peninsula. The sun was just beginning to dip behind the mighty waters on the horizon, and I steered the kayak safely behind a large bluff that stretched out across the water. I took out the fishing pole that had been strapped, virtually unused, to the poles of the outrigger, and baited the hook with an artificial lure. This was one of the poles Gary had given me in Punta Final.

"Maybe you'll help me catch a big fish tonight, Gary!" I said out loud. I'd been talking to myself more frequently lately, and I found I enjoyed the one-way conversations. No arguments that way.

I grasped the rod between my knees, and with the line trailing several yards behind, paddled slowly toward the shore. The beach was still fifty yards away.

After only a few minutes, I felt a tug. I picked up the rod. The reel shot forward, rotating around its axis with incredible speed. I waited until the line was almost out and then grabbed it with my right hand.

"This one's gonna be huge!" I cried out in excitement.

After several minutes of letting the fish swim in and out of the currents, I reeled him to the boat. It was a dark colored fish, most likely a bonita.

Now, though, I had a predicament. The fish was thrashing against the side of the boat with great force.

"Should I kill you now with my knife?" I asked the fish as it continued to try and free itself from the line. "Or should I try and bring you to shore first?"

I didn't want to attract sharks with the blood, but being so close to shore, I decided to kill it in the water. Not as messy that way. I unsheathed my Bowie knife and waited until the fish tired of its struggle. Finally it swam close to the boat and stopped its movements completely.

Solemnly, I brought my knife close to its head. As quickly as possible, I brought it down with great force, splitting its skull. The fish thrashed only for a moment, and then died.

I picked up my paddle. Blood was already flowing into the waters around my kayak, staining the blue to a crimson red. There were no sharks yet, and I did not wait to find out if they would join my feast. I was soon on the shore, hauling the bonita out of the water. It was dark, almost black, a foot and a half in length. It probably weighed close to ten pounds.

There were several pieces of driftwood scattered across the beach. I set the fish down and quickly gathered enough wood to start a fire. After I had built a small triangle with dried wood, I took out a few waterproof matches that had gone virtually unused until now. It took several tries, but eventually, the fire caught hold of the smaller branches, climbing upwards along the wood.

While the fire burned, sending a trail of smoke curling into the air, I went back to the fish. After cleaning out the guts and washing the carcass in the waves, I cut several large filets, an inch thick. I found a small tree with branches still small enough to break off, yet sturdy enough to whittle the tips down to a sharp point. Soon the fish steaks were cooking, three deep, on the tips of the skewers. I roasted a total of six filets, and as the smell wafted through the calm night air, I was ravenous with hunger and delight.

I burned my fingers slightly in anticipation of the feast but hardly noticed. I was so hungry I pulled the first piece off while the center was still nearly raw. I swallowed the half-chewed piece like an animal, grunting in satisfaction. Leaving the other pieces to cook, I went down the beach to find some coconuts.

The sun had completely set, and dusk draped over the coast. My bonfire rose cheerily, a stark contrast to the dark horizon. A passion rose within my breast, so violent, so clean, so primal, and so pure that I thought I might never leave this spot.

So uplifted was I from this little fire, that I gathered more wood from the forest and built it up to a blazing bonfire. I sat down and felt the heat from the fire, and I was happy. I ate the rest of the fish and threw the remains back into the ocean for the scavengers to finish.

I sat back down and brought my knees up to my chest. Looking out through the fire and into the darkness of the vast waters where I had spent so much time, I felt completely satisfied. My watch, I realized, had stopped at 7:29 PM, February 10, 1997. That was the last time I would know the time of day, the date, or even the month. Lost in a sea of memories, adventures, rain forests, and rhythm, both of the ocean and myself, I would gradually slip, over the next few weeks, into a state of absolute bliss and oblivion.

Spiritually, something was also stirring inside of me. In the beginning, I had wanted to become a better person—mentally, physically, and spiritually. Sure, I had also yearned for the attention that would come when I broke the world's record. I knew before I left the States that I would be encountering many hardships and trials over the next six months. But stopping was not an option, and that bull-headed obstinacy had not only almost killed me, it had also kept God at a distance.

Five months later, in February, I'd learned that my only key to survival was my reliance on God. I no longer waited to pray at night, or in the morning. Instead, I prayed all day, every day. In much the same way as my thoughts rambled on without stopping, I prayed without ceasing.

I remembered two distinct times before I'd left, when a fear so powerful gripped me that I thought I might never leave. Once, about a week before I left, I'd traveled down to Laguna Beach. I'd walked along the beach, looking out over the blackness that blanketed the ocean. Doubts about my ability to persevere frightened me almost to a point of anger. *I have to do this*, I told myself, *no matter what happens.*

Also, as I've mentioned, the night before I left San Felipe, I saw the ocean for what she truly was—a powerful, all-encompassing creature, waiting for me with open jaws. I had gripped Heather's hand tightly, wishing to never let go.

But in September I had set off, on a voyage to prove myself and to prove to others that I follow through on my boasts, yet also eager to get it over with and return home.

Now in February of 1997, I refused to look to the future. Home was not a place I would return to. I was already there.

THIRTY-THREE
A Scream Ripped Through The Silence Of The Night

The morning sun woke me early. The fire had long since died, and I rose slowly, stiff from the cool night. The ocean looked rough, the blue waves speckled with white.

By the evening I had paddled more than forty-five miles. The city of Puntarenas was just ahead. A ferry passed by on my right side, welcoming me to civilization. It was the first time in a week I had seen any sign of human life. I waved to the passengers, but doubted if they saw me.

"Hey, guys! Look at me!" I cried happily. "Yeah, I'm a free man!"

Soon I saw the beach next to the city. It was at least four miles in length. There were many boats around me now, on all sides, and I continued slowly, watching their every move. The people on board waved to me, and I returned the gesture happily.

The water didn't look clean, and I noticed that nobody was swimming in the gentle surf when I landed ashore. The city was not so populated as to force itself upon me, and I left the shore to find a pay phone.

"You remember Liz Brea, don't you?" my mother asked when she accepted my call.

"Of course. We knew her about twenty years ago," I said.

"Well, she married a man from Honduras. I just talked to them a few weeks ago. They said if you were anywhere near them to call and see if you could arrange a visit."

"I don't know about that, Mom," I said reluctantly. The last thing I wanted to do now was a visit an old friend, especially if it meant backtracking away from the ocean.

"I really think you should, sweetheart," my mom said again. When she called me that, it made me feel loved again.

"I'll see what I can do. This will be the last time I call you."

"Are you almost done?"

"Yep. It's almost over. But I don't know if I want to come back home."

"Well, I think you should. Aren't you tired of the traveling?"

"No, not at all," I said with a confidence I now felt whole-heartedly. "Anyway, I love you, Mom. Tell Dad, too."

However pleasant the conversations were I had on the phone, my heart belonged to the ocean. How could I give this all up to go back to society? Would I ever be content to stay ashore, and not become restless?

Back on the beach in Puntarenas, I unchained my kayak from the sloop in the harbor and was off before noon.

That night I camped on a small beach thirty miles south of the city. The forest behind the sandy shore grew thick and coarse. It was more humid every day, and the mosquitoes whined noisily around my ears as I hastily set up the tent. One of the rods broke again as I was nailing it into the ground. No matter how much tape I wrapped around the crack, I could not get the tent to stand up straight. There was not much hope in prolonging its life much longer, and I knew that the next port would be its last.

The jungle was alive, just feet from my sleeping bag. I heard the shrieks of monkeys and various night fowl. Insects buzzed so ferociously that I sat up several times in the night, wondering if they had crawled inside my ears. More than once I heard small rustlings in the low ferns nearby. I breathed deeply but quietly, not wishing to alarm any animal that nosed about.

* * *

I woke up wondering what day it was. I had not read the Bible out loud for several days and thought perhaps it might be Sunday. It didn't matter much, since I prayed all the time anyway. I didn't look at my journal, which would tell me the date if I counted from the last few entries. Instead, I packed everything up in the kayak and took off from shore.

The first wave crashed overhead, and I calmly held my breath, braced my back against the seat and dug into the swirling waters with my oar. The muscles in my arms responded with great strength. I broke through the first wave and shook my head vigorously, clearing my ears and eyes. I sailed up the face of the next breaker, relishing the thrill of crashing through the hands of the ocean. I was soon over the top of the next wave, and was gliding down its back.

"I love this!" I exclaimed at the top of my lungs. "Have you got anything else for me today? Let's see what you got!"

The open waters called to me, and I rolled up and down each swell. I crested down the back of each mountain, which added an extra push to my stroke, increasing my momentum. The sharp front bow of the kayak cut sharply through the water. Ripples of white foam parted, leaving little waves to form and head back out, away from my craft.

At midday, with the sun directly overhead, and after about four hours of steady paddling, I stopped for lunch. I noticed again that I didn't have much. I had bought a few items at my last stop, but only enough for the next few days. The lack of food didn't bother me much.

Before I started again, I looked down at the chart in my lap. I sometimes looked at the charts, kept in a waterproof plastic bag, a dozen times a day.

I was only a few miles off shore. The closest guess I could come to my location was that Quepos lay ten to twelve miles ahead. Judging by the location of the sun, I figured it must be past noon. I should reach the city by nightfall.

The day went by smoothly, and I was fairly comfortable in my little seat. The only deterrent of the past few days seemed to be the weather. I hadn't seen rain for several days, and the sun beat down mercilessly on me. The temperature must have been in the high eighties, and the glare from the sun came off the water with such force that I was continually squinting my eyes and wiping the sweat from my brows. I pulled the brim of my wide hat down lower on my forehead. At times I closed my eyes completely, shutting out the penetrating heat and glare. I let the ocean lift me up and down; the direction I was headed didn't seem to matter much.

I reached Quepos ahead of schedule. The sun had not yet begun its descent when I reached a small canal that led to the city. The surf broke abruptly against the sandbars that surrounded its entrance, and I was almost overturned. But the water in the canal was smooth, and once I reached its quiet domain I glided easily over to the shore.

As I pulled the kayak to the beach I wondered if the map had misled me. I saw no city. In fact, the only thing that met my gaze was a long, tall sand dune.

Then a sound reached my ears and I realized that a street must lie just beyond the sand, for it was a car engine that had just caught my attention. Nobody was on the beach, and after throwing a line over one of the tall trees I climbed on all fours up the bank.

Sure enough, when I reached the top of the dune I blinked in surprise. There, spread out before me, was the modern city of Quepos. There were little surf shops everywhere, and several of the streets were dotted with small hotels. My stomach growled at the smell of roasted meat, which wafted by on a small breath of wind.

Across the street I noticed a rather fancy restaurant. The sign over it read El Grand Escape. That sure sounded promising. After looking both ways, I quickly crossed the street, walked in the front door and took a seat at the first table I came to.

A magnificent breeze blew in and through the restaurant, and I sat back to relax. The cooler temperature felt great; I took off my hat and placed it on the table. There were a few waitresses near the back, and one smiled at me and held up a finger. I took the time to look around and noticed thousands of pictures hanging on the walls. Most were of men with big fish, undoubtedly caught in nearby waters.

"There should be a picture of me up there," I said softly. I thought fondly of my own catch of the previous day and smiled.

After picking up a menu, I checked my wallet and found that I still had more than $150 left. For once I didn't have to worry about money.

Memories of all the help I'd received flooded my mind. I leaned back in my chair and reflected. Gary and Carl had given me everything they could spare, from fishing rods to maps. That information had been lifesaving, and I was still reaping the rewards of their generosity. Edward Guzman had given me so much as well, including countless dinners and even the plane ticket to Mexico City. Finally, Brad Jordan, my cousin, had given me most of the money I now possessed, and I shuddered to think what I would have done without it.

It was ironic how I was still, despite all of my efforts, connected to society. Would I ever really be completely independent? Perhaps now, with all of these experiences changing and shaping my character, I could live without the assistance of civilization. But did I want to?

Seeing all those smiling faces in my mind and remembering all the good times along the way, caused some doubt. On the one hand I cherished my relationships with people who had sacrificed so much to make my journey successful. But my soul now longed for the freedom of the outdoors, away from people, away from hassles, and away from boundaries. It was a dilemma I would face throughout not only the rest of my journey, but the rest of my life as well.

I knew I needed to save some of this money for the long trip home. I still wasn't sure of the logistics. For example, how would I get my kayak back to the States, or myself for that matter? I couldn't possibly have imagined how much of a struggle it would be to get back. At the moment I was blissfully ignorant of the hardships ahead, so I nonchalantly ordered the biggest steak on the menu.

(Several weeks later I would pass through this same town, eat at the same restaurant, and meet Margo, the owner. Margo, who was not present at this time, would take a certain liking to this hungry wanderer, and sponsor all of my meals there. She was a nice, friendly lady, who lavished her attention on me and let me eat anything on the menu I wanted. Although we only spent a few days together, she understood my plight and helped in any way that she could. That would be the last haven and comfort I would see for more than three weeks, the time it took me to get the rest of the way home. But that's the beginning of my next adventure and I wouldn't dare spoil that story by talking too much here.)

After I ate the steak I let it digest for a few minutes, then walked back down to the beach. Soon I was back in the canal, paddling vigorously toward the shallow breakers. Going out was much easier than it had been coming in, and my kayak split the waves smoothly as I headed for the open ocean.

It was getting late in the day now, so I paddled for only an hour before I headed for the shore. After rounding Punta Quepos, which was covered with a thick rain forest, I headed south, past several shady beaches. I saw a few people walking along the shores there, so decided to press on for a more isolated spot. There were several tiny islands spread out to my right. I paddled between them, counting a total of six islands, before I saw a larger point in the distance. The sun was setting, and I decided that, people or not, I would camp there for the night.

My charts indicated that I was just south of Playa Puerto Escondido. The jungle was so thick I couldn't step on the shore without lowering my head to dodge a few overhanging branches. The white sands penetrated the rain forest only for a couple of yards. I felt like I was conquering the Amazon jungle.

I made another bonfire and curled close to its warmth on the soft sand. Before falling asleep, I took out my clothes, food and sleeping bag, which were all soaking wet, and spread them by the fire to dry. I lay down again, turned my back to the warmth, and was soon asleep.

* * *

A scream ripped through the silence of the night. I was instantly awake, hardly daring to breathe. I turned over slowly to face the jungle, from where I thought the sound had come. There were still a few burning embers in the ashes of my fire pit on the sand. Several of the branches overhead moved, giving way to some animal, the rustling of leaves catching my attention at once.

My heart pounded in my chest as I forced myself to lie still. Whatever it was, I didn't want to announce my presence. Hoping to hide from view, I pressed as flat as I could against the cold, hard sand.

The moon came out from behind the clouds, casting an eerie light toward the jungle. Long shadows stretched from the taller trees to fall silently on the beach, some directly over my campsite. Even the crickets and the other insects of the forest had stopped their chirping, and a dead calm fell over the entire area.

I continued to lie still, waiting for something to move. Had the animal, whatever it was, seen me? Was it at that very moment watching my every move, aware that my eyes too were searching? I couldn't tell, but I felt its presence.

Another scream broke through the air, and I jerked involuntarily. The branch overhead swayed in the still air, and I knew the sound had come from them. I realized that my fists were clenched tightly and my lungs were gulping in as much air as possible. I looked up to see if I could distinguish the animal that moved among the trees.

I heard another movement, still overhead, but farther off to the left. More now to the right. Then, in a wild flurry of voices, several monkeys screeched at once. I caught a glimpse of one, less than twenty feet away, swinging madly from one branch to the next. All of the monkeys imitated the first, and in a kind of dance made their agitation known. They were white, making them stand out against the dark background of the forest.

I noticed they kept their eyes on the ground. Whatever it was that had caused them to erupt in such violent screaming must be close to where I lay. It was not I that had disturbed their night.

Another movement in the undergrowth of the jungle caused my breath to stop abruptly. By the sound of the branches breaking and leaves crackling like paper being ripped, I guessed that whatever was moving around was fairly large in size. No wonder the monkeys were agitated.

A low, heavy breathing reached my ears.

What was it? The only animals that hunted on the ground at night were the giant cats that frequent this coast.

Could I jump up and run down to the kayak in time to get away? Then I remembered that the safety line was tied to a nearby tree. It would be impossible to untie it, run down to the shore, jump in my kayak and paddle away without being noticed.

I reached down slowly and felt the large knife that was half buried in the sand, close to my leg. But who was I kidding? The blade, no matter how sharp, would be no match for a jaguar or puma.

More rustling ahead. The monkeys had grown quiet, and I wondered if they had scurried away to safety, leaving me feeling very alone and vulnerable.

After a while, another monkey screamed, and I started again at the intrusion of silence. No others joined its cry, but I knew they were still there, up in the trees, guarding their homes. For some reason I felt better knowing that the little creatures shared my plight.

After what seemed like hours, the larger animal on the ground moved again. This time the noise sounded farther off, and I breathed a sigh of relief. The monkeys continued to hop from limb to limb, until their rustlings faded away into the night. They would probably follow the hunter until it was definitely out of the area.

Thankful that they had alerted me to the danger, I sat up and stoked the fire again. The blaze would keep off other animals that prowled in the night—I hoped—and soon the fire was roaring. I still had a few pieces of driftwood beside me, and at different intervals over the next several hours, I threw them into the flames. I can't say that I remained awake for the rest of the night, because after a while my exhausted mind slowly shut down. I kept watch with my back to the fire, but eventually dozed off.

* * *

I woke up late the next morning, wondering if I'd experienced another nightmare as the events of the night came quickly back to memory. Thankful that I was still in one piece, I ate a quick breakfast and packed all of my dry supplies back into the compartments. I was standing at the water's edge, knee deep in the surf, when I looked back at the jungle. Something white, moving about in the trees, caught my eye and caused me to stop. I looked closer and saw the tiny face of a monkey.

"Hey, little guy," I said, calling to it.

It cocked its head to one side when it heard my voice and let out a low whoop.

"Did you save my neck last night, little guy?" I asked.

I walked back up on the beach, hauling my kayak behind me, then left it on the sand. As I neared the jungle the monkey moved away, farther into the trees. I stopped, not wishing to frighten it.

"I'm not going to hurt you," I said softly.

More movement overhead, and soon there were more than a dozen monkeys, all white-faced and about a foot tall, hopping from tree to tree. There was a little path that I'd not seen the night before, just off to my left. I looked back at the kayak to make sure it was far enough out of the water. To be on the safe side, I walked back down, pulled it another few feet up the beach, and placed my paddle in the cockpit.

The monkeys were watching me inquisitively, so I decided to investigate the jungle for a few minutes. I put my sandals on and walked up the beach to the head of the trail.

The dark forest quickly enveloped me, and it took a few minutes for my eyes to adjust to the change in light. I had walked only a few feet into the jungle, but its dense vegetation left little room to move about freely. The only relief in sight was the thin trail beneath my feet, which wound up the hill, disappearing several yards ahead in a mass of vines, ferns and tree trunks. Insects were flying around my exposed skin, and I swatted constantly at them. In minutes I was covered with dozens of tiny red bumps. I hoped none of the mosquitoes carried malaria.

There were now fifteen or so monkeys overhead, and I watched as they danced around in circles, their eyes on me. I continued through the thick undergrowth, attempting to follow the winding path that disappeared and then reappeared every several steps. There was movement to my left, and something scurried quickly away. The jungle was incredibly alive with movement. I saw rodents and other mammals foraging for food. Some moved away, scared by my intrusion, others remained still, curious about me.

I couldn't imagine anyone ever passing beneath this canopy of life and remaining untouched. The path now climbed upwards and I looked back to where I'd come from, hoping I'd be able to find my way out again. Something about the jungle, much like the ocean, was drawing me deeper into its grasp. Through the tiny patches in the forest I could just make out the blue of the water near my campsite. I continued my explorations.

More monkeys came overhead, this time playing with each other. They kept their eyes on me, but seemed more comfortable now with having me near.

The path grew wider and the trees drew back to let me pass. Overhead they arched their branches to form a canopy twenty feet in the air. Very little sunlight penetrated through the mass of vegetation above and the air was heavy with humidity.

I heard a loud, raucous "caw" several yards ahead. Cresting the hill, I scanned the branches for more signs of life. A brilliant flash of red appeared briefly, then retreated back into the forest. I left the trail, listening for more signs of movement. Another raspy cry, which I knew was some sort of tropical bird. I saw a blur of blue and yellow, and could just make out the vanishing traces of a parrot.

The monkeys must have been busy playing somewhere else, or maybe I had walked out of their territory. More birds fluttered overhead. My head jerked back and forth, trying to catch the beauty of their movements. An enormous, bright red macaw landed on a branch twenty feet above my right shoulder. It was a foot and a half in length, with long tail feathers hanging down over the branch where it sat. Another macaw, possibly the mate, fluttered near the same branch.

Slowly I took out my camera and began to take pictures. Startled by the bright flash, both birds let out a few strident cries before swooping off to a safer branch. I closed my eyes and listened to the sounds of the forest. Far off in the distance I heard the gurgling sounds of a stream. I continued to follow the trail and was soon kneeling down at a small river, dipping my hands and head in the cool water.

When I rose again to my feet, the water swirled about my ankles, forming small pools and eddies. It was flowing to the south, leading out to the ocean from which I'd just come. There were no animals presently drinking from the stream, but I knew that if I waited long enough I'd catch a glimpse of renewed activity.

Overhead, a few small chinks of sunlight burst through the thick canopy of the forest, flickering across the leaves and trunks of the trees. It was now quite muggy, and I kept busy slapping the insects from my legs, back, neck and face. It was time for me to head back to the beach.

I retraced my steps along the trail, followed by birds and monkeys alike. I ducked my head down under the last few branches that hung over the beach, but not before looking back at the variety of wildlife that thrived there. I waved goodbye to the creatures, talking to them without embarrassment.

"You're so pretty and red!" I called to the birds of paradise. "Hope to see you soon, down the coast. Goodbye, little monkeys. Thanks again for last night." With no other human beings around, it felt completely natural to talk to the animals.

I waved again and turned back to the ocean.

It was now close to midday. The air was still and hot. I pushed my kayak to the water and climbed in. As soon as I was on open water, I jumped in for a swim, washing off the dirt of the forest in the clear blue sea.

* * *

By dusk I saw the lights of a small city called Dominical. I rested for a while, letting the swells carry my kayak closer to South America. The current was still going with me, and I was traveling close to fifty miles each day. Still, I didn't bother to check what day it was. What did it matter, anyway? I slept with the night's darkness blanketing my eyes and woke with the sun's warming rays. What else could tell me, as perfectly as the sun, when I needed to do things? My stomach told me when to eat, and the heavens told me when to sleep. Nothing could have been simpler than that.

Thousands of stars covered the sky. I winked back at the ones I knew, calling out their names one by one.

"Hello, Mr. Dipper. Good to see you tonight," I said to my friend. "How do things look from up there? I'll bet you didn't think you'd be seeing so much of me. Well, I'm still here."

I looked over my shoulder briefly and added, "You either, eh, North Star? Can't say I blame you. Don't know if I'm gonna stop. Just love being out here with you guys, night after night."

I stretched out, content. I was no longer alone. My friends looked out for me from above; the ocean gently held me in her arms, rocking me. The coast invited me to shore each day, presenting new gifts at every turn. I talked to everything, and God smiled down on me from above. There was no need to close my eyes and pray, either. All I did was open my mouth to talk, and I knew that He was right there listening to every word I said.

"If this is a dream, let me never wake, and if I am awake, let me never close my eyes," I said, before I nodded off to sleep, drifting on the open ocean.

THIRTY-FOUR
A Dark Form Lifted From The Water

A wave came over the bow of my kayak, crashing into my lap. I woke with a start and sat up coughing. I picked up my paddle. Had a storm come up in the night without my knowledge? My eyes focused to the moon's pale light. The ocean was a bit rough, but the sky remained cloudless.

"Well," I said with a laugh, "I'm awake now. Might as well start paddling again."

I stood up briefly and stretched my tired muscles. Several miles in the distance, I thought I saw a shoreline. I had no idea where I was, or how far out to sea I'd drifted, but I was not overly concerned.

The night air was warmer than it had been for several weeks. I was nearing, if not already on, the twentieth parallel, and could feel the change in the weather as it became hotter and more humid each day. More clouds formed on the horizon during the long days, but it hardly rained now. The official ending of the wet season had occurred in December.

I continued to paddle through the night, for about another hour. After a while I closed my eyes again and relaxed. With my paddle still gripped firmly between both hands, I dozed for a few minutes. When I woke again, and with my eyes still closed, I paddled out of habit. This happened several times—sleeping, paddling, eyes barely open, eyes closed. Half awake, half asleep.

By the time I opened my eyes for good the sun had risen. I was quite close to the coast. My stomach growled impatiently, and I took out several bags of oatmeal. I poured a little water into the pouch, and then swallowed its contents. I had a gallon and a half of water left and made a mental note to drink sparingly. Though I was still getting coconut milk when I could along the way, I couldn't afford to be careless with my rations.

For the entire day I paddled without seeing any cities on the shore. I was passing through the Bahia de Coronado, but the water there didn't seem any calmer than the open ocean. The swells still crested twenty feet over my head, and I leaned forward in anticipation of each new wave.

I steered the kayak farther out to sea, perpendicular to the coast. The compass reading pointed almost due south, and I remembered that the coast of Costa Rica curved sharply to the east. I kept a keen eye on the waves that crashed towards the shore, careful not to be drawn too close. My stroke quickened, my arms grew extremely tired, but finally I was out of reach of the whitecaps.

I again headed east, parallel to the coast. I was now several miles out and the shore looked small, off in the distance. Most of the time, unless I climbed to the top of one of the rolling swells, I saw nothing except the ocean all around me. It moved constantly, shifting here, breaking into a small wave there, and my eyes never rested on any particular spot for long.

Eventually I spotted a town on the horizon. I steered diagonally towards the cluster of houses and huts, and by dusk I was surfing the waves to shore.

Once my kayak was secured, I pulled a shirt over my head and walked toward the town. There were only a few people on the beach, and none had seen my arrival. I welcomed the anonymity.

There were several small hotels, which looked expensive, at the edge of town. I walked through the front doors of the first hotel that caught my eye, and took a seat in the restaurant.

A waiter, neatly dressed in a white cotton shirt and pants, came over.

"Evening, sir," he said, with only a slight accent.

"How are you?" I asked after a moment of uncertainty. This was the first human being I'd talked to in more than a week. It felt odd to converse with something other than the stars, the sky, the ocean, and God. Oh, yes, and the animals of the jungle.

"Fine, thank you." He was middle-aged but looked as though he might be a surfer.

"What's the name of this place?" I asked.

"The Cocalito Lodge, sir," he said with an air that told me it was probably the nicest place in town.

"Let's see," I said, looking down at the menu. "Nice menu. Fish, chicken, shrimp. What shall I have? Haven't eaten a lot lately. Haven't really felt like it. The water was pretty tough lately, so I haven't been able to fish as often as I would like. Maybe I'll have some fish. Fresh here. Should be. Is that what I want?"

"Excuse me, sir? I don't understand." The waiter, obviously puzzled, interrupted my monologue.

I looked up at his face, which was a mass of confusion. I looked again at the menu in my hand, which I had quite forgotten, and saw the white tablecloth spread before me.

"Oh, sorry," I said, embarrassed. Was I crazy? He must have thought so. I'd spent so long by myself that I'd forgotten my habit of talking out loud. Now, without knowing, I had let my thoughts evolve into words. "Yes, right," I continued hastily. "I'll have the *dorado*." (Spanish for mahi-mahi, a fish I was particularly fond of.)

He nodded his head and smiled.

I was so ravenously hungry that I barely tasted the meal. When I was finished I motioned again for the waiter to come over.

"What city is this?" I asked. There had been no clear indication on my map.

"Drake, sir," he said.

"How far am I from the next national park?"

"About four miles. It is a rain forest."

"Corcovado?" I asked, pleased with my progress.

"That is correct, sir," he said, smiling.

"Is there a place here where I can clean up? An outdoor shower or something?"

"Um, yes." He looked around before he spoke. "There is. We have facilities to rent. They are eight dollar a night, but you can use it for free if you hurry"

I smiled, grateful for his kindness, and left him an extra big tip.

I practically ran back down to my kayak. After grabbing my toothbrush, razor and soap, I hurried back to the shower he had pointed out to me.

The water felt wonderful, and I scrubbed vigorously at the salt that caked my body from head to toe. I stepped out refreshed, clean, and feeling like a new man.

At a nearby store I bought a few groceries. I packed the bananas, six gallons of purified water, and bread in my little backpack.

I walked back down to my kayak, watching as the waves slowly broke onto the shore. A great calm had fallen over the ocean, since I'd landed, and I could see the moon reflecting brightly off its smooth surface. I put the groceries away in the kayak and found a spot on the sand next to a giant palm tree, where I slept again under the stars, curled up on top of my sleeping bag.

* * *

I was still skirting the Parque Nacional Corcovado late the next morning, when the surface of the water churned a dozen yards to my right. The ocean was fairly calm, and the breeze that lifted off the shore made no sound except the slight rippling effect it had on the water. The air was hot, humid, and still, and I looked over in startled bewilderment. What had made the surface move like that?

I was soon to have my answer.

Again, now farther off in front of my kayak, I saw the waters swirl in a great circular motion. Suddenly a dark form lifted from the water, blowing an enormous jet of air up into the sky. With incredible excitement, I saw the top of a whale's back lift slowly from the ocean and disappear again beneath the surface.

I paddled faster, toward the spot where the whale had come up for air. I passed over the area and saw that all around me the ocean was moving. I looked from side to side, searching for any signs of the great beast. A shadow passed by directly underneath my kayak and I slowed my stroke, gliding silently through the swells. Another movement caught my eye over my left shoulder. I turned my head just in time to see the whale rising to the surface again.

"Oh, my goodness," I exclaimed under my breath, for the whale, a humpback, had emerged from the ocean a scant fifteen feet from my kayak. Its eye stared directly into mine.

"Mr. Whale. I can't believe what I'm seeing. You're huge."

Was I talking or just thinking? I shook my head and paddled again. The giant beast had again submerged, but the water all around continued to ripple and break in all directions. I knew it was still just beneath the surface, eyeing my slow, rather pathetic movements.

"Please, come up again," I cried.

The sun beat down hot, and the slight breeze that had attempted to cool me off now ceased. I was alone in my little boat, a few miles from the shore, with the biggest whale I had ever seen just beneath the waters. My heart beat fast in anticipation, and I continued to scan the horizon. When the water became still I thought I'd seen the last of the humpback, but then, with a burst of speed, the whale came rushing up to the surface.

I stopped paddling and leaned back in my seat. Twenty yards away, in a rush of sound and speed, the whale burst out of the water. I looked straight in its eye, trying to understand what it must be feeling. Free, happy, grand, proud. Its tail, speckled with black and gray spots, flipped high out of the water. It paused for a second, and I found myself holding my breath until it came back down. The huge tail landed hard, scattering the water high into the air. I closed my eyes as a few drops headed my way.

The entire ocean seemed to lurch forward. For a moment I thought the whale had swum underneath my kayak and was lifting me into the air. My kayak, with me in it, rose to a great, dizzying height. Then, just as gently as if I were an infant lying in my crib, the wave set me back down, breathless, ecstatic, and in one piece.

For the next hour I continued to scan the waters, longing—wishing—for another such encounter. Far off into the horizon, I thought I saw the spouts of more whales, but was too far away to be certain. I sat stunned by the magic I'd too briefly experienced.

Finally, still lost in a daze, I paddled halfheartedly for the rest of the day.

THIRTY-FIVE
Did I Really Have To Go Back?

At nightfall I camped out on a small beach near the entrance to the Golfo Dulce.

I walked up the beach to the forest and foraged for coconuts. After chopping off the top of one, I tilted the small opening up to my mouth. The cool liquid spilled over my chin and dribbled down my chest. It was so sweet and refreshing. When I'd had my fill I sat down and cut a larger opening in the top of the shell.

Several bags of dried oatmeal fit neatly into the coconut bowl, mixing with the last of the milk.

I stirred it vigorously with the plastic spoon I carried with me and swallowed the gruel. Again I took out my knife and cut several chunks of the tender white meat from inside the coconut. I ate until I was full.

I stretched. My body was tanned, lean and strong. I took in a deep breath, feeling the power of the moment. The sun was setting over the water, and I noticed a small island on the horizon. I was camped on a large point just south of Montezuma. The sun dipped down behind the island, illuminating its shape and blurring it slightly with shimmering radiance. I closed my eyes, blinded by the spectacle in front of me, and began to sing. Softly at first but then loud and clear.

I sang a song that I wish now I could recall. If only I had written it down, to sing to the world. It was a song of the sea, clear and blue. Of the waters that leaped about on all sides and of the coast that produced such wonder and amazement. It was for the animals that swam so freely in the ocean. It was about my God who, under great and many circumstances, had helped me every step of the way.

I sang whatever words came to my lips, but they came straight from the heart. I cried a little as I lay down to sleep, wondering why

I had been so blessed. Not only with safety, but also with beauty and adventure. I felt like the luckiest man alive.

* * *

I looked out across the great expanse of water, towards the other side of the Gulf. With a deep breath, I shoved off into the water. My compass was set on 120 degrees east. Hopefully, without much of a current, I would see land by that afternoon. Several boats passed on the horizon, in front and in back of my kayak, but none came close enough to cause concern.

By mid afternoon I'd crossed the Gulf and passed a small beach called Esterillos. By nightfall I spotted an enormous point that jutted twenty miles out into the ocean. This was where Panama began. The point was called Punta Burica, and I set my eyes solidly on its massive form, paddling well past nightfall.

The moon came up, lighting my way. Encouraged, I put my head down and paddled with even greater fury. After a few hours of such exertion, I was exhausted and forced to stop. I took out my windbreaker and huddled in the cockpit, watching the swells roll and the moon reflect their movements. Soon, my eyes—too heavy to keep open another minute—closed.

I slept until morning and woke with the sun. I was amazed at how well I'd slept. The morning air was cool, but I jumped in the water to refresh, and to stretch my cramped muscles. The water was invigorating.

Still a few miles from Punta Burica, I adjusted my direction slightly to counteract my drift during the night. Soon I reached the calm waters of the Golfo de Chiriqui.

I still had four gallons of water left, so I decided to bypass the city of David, third largest city in Panama. It would be better if I didn't clutter my mind and body with the distractions of a large city. I paddled between several islands that rose high enough to not only block my view of the coast, but of the open waters of the Pacific, as well.

I stayed clear of the islands' shores. At times the ocean hurled itself with such force against their rocky coasts that I could hear and feel the thunderous activity. Yet the waters around were without whitecaps. Strange that the surf should remain so strong against the islands, while the rest of the water around me rose and fell almost lazily.

Once past the island, I headed out to sea, veering off at an angle to head for Punta Jabali.

While the sun set behind my back, I saw a black object floating in the water. I paddled toward it, realizing while it was still some fifteen yards away that it was a sea snake. I watched as it slowly glided by. It paid no attention to my paddling. Its head was bent slightly, its muscles curving elegantly in the water, leaving small ripples behind. The body was entirely black except for a bright yellow streak that ran across its brow. I turned in my seat and let it pass, watching its head move back and forth, back and forth.

* * *

I awoke the next morning slightly disoriented. A low fog had rolled in over the ocean, and I could see only a few yards ahead. There was a ghostly, eerie calm over the water. Waves crashed somewhere in the distance, the sound muffled. I picked up my paddle.

The fog was so thick I couldn't even tell in which direction the sun was positioned in the sky. I still didn't know the date. Was it February still? Or maybe March? Without the sun, I couldn't even estimate the hour of the day.

There was a sharp noise somewhere to my left, and I turned to see if I could make out anything in the shadows. It had sounded almost like a dolphin surfacing for a breath of air, but in this gloom, I could only imagine. My mind, after a long stretch of sanity, now began to conjure up all kinds of ideas. Another shark? A whale? Or had I drifted too close to the shore?

Unable to see, I felt quite helpless. For some reason, this was different than the darkness I experienced at night. With my mind playing tricks on me, I imagined strange forms peering out of the mist, coming menacingly toward me. My imagination clearly enjoyed torturing me with fear and doubt. I shook my head, telling myself repeatedly that it was only the morning fog, and it would soon lift.

Without any serious incidents—except for those played out in my head—the sun finally broke through. First it was a thin ray of sunlight that sparkled on the water, then the air lightened and I could see several hundred yards on all sides. I heard the cries of seagulls near the shore and the rumble of the waves. I looked at the charts and saw that I was nearing the Isla de Coiba to my right, with Punta Jabali to my left.

The day passed slowly, and by late afternoon I was ready to head to shore. I had traveled over a hundred miles in two days, and was ecstatic at the increased endurance and strength my muscles possessed. The Azuero Peninsula bulged out ahead, its great mass jutting out into the Pacific Ocean. The water ahead grew anxious, anticipating the change in the coastline. White streaks of water dotted the horizon and the surf rose to new heights from the intrusion of land. Just past Cebaco Island, I decided to spend the night in a small cove that emerged on my left.

Punta Mariato, on the far tip of the Peninsula, took most of the Pacific's power and fury, which left room for calmer waters beneath its protective wing. The point stuck out into the open ocean for several miles, and I paddled quickly into the bay it provided. Just before the sun dipped below the western horizon, I surfed the small, three-foot waves to shore.

The water was clear, the beach nice and flat. I took out my sleeping bag. The loss of the tent no longer mattered, for the nights were calm and the animals were now my friends. No harm would come to me while I slept.

Too tired to light a fire, I lay down on the soft sand. The night breeze tousled my hair and whispered softly into my ear.

I knew in my heart that I did not want this experience to end. I wanted to paddle into the sunset forever, never looking back. This life on the ocean, with all of her power and beauty, could not be matched on land, and the splendor of any city did not compare to the ocean's riches.

Did I really have to go back? Or could I live this way while I grew old?

The clouds rolled by and the stars, peeking out from beneath, winked at me. I smiled at their return to the sky. Here were my friends. I was home, out here in the open, and I would never go back.

THIRTY-SIX
My World Turned Upside Down

With the rising of the sun, I still wore a contented smile on my face. My body had turned toward the ocean, and I watched the waves rise and crash onto the beach for a while before I stood up. I stretched slowly, letting the blood circulate to all of my muscles.

Then I frowned slightly, because I knew that it couldn't last. All dances must end, and even though I didn't want it to, I knew it was inevitable. I was not drawn to civilization for its comforts, but by the relationships, my family and friends. My love for them was no less important than this ongoing affair with the ocean. Still, it saddened me to realize I was nearing the end of my journey.

I saw no cities as I paddled past Punta Mariato. The ocean surged forward just south of the point, and I braced myself as the swells rolled quickly toward the coast. I paddled furiously up their faces and held my hands over my head in triumph as I soared down the back of each new wave. It was an incredible sensation of speed and motion as the wind whipped across my face and the waves smacked across my bow. I tasted salt, and the ocean rose and fell as if breathing deeply in conjunction with my own lungs.

The swells evened out once I was past the point, but they were still well over fifteen feet. The land appeared and disappeared several times that morning before I decided I'd seen enough.

Turning my face toward the already risen sun, I quickened my stroke and yelled loudly into the wind, "South America, here I come! I can almost see you there on the horizon."

I was still over two hundred and fifty miles from the shores of Colombia, but with each passing hour I sensed her coming closer. When I thought of landing on her shores, which was often now, my heart would beat fast and my breath would come sharp and deep.

Each wave pulled gently at my kayak, inviting me along for the ride. I turned my head and saw a wave arching several yards behind.

As it came closer to my kayak I put my paddle in the water and thrust myself forward. I felt its draw, sensed its power. I continued to paddle, but the strength of the wave made me feel like I was going backwards. The top of the wave began to curl, which produced tiny flecks of white foam that danced down the face and around me on all sides.

The front bow of my kayak cut through the water as I raced down the face of the wave. Several feet below, the ocean leveled out. In a matter of seconds I was in its trough. I had the rudder jammed to my left, but once I was out in front of the wave the kayak began to slowly curve to my right, toward the inside of the wave.

I dug my paddle into the water on my right, attempting to keep from rolling into the breaker's vacuum, but I was powerless. The kayak turned sideways into the curling vortex, the saltwater hitting my face. As the kayak rolled I took a quick gulp of air and felt the swirling water engulf me.

My world turned upside down. I pushed off the floorboards in the cockpit to clear myself from the boat, but it was too late. The force of the wave pushed me down, headfirst. The undercurrent flipped me over, and with a rush of motion, sound and light, my body lurched forward again. My head snapped violently forward as the kayak's Kevlar hull ran into the back of my skull. For a moment everything was black, but I forced my eyes to open, searching for the light on the surface of the water.

During the fall I had tensed my muscles, waiting for the moment of impact. Now I relaxed and let the ocean take me where it would. Briefly I resurfaced, and I saw the kayak only a few yards away, gliding toward the shore.

Another wave crashed down on my head, but I swam with the white water this time, toward shore. I was farther now from where the breakers began their descent, their power somewhat lessened, so it was only a few seconds before I resurfaced.

I swam to the kayak and, with a few powerful strokes, reached the safety line. The cockpit was completely full of ocean water; it would be useless to try and climb aboard. I grabbed the safety line and swam out in front of it. The back of my head was throbbing. When I touched it gingerly I was relieved to find no blood.

As soon as I felt the hard surface of the sand beneath my feet, I scrambled to shore, dragging the kayak behind. Though I'd lost a few of my supplies, including the radio, I felt lucky to be alive, and with my kayak intact.

Next, I needed to get the paddle. It was bobbing up and down in the water, fifteen feet from the shore. Caught between the wave's rhythms, at times it disappeared from sight. Down the shore a few yards I ran closest to where it floated, and jumped in. Ducking under the surf, I grasped the paddle with my left hand, turned over on my back, and caught the next wave to the beach.

A welt the size of a golf ball had risen on the back of my head. It throbbed, and I felt a little dizzy. I sat down on the beach, then lay back to soak up some of the warmth radiating off the beach. Closing my eyes, I took in a deep breath and sighed, coming down from the adrenaline rush I'd experienced. I hadn't been on a wave that size since October.

* * *

When I woke up the sun was lower on the horizon. The beach was long and wide, with a thick forest on the hills beyond. Several palm trees were nearby, from which I gathered fruit. Once my fire was built, I spread my final chart on the sand, the corners lifted by the breeze that blew across the water. I placed four coconut husks on the corners to keep the map from blowing away. The sun had set, but I could make out the details by the light of the fire.

I had landed near Punta Mala, and from there I calculated out the distance to Colombia to be roughly two hundred miles. I had decided to cut across the Gulf of Panama and head in a diagonal line to South America. There were several reasons behind that decision.

"Well, I don't want to go near the Panama Canal, that's for sure," I said, continuing my new habit of talking out loud to myself. "Too many boats. Of course, that means I'll have to go way out in the middle of nowhere, a hundred miles from shore. How much water do I have left?"

A quick inspection told me I still had two and a half gallons left. Enough for three days if I rationed it. If I paddled fifty miles a day, it would take four days to reach Colombia.

"Not enough water," I said, brushing away the sand that had blown across the map. I looked hard at the chart. "But I could collect liquid from the coconuts and fill the two empty gallon containers. That'll give me five."

The coast of Colombia appeared tantalizingly close. I folded up my map before I could change my mind again.

"I'm gonna head straight for South America," I said.

* * *

The ocean rolled out before my eyes as I stood at the edge of its great mass the following morning. My heart beat faster, as I anticipated the next several days. For the most part, I would spend them on the open waters, without the comforting sight of land.

I pushed my concerns aside and turned my attention to my water supply. I'd gathered eight coconuts, and now I patiently extracted the milk from each one. After I finished pouring the last drop from the last coconut, I had four gallons of liquid. I gathered more coconuts and managed to fill the last gallon. I then sliced off as much of the white meat from inside the shells as I could and placed it in plastic bags. My food supply was getting dangerously low, but I hadn't seen a city for days.

It was late in the morning when I finally secured the gallon jugs on the outrigger poles, packed the coconut meat, with ten bags of oatmeal, a half empty box of cereal, and three slices of sweet bread, all I had left.

The waves were still cresting over seven feet. I swam out a few yards, holding onto my kayak. When there was a small lapse in the rhythm of the breakers, I pushed off the bottom and jumped into the cockpit, which was now nearly half full of water, and began to paddle.

I cleared the next several breakers, paddled out a hundred more yards and then bailed out the water in the cockpit.

The land was slowly drifting away. I thought of the fire from the previous night—the last I'd have for many days. Standing in the kayak, I turned for one last look at the coast. I waved my hand high above my head in a farewell gesture, then sat back down and began to stroke.

It would be the last time I'd see land until Colombia.

THIRTY-SEVEN
"I got you now, fish!"

I began to grow worried the very first evening, when I stopped to eat supper. Though I had enough liquid for several days, my food supply was already running out. My muscles were weak from lack of protein. I had eaten four bags of oatmeal around noon and several handfuls of the Frosted Flakes. Why hadn't I stocked up when I'd had the chance? Because I'd been in too big a hurry.

There was no land in sight, but there'd be no turning back now.

For the first time in months I felt truly alone. The waves rolled endlessly by. I couldn't judge my progress without a coast for reference, and I wondered if I was even moving forward. But the compass on my kayak pointed southeast, so eventually, whether I was alive to see it or not, my path would have to run into South America.

As the sun cast its final rays across the heavens, several things bothered me. I didn't have enough food to last past the next day. I couldn't believe I'd been so nearsighted. Another thing that worried me was my inability to calculate the miles I traveled per day. Even with my compass pointed toward the coast, I might be pushed farther south and never hit anything. If I drifted farther west, away from Panama and Colombia, I'd never know the difference until it was too late. The Pacific Ocean stretched out for thousands of miles in that direction, and there was no telling what would happen if the currents grew too strong.

I tried, rather unsuccessfully, to push those morbid thoughts from my mind. Part of me said to turn around and go back to shore, but at this point I was far from rational.

I opened the front compartment to put on my windbreaker. The moon rose high in the night sky, then the stars came out. I smiled weakly and began, once again, the ritual of welcoming the ones I knew by name. The moonlight reflected off the surface of the water. It looked like I was traveling on a road to the moon.

* * *

In the morning, I ate another two bags of oatmeal, which left me with just three, plus a little cereal. I cast my line out from the back of the kayak, wedged the fishing rod between the outrigger poles and the cockpit, and hoped for the best.

One day moved seamlessly to the next. I was cramped, cold, wet, tired and hungry. With growing lethargy, I paddled toward the southeast, hoping that I was still headed in the right direction.

My line had received not so much as a nibble.

"Come on, you stupid fish," I croaked at one point. "I know you're down there."

It was no use. The water rolled on, the sun beat down on my back, and my paddled dipped slowly into the waves.

My eyes closed. I dozed.

My head jerked sharply, and my eyes flew open. There was nothing to see except the endless ocean. I shook my head to clear it, and opened another gallon of water.

I felt a fever coming on. I forced myself to look ahead and focus on the bow of my kayak. It bounced up and down and sometimes side to side as each new wave crashed over the hull. There was a splash to my left, but when I looked there was nothing there. Overhead was only the deep blue sky, void of anything except a few white clouds in the distance.

I ate the remaining bags of oatmeal and the last few chunks of coconut in a daze. I pulled out my final chart, which really did me no good now, and wondered how edible it would be if I soaked it in saltwater. I laughed at the thought, but knew that if I didn't catch something soon, I'd be hungry enough to eat just about anything.

* * *

There was a whisper in the wind, and slowly I opened my eyes. Again. . . soft, but still audible. Groggily, I looked around, but saw nothing. My head drooped forward and I was about to doze off when the wind picked up again.

"What is that noise?" I asked out loud.

As the swells of the ocean settled a bit, my kayak gently rocked back and forth. I stood up to breathe in deeply, almost panting in an effort to clear my head. My heart hammered in my chest, perhaps brought on by my increased fever.

"Enjoy this creation."

Was that a thought, or had I actually heard it? I couldn't tell. But now I dared to barely breathe, waiting for something else to happen. And then, as if a fog had rested lightly over my eyes, I felt a peace flood through my whole body. I sat back down and closed my eyes, feeling my body relax. My breath resumed its normal pace, as did my heart.

"I've been on this ocean for more than five months," I said to the waves around me, "and you have not forsaken me. I've prayed this entire time, and God has not turned his back on me either. Why should I not enjoy this time alone, like the rest of my journey?"

Turning around in my seat, I watched the sun disappear slowly beneath the waves. The wind continued to whisper across the water. I sat back and savored the moment, knowing that somehow, everything would work out.

I might have slept, but I don't remember it. Images floated through my mind, and a couple of times I thought I saw the shore. Bright flashes of light exploded at the corners of my vision, and I wondered if I had taken off my sunglasses. Was I going blind?

. . . I felt her breath, and my body heaved as I caressed her smooth skin. My eyes were closed. At least I thought they were. Was I dying? My body remained limp. The images that surrounded me and encompassed my mind brought a silent calm that passed through my soul, and my breath was a soft purr, joining in with the rolling water. "What a beautiful slow dance," I murmured, and reached forward to quiet my partner. "Don't worry, my love, I am right here. I'm not leaving you. We will be together forever."

I smiled as I continued to feel the rhythm of the ocean, powerful, majestic, and still captivating me, to the end. Tomorrow was forgotten. The world vanished. I remained calm, knowing that everything was going to be okay. The only thing that was real existed now, not yesterday or the day before, nor even in the future.

The only thing that mattered was the state of absolute bliss that I encountered with each new breath . . .

* * *

A high-pitched whining woke me abruptly from my dream. Annoyed, I swatted the air behind my neck, thinking it was an insect of some sort. I struggled to open my eyes. When the haze finally cleared, and my vision returned, all I saw was water. Still, the buzzing persisted. To my right, something was moving. I was going to find out what was making such an annoying sound.

A lever of some sort was moving in a circle. It was black, small and had a handle on its end. It was just my fishing rod.

"Oh, crap!" I yelped, blinking my eyes. I'd been deep in the grip of a dream or hallucination, I wasn't sure which, but now reality came flooding back. I sat bolt upright in the cockpit. I saw my kayak, the small fishing pole, and the mighty ocean all around.

"I think I've got a bite!"

Indeed I had. The line of the reel was almost out. My hands fumbling, I reached out to grab the pole. I set it in my lap, and slowly tightened the tension in the reel. Something was on the end of the line. I was lucky it hadn't dragged the pole overboard.

"I got you now, fish!" I cried triumphantly.

My stomach, awakened by the anticipation of a meal, rumbled noisily, reminding me that it was at the top of the priority list. I had to turn around and sit on the lip of the cockpit in order to see which way the line moved. Several times it swerved to the left and then back to the right. I reeled the line in, hoping it wouldn't break under the tug of the fish.

There were flashes of movement as the line drew closer to the kayak. The fish grew tired, and I hauled it in close to the boat. After locking the reel, so it couldn't get away, I clutched the fishing pole in one hand and jabbed the knife into the fish's skull with my right. After a few quick, powerful jerks, it lay still.

There was blood everywhere. The water was quickly turning crimson around my cockpit as I grabbed hold of the fish. It was extremely slippery and must have weighed over ten pounds. Eventually, after much pulling, grabbing and cursing, I heaved the entire thing over the rim of the kayak and onto my lap.

Slicing at it with my knife, I cut off the head and tail of the fish and threw them overboard. Now there was blood all over my hands, lap, and the floorboards of the kayak. The strong smell of it filled my nostrils. Had I not been so hungry, I would have vomited.

Next I held the body of the fish over the water. I used another knife to skewer its body because my fingers were too slippery to hold it steady. If I had dropped it back into the water, there's no telling how I would have reacted. Probably I would have jumped in after it.

I held the fish over the water. With the knife in my right hand I sliced open the gut, emptying the kidneys and other organs into the ocean. I couldn't tell what type of fish I'd caught. It was dark, almost black in color, with a few flecks of white along its head and back. I dipped it briefly into the water, then set it down again between my legs. Without waiting to clean myself off, I picked up the paddle and dug into the water. All this blood would certainly attract sharks, and I wanted to be as far away from the killing spot as possible. No telling how big the marine life was at this depth. There might even be some great whites nearby.

I looked around as I paddled, my heart beating faster. With every wave that broke and every stroke I made, I turned in fear, half expecting to see a fin break the surface of the water. But there was none. After about a half an hour, I stopped, looked around again, and convinced myself that I'd gone a safe distance.

There was a piece of mesh plastic between the outrigger and myself. The gallon jugs of water were tied there, constantly bobbing in and out of the swells. I placed the remains of the fish in the mesh, and then jumped into the water to wash off the blood that still clung to my skin and shorts.

After swimming around for a couple of minutes, I climbed back in, careful not to upset the kayak and send the fish flying into the water. I placed the fish in a thick plastic washbasin—the same container I used to shave—and it proved most useful. I splashed some water over the fish, cleaning off the rest of the blood, and then scrubbed the floorboards with my hands. Soon I was reasonably clean.

Now I turned my full attention to the fish. With my knife, I cut off five thin steaks from the middle of the carcass. I was tempted to eat the pieces raw, and I don't think my stomach would have minded much. But I had another idea. There was still a book of waterproof matches left in one of the compartments. I found the box and lit a small blue candle that I'd saved. At first it was hard to keep the candle lit, for the waves wanted to push over the sides and snuff it out.

Eventually, though, with the paddle balanced under my forearms, the candle in my left hand, and two pieces of fish on the tip of my knife, I was able to devise a crude cooking method. The swells pitched me back and forth, but I continued to focus on the small morsels of fish that would soon satisfy my hunger.

After both sides of the pieces were black, I took a big bite from the top portion. It tasted a little charred and smoky, but I didn't care—I'd soon swallowed both pieces whole. If the insides were raw, I hardly noticed. A few drops of water landed on the wick, putting out the fire. When I'd managed to light the candle again, I put the remaining three steaks on my knife and, in the same manner as before, cooked the rest of the fish.

After the other pieces were done, I sat back and swallowed the last bite. Then I thanked the ocean and her Creator for their provision. Everything would be just fine. There was still, I estimated, over a pound of fish left. I placed this in a small bag to eat the next day. With my stomach full and my strength returning, I got out my sleeping bag and curled up for the night.

The familiar faces of the stars that stretched out above the heavens seemed particularly bright that night. It seemed I could almost reach out and pluck some of the closer ones from the sky.

Within a matter of seconds I'd drifted off, and I slept for most of the night without any disturbances.

THIRTY-EIGHT
I Had Dreamed Of This Moment For Six Months

I had not the faintest idea how long I'd been paddling or what day it was. Regardless of my lack of knowledge, my spirits could not have been higher. I looked across the water, searching for South America.

A school of whales broke off to my right side, about fifty yards away. I waved to them, but they didn't see me or wish to approach. After a breakfast of cold fish my energy level had risen, and I felt like a new man. The water was rushing by, and my stroke quickened with each second. I felt that the end was near.

I continued to paddle furiously. The dance was sweeping over my entire body, and I was not thinking of its end, or even of its beginning. All I could focus on was the sweeping movements that carried me across the floor. I held my partner close, feeling her breath and tasting her sweetness spray across my lips. We were joined in a seemingly endless circle of spectators on all sides.

Now we were apart, and I watched her movements with fascination, feeling proud of our relationship together. She was watching me too, feeling my rhythm, and enjoying the strength of my muscles. We would embrace as I rushed down her back, and our passion was unbridled with enthusiasm. And then we would tear away from each other, and I would rise high on her waves, ready for us to join together again.

I had never felt more alive.

Ever alert, I heard each wave crash against the hull. My eyes were sharp and focused, scanning the horizon for any sign of life or land. I still tasted the fish on my tongue and the salt on my lips. My muscles rippled with each new stroke, and my skin was tight and tan and lean.

The sun beat down on my shoulders, but my hat provided shade for my face and neck. I'd never felt better in my life. The past few days, which had passed with little food or hope, faded away as the morning progressed. Now I felt not a trace of my past exhaustion.

At one point I said, "I think I could go all day without stopping."

Sometime in the late morning, a sound came to my ears that made my heart jump. At first I thought I was imagining things.

Then again. No louder, but more persistent. A distant rumbling. Was it the waves near the coast of South America?

I stood up in my kayak, straining to see land. With the clouds on the horizon, I couldn't tell for sure. Then a dark form, far off in the distance, emerged slowly and I hoped my eyes were not deceiving me.

The swells of the ocean changed direction, barely noticeable at first. I thought I'd gotten turned around, but after checking my compass and assuring myself that I was still on course, I knew for sure that the ocean was now rolling to the east. That could only mean one thing. The floor beneath, no matter how deep, had been rising. The coast of Colombia was near.

I sat down and tore into the water with new fury in the hope of seeing land before the day was out.

A distant cry, sounding like a seagull. In the sky, a hundred yards from me, several black dots circled in the sky. I blinked and rubbed my eyes and saw that it was no mistake. My heart leaped with joy, for I knew that I was indeed drawing close to my final destination.

Again I strained my neck, hoping to see some type of outline on the horizon. Nothing yet.

The sun was beginning to move down in the sky when I saw it. Less than twenty miles away, barely visible, but without a doubt— the dark form of a mountain rising above the ocean. I stopped paddling, frozen by the possibilities.

Standing up again to get a better viewpoint, I knew there was no mistake. The coast of South America lay directly in front of me. I let out a tremendous cry of joy, hope, and relief. I could scarcely believe my eyes.

My breath was short, my heart was pounding, and my stroke doubled in its intensity. Images floated by. I shook my head, remembering all of the trials, the hopes, the fears and the obstacles I had overcome to get to this point. It almost didn't seem real. Could it be a dream? No! I had dreamed of this moment for six months, and now, at last, it was upon me.

I stopped paddling and jumped out of the cockpit, into the water. Lifting above the surface and shaking my head vigorously, I swam quickly to the front compartment. After crawling on top of the kayak, I opened the hatch and took out my journal. I slid back to my seat and opened up the cover.

Tearing furiously at the pages, I looked for my last entry. I knew that this was a day to be remembered for the rest of my life. Lately I hadn't bothered to write the day or month in my journal, but now I must.

I counted the last dated entry, which was February 10, 1997. There had been sixteen small entries since that date, some only one sentence long. Just two days prior I had written simply this:

No food. Can't go much longer. Where is this South America? I think I shall never find it.

Others were more elaborate, but that was all the information I needed. I knew the day and the month. I couldn't believe that it was almost over. Here is what I wrote that day:

February 27, 1997
I cannot believe that my long struggle is almost over. Here, standing immovable in front of me, is undoubtedly the coast of South America.

It has been almost six months now since I first pushed off the sand at a small beach called San Felipe in Baja California. It seems like I have been here on this beloved Ocean called the Pacific for more than ten years. This is my life. This is my love. I don't want to ever leave. But, I have made it, alive, to the continent of South America. I always believed in myself, and now it has become a reality.

With each stroke the land grew closer. Soon I saw the rugged mountains that shadowed the shore, and my surroundings faded slowly away. On all sides my vision grew darker, and a bright, brilliant light shone across the waters and onto the shore. The waves slowed down, as did I, moving up and down in a trance-like state. I was dancing slowly now, taking my partner's hand softly in mine, smiling at her beauty, and counting our final moments together. She held me close, gathering me up in her arms like a child, and I bowed my head one last time to weep.

A sadness that I'd never before experienced came over me, and I mourned. The time was approaching when we would not be together. The seagulls cried louder overhead, gathering to see this new spectacle on the water. They swooped about overhead, but I kept my eyes on the swells around me.

Here I had seen safety, majesty, beauty, danger, death, promise, hope, failure, disaster, heartache, loneliness, comfort, devastation, suffering, pain, success, glory, loss, and pride.

I could write pages on each of these emotions, which, through the testing of my inner strength, had molded me into a softer, yet more chiseled man, with many newfound characteristics. I felt much closer, not only to myself but to God. The ocean had taught me great wisdom—at a price that had at times been difficult to pay.

But it had been well worth the cost in the end.

* * *

The land drew closer now, and my eyes were turned upward, to the heavens. I couldn't see clearly—whether it was because of the tears in my eyes or an incredible feeling of awe as I neared this new continent.

It seemed I was completely out of touch with reality. Or perhaps I was simply more deeply involved with the circulation of life on this planet. Either way, for the remainder of that day I seemed to be in a trance, surrounded by a cloud of euphoria. I soared higher, just off the surface of the water, heading south.

Sounds echoed all around. The wind whispered over the surface of the water, and the waves thundered toward shore. But these sounds barely reached my ears. The ocean glistened brightly in the afternoon sunlight, and the swells continued to roll south, but I couldn't focus on any one thing.

"Look there," I told myself.

I thought I saw Heather. She was coming toward me over the water. I stood up, my arms outstretched. She looked so beautiful; I almost began to weep again. I had not lost her after all.

The kayak reached the top of a wave. As it began to ride slowly down its back, I slipped and began to topple over. I caught myself just before I would have tumbled in, and I blinked in surprise.

I scanned the horizon for Heather, but of course she wasn't there. The sun winked at me in amusement. I shaded my eyes with my hand, blocking out its mirth. I dropped back down, numbed by this turn of events. Slowly I picked up the paddle and began to do the only thing I knew how.

I closed my eyes for a moment, letting the slow rhythm of my muscles striking the water's surface carry me back into a trance. Although I couldn't actually see them, I imagined all kinds of life under the sea, following my progress. Dolphins swam on all sides, whales moved powerfully just beneath the surface, and we all watched the sun set over the horizon. I imagined all of the people I had met along the way; imagined them watching my progress, waving as I looked to each one. Americans, Hispanics, and even my family were there, cheering on my progress. I smiled—not at their approval, but at my own. I had *not* turned back. I had succeeded in doing what everyone had said was impossible.

Though it almost cost me my life, I had overcome insurmountable odds to reach this coast. I'd almost listened to the whispers of doubt and failure, losing sight of the eventual goal. But through the strength of God, and perseverance, which produces patience, which produces character, I had made it six thousand miles to the coast of South America.

I paddled with the giant waves one last time, feeling the power sweep beneath me. They crashed loudly behind my kayak, but I was well in front and I reached the calmer waters safely. Soon I was stepping out of the kayak and kneeling on the beach. I kissed the sand and let the waves sweep over my feet.

Crouched there, with the sun just beginning to set, I lifted up my hands and head and cried out as loudly as I could. There was no one there. No city, no crowds, no press and no other boats. This was just the way I would have preferred it to end.

No people, but plenty of friends.

The surf thundered onto the beach, cheering loudly its approval. The dolphins and whales and even the sharks swam beneath the surface of the ocean, no doubt still keeping an eye on me, congratulating me for my efforts and guts. The sun waved goodbye, far off on the horizon, and winked at me as if he'd known all along that I would arrive here safely. Soon the stars would be out, filling the huge amphitheater of the heavens, singing their praises for the God who had seen me through my many perils, who had stayed with me during my long journey. Even this beach lay still in awe. Though stranger to each other, we shared the companionship that I had known with many along the way.

The wind whispered into my ears, caressing me with her arms and comforting my tired body, lifting me off the sand, away from the coast. And finally, the ocean rolled and waved and thundered and wept great tears onto the beach. The sun was now casting a magnificent orange glow across her surface, and I knew then that I would always be welcome on her breast. It was where I belonged. It was there I called home. It was within her reach that I found my happiness and the answers I had so desperately sought—about myself, the world around me, and my future.

On Thursday, February 27, 1997, I climbed the rocks near the cliffs at Punta Charambirá, Colombia.

With my eyes closed, I lifted my arms over my head, overwhelmed by the feelings of pride and strength that come with personal victory. I took in several deep breaths as the blood pounded through my head and chills rushed up my spine. A flush of red covered my face, and my passion for this beautiful ocean rose upon my breast and consumed my soul.

Then, in a loud voice, I cried out, "*It is finished!*"

I said this until the walls of rock echoed with my cries, and the seagulls, waves, wind, and breath of the ocean joined in with my song, filling the evening sky with our voices lifted together in harmony.

"*It is finished, now!*" I cried one last time.

Little did I know, I could not have been further from the truth.

The adventure had just begun.

EPILOGUE

When I had reached the shores of Colombia, South America that day, I figured that my adventures were over. Of course, they had only just begun. It took me three weeks from that day, just to get back into the United States. I could write an entire book on those adventures alone, but like I mentioned earlier, I do not want to give away too much of that story. I will say, however, that along the way home, I was reunited with many of the same friends that you have become familiar with. The people who were able to assist me in my dream to do the impossible.

I will never forget the lessons I learned. I'll always cherish the memories of golden sunsets, beautiful beaches, and bold and brash thoughts and dreams. The adventures and dangers still cling to my soul, strengthening me in times of trial, and I know the person I have become will never change.

My next journey is around the corner, and it will begin where this one has ended. I could not turn my back on my love for too long, and I will leave you with my last journal entry, one month after I had reluctantly rejoined society.

> *April 13, 1997*
> *Sometimes, at night, when I feel that the world is pressing in on all sides, I stand outside my front door and look up into the sky. My friends in the heavens are still watching me, and sometimes I turn to face the Ocean, straining my ears to hear her voice calling my name softly. I cannot hear the thundering of the breakers, but I know that they are there, restless for me to join them in another dance soon.*
>
> *Last night, I did just that, and smiled at the thoughts that danced through my head. I*

whispered her name softly, hoping to receive some response, and I knew then, without a doubt, that it would only be a matter of time before I would come back to her shores. And there, like always, she would welcome me with open arms.

25-year-old breaks world kayaking record in Gulf of Fonseca

March 1997
Posing for
LA Times Article

ABOUT THE AUTHOR

Benjamin Wade was born in Knoxville, Tennessee. At an early age he felt a strong affinity for music, and by the age of sixteen he was being called one of the best young trumpet players in the world. He has played with the New York Metropolitan Opera, and the Indianapolis and Knoxville Symphony Orchestras.

In 1996 he decided to embark on a 6,000-mile kayaking adventure, to prove to himself, as well as to others, that he could meet any challenge set before him. The journey took nearly six months, after which he emerged the record holder for the longest solo kayak trip, and was recognized as the first kayaker to solo navigate the Orinoco and Amazon Rivers.

No Turning Back: The South American Expedition of a Dragon Slayer, comes from the journal he kept during his trip. It's a story not only of adventure, but also of deep faith and redemption.

Upon his return he began a career coaching college soccer, where he earned the apt nickname "Coach." Now entering into his 17th season as a collegiate coach, his teams, from the NAIA to the NCAA, have won 16 conference championships during that time.

In 2003 he co-founded the Susanville Symphony, an accomplishment for which he holds the greatest pride. The documentary "Small Town Big Sound," filmed in 2006 by his brother, Peter Wade, premiered on the Documentary Channel.

Wade's groundbreaking contemporary ballet, "The Four Elements," premiered in 2011 and is also available on DVD.

Coach, Maestro, philosopher, businessman—however you describe him, Benjamin "Coach" Wade has proven to be an accomplished man and an unforgettable character. As a three-time contestant on the top-rated CBS primetime reality television show *Survivor* (*Survivor: Tocantins*, 2009; *Survivor: Heroes vs. Villains*, 2010; and *Survivor: South Pacific*, 2011)—you either loved him or hated him, but either way he's been a standout contestant who has never failed to surprise, delight, and sometimes even infuriate an audience.

Coming next: *The Wisdom of Coach*, due out in 2012.

9453903R0015

Made in the USA
Charleston, SC
13 September 2011